In the Light of Truth:
A New History of India

BY THE SAME AUTHOR

Arise Again, Ô India!

A Western Journalist on India: The Ferengi's Columns

A New History of India

A History of India as it Happened

In Defence of a Billion Hindus

Hindu Power in the 21st Century: Resistances, Fears and Obstacles

In the Light of Truth: A New History of India

François Gautier

HAR-ANAND
PUBLICATIONS PVT LTD

HAR-ANAND PUBLICATIONS PVT LTD
E-49/3, Okhla Industrial Area, Phase-II, New Delhi-110020
Tel.: 41603490
E-mail: info@haranandbooks.com/haranand@rediffmail.com
Shop online at: www.haranandbooks.com

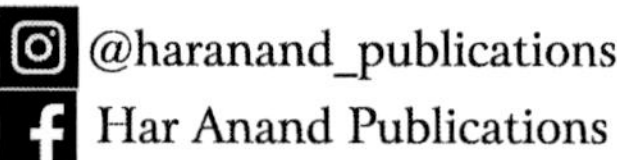

Published by Ashok Gosain and Ashish Gosain for
Har-Anand Publications Pvt Ltd

Printed in India at Megha Enterprises

Dedicated to
Mother India,
who took me in Her arms

Contents

Prologue
Why should Indian History Be Rewritten

Indian history must be seen in the light of truth. It must be therefore rewritten, because the way a nation tells its story deeply shapes its identity, confidence, and the way its people understand themselves. History is not just about the past—it influences how we live today and how we imagine the future.

Much of the history that is taught in Indian schools was originally written by British colonial historians. Their goal was not to celebrate India's legacy, but to portray it as disorganized, primitive, or in need of civilization. This narrative helped justify their rule. Even today, many of those colonial biases shape the way history is taught. Rewriting Indian history means telling the story from an Indian point of view, with balance, dignity, and cultural pride.

India's history is full of forgotten heroes, such as Shivaji Maharaj, Maharana Pratap, and heroines, like Rani Durgavati or Rani Abbakka Chowta that have not been given space in mainstream textbooks. From tribal resistance leaders to women warriors, from regional reformers to spiritual figures, so many lives and contributions remain in the shadows. Writing history accurately means giving these individuals their rightful place in the national memory. India also holds one of the richest cultural and philosophical heritages in the world. From the Vedas to classical dance, from ancient universities like Nalanda to great epics like the *Ramayana* and *Mahabharata,* our contributions are vast. If we do not take the time to write and preserve this legacy, we risk losing it—or having it misrepresented by others. History also includes pain—invasions, colonial exploitation, religious conflicts and social injustices. Writing history truthfully allows us to face these wounds with honesty, not to remain stuck in the past, but to learn from it and grow wiser. It helps us mature as a society. Telling our own history also strengthens India's image globally. When the world sees India only through outside eyes, it misses the complexity, depth, and beauty of Indian civilization. A well-written, self-aware history shows India as a land of great ideas, resilience, and innovation. Finally, we see more and more today that Indian History has to be rewritten according to the latest linguistic, archaeological, and even genetic discoveries. Not only that, but British and Marxist historians, eager to highlight the Congress party—which was originally a British institution—have erased from history the true roles of spiritual giants like Sri Aurobindo, who, besides being the avatar of the 'Supramental' age, was also an early prophet of Indian independence, at a time when Congress merely sought a few crumbs from the British. As a result, very few Indian children know about Sri Aurobindo today.

If you visit the new Museum of Indian History, situated in the Lok Sabha annexe in Delhi, which was conceived by Somnath Chatterjee, Speaker of the Parliament till 2008, you will be extremely surprised to see that for the Congress, Indian history starts with Ashoka, a politically correct king, because he was supposed to be Buddhist. It then passes on to Akbar, another acceptable figure to Marxists and Muslims, as he was an 'enlightened' emperor (but pretty ruthless in his early reign), then practically jumps to Subash Chandra Bose, Mahatma Gandhi, and Nehru, who are given prime importance in this museum. There's not a word about Sri Aurobindo, Tilak or Bipin Chandra Pal, the real revolutionaries of the Indian Independence Movement. The sad thing is that this beautiful museum, with state-of-the-art facilities, such as the re-enacting of Nehru's 'Tryst of Destiny' speech, with animated wax figures, is seen by so many Indian school children and college students. Hence the need for this book, which we hope will set the record straight.

CHAPTER 1

A Brief Outlook on Indian Protohistory

PALEOLITHIC INDIA (2 MILLION YEARS BCE): THE INDO-FRENCH DISCOVERY THAT REDEFINED HUMAN HISTORY

In the dusty plains of Attirampakkam, near Chennai in Tamil Nadu, a quiet revolution in our understanding of human history began to unfold. In 2011, a team of Indo-French archaeologists, led by Dr. Shanti Pappu and Kumar Akhilesh of the Sharma Centre for Heritage Education, in collaboration with French geochronologist Dr. Yanni Gunnell and other international researchers, made a discovery that would shake the foundations of prehistoric chronology. Through meticulous excavations spanning over a decade, the team unearthed a remarkable collection of over 7,000 stone tools. These tools, crafted with skill and intention, were identified as belonging to the Acheulean tradition—a tool-making culture associated with early hominins such as *Homo erectus*. What stunned the scientific community was the age of these artifacts: they were dated to approximately 1.5 to 2 million years ago, based on advanced dating methods including cosmogenic nuclide burial dating. Until this discovery, most history books stated that human presence in India could be traced back only to around 300,000 years BCE. But the Attirampakkam findings suggest that early humans—perhaps even the ancestors of *Homo sapiens*—inhabited the Indian subcontinent nearly a million years earlier than previously believed.

This Indo-French collaboration was more than just a scientific triumph—it marked a turning point in how we view the global migration of early humans. For decades, Africa had been considered the unquestioned cradle of humankind. While that remains true, the

Attirampakkam site positions India not just as a stop along the way, but as an early and long-standing center of homin in activity. The key aspects of the discovery include: advanced stone tool technology that reflects cognitive and motor skills comparable to early humans in Africa and Europe; stratified archaeological layers showing a continuous evolution of tool-making over hundreds of thousands of years; evidence suggesting that early humans adapted to changing climatic and environmental conditions in the Indian subcontinent.

This finding has profound implications. It challenges older Eurocentric narratives that saw human advancement as something that spread outward from the West. Instead, it affirms that South Asia played a central and continuous role in the saga of human evolution. Attirampakkam is now recognized as one of the oldest Paleolithic sites outside of Africa, comparable to key sites in East Africa and the Levant. Moreover, the Indo-French team's approach—blending archaeological rigour with cutting-edge geoscientific techniques—has become a model for international collaboration in heritage science. Their work demonstrates how history is constantly being rewritten, not through fiction, but through the slow, patient uncovering of the earth's ancient memories.

PROTO-HUMANS IN THE SOAN RIVER VALLEY (500,000 BCE): THE EARLIEST FOOTPRINTS OF HUMANITY IN THE INDIAN SUBCONTINENT

The story of human presence in the Indian subcontinent begins deep in prehistory— long before the rise of civilizations or even agriculture. One of the most important sites that sheds light on this remote past is the Soan River Valley, located in the Pothohar Plateau of present-day Pakistan, near Rawalpindi. This region has yielded some of the oldest evidence of proto-humans in South Asia, dating back over 500,000 years, and possibly as far back as 700,000 years. The early inhabitants of this region are associated with what archaeologists call the Soanian culture—named after the Soan River. These proto-humans, likely belonging to the species *Homo erectus* or early *Homo sapiens*, lived during the Lower Paleolithic period, and left behind a rich legacy of stone tools, such as hand axes, cleavers, and choppers. These tools were made using simple yet effective techniques, often from quartzite or other local stones.

The significance of the Soan Valley lies in its continuous archaeological record of human activity, which stretches back hundreds of thousands of years. The Siwalik Hills, which flank the valley, are a treasure trove of fossil-bearing sediments, including not only early human tools but also bones of now-extinct animals—elephants, rhinoceroses, and hippos— indicating a lush and varied prehistoric ecosystem. Although no complete hominid skeletons have yet been recovered from the Soan Valley, the stone tools and fossil remains strongly suggest the presence of proto-human populations who lived by hunting, gathering, and adapting to a changing environment during glacial and interglacial periods. The discovery of the Soanian sites challenges the earlier belief that India was just a "corridor" for human migration. Instead, it shows that South Asia had its own distinct and long-standing tradition of human occupation, possibly parallel to the better-known Acheulean culture of Africa and Europe.

In summary, the Soan River Valley represents one of the earliest cradles of humanity in South Asia, providing criticalinsights into the earliest ancestors in this part of the world. It reminds us that the roots of Indian civilization stretch back not just thousands, but hundreds of thousands of years—into a time when proto-humans first began shaping the world with their hands, their tools, and their emerging minds.

THE MESOLITHIC PERIOD IN INDIA (C. 10,000 – 6,000 BCE): LIFE BETWEEN TWO WORLDS

The Mesolithic period, also known as the Middle Stone Age, marks a fascinating transitional phase in Indian prehistory—a bridge between the Paleolithic world of hunting large animals and the Neolithic age of farming and settled life. Spanning roughly from 10,000 to 6,000 BCE, this period saw early humans adapting to a changing world after the last Ice Age.

As the climate warmed and forests expanded, the giant animals of the Paleolithic began to disappear. In response, Mesolithic communities in India began hunting smaller animals, fishing, and gathering wild fruits, seeds, and roots. Their tools also evolved: instead of the large hand axes of earlier times, they began to use microliths—tiny, sharp stone blades often mounted on wood or bone handles to make arrows, spears, and cutting tools. These tools were more refined, more portable, and suited to quick, efficient hunting and food processing.

The Mesolithic people were mostly nomadic or semi-nomadic, living in temporary camps or natural rock shelters. Some of the most famous Mesolithic sites in India include Bhimbetka (Madhya Pradesh), known for its vivid rock paintings, Bagor (Rajasthan), one of the earliest known evidence of animal domestication, and Sarangpur, Mahadaha, and Langhnaj in Gujarat and Uttar Pradesh. Their cave art provides a rare insight into their world, with scenes of hunting, dancing, rituals, and everyday activities rendered in natural pigments that still survive on rock walls. Such imagery reflects both creativity and a deep spiritual engagement with nature and community.

Though they did not yet farm extensively, some Mesolithic groups began experimenting with early agriculture and domesticated dogs and cattle. They buried their dead with care, sometimes along with tools or ornaments, suggesting the beginnings of rituals and belief systems. The Mesolithic period shows us a flexible, intelligent human society learning to live with nature in new ways. These were people who adapted their tools, lifestyles, and thinking to a changing environment. They were still hunters and gatherers—but also inventors, explorers, and artists. They represent the dawn of cultural practices that would eventually lead to permanent villages, farming, and civilization.

THE NEOLITHIC PERIOD IN INDIA (C. 7000 – 2000 BCE): THE FIRST FARMERS AND VILLAGERS

The Neolithic period, or the New Stone Age, marks one of the biggest revolutions in human history—the transition from wild to domestic, from roaming to settling, from surviving to building. In India, the Neolithic Age began around 7000 BCE and lasted until roughly 2000 BCE, depending on the region.

This period saw the birth of agriculture, the domestication of animals, the building of permanent homes, and the rise of village life. People began to grow crops like wheat, barley, and lentils, and to rear animals such as cattle, sheep, and goats. For the first time in Indian prehistory, humans were producing food rather than just collecting it from nature—a fundamental change that shaped the entire future of civilization. Tools became more advanced too. Neolithic communities used polished stone tools—axes, sickles, and grinding stones—that were stronger, smoother, and more effective than earlier microliths. They also began to make pottery to store grain and water, often decorated with simple patterns or shapes.

The earliest known Neolithic site in the Indian subcontinent is Mehrgarh, in present-day Pakistan (Balochistan), dating back to about 7000 BCE. Here, archaeologists found mud-brick houses, granaries, beads, figurines, and evidence of dental surgery—showing a surprisingly advanced way of life. In Kashmir, at sites like Burzahom, people lived in pit dwellings, used stone and bone tools, and painted animal motifs on pottery. In South India, especially Karnataka and Tamil Nadu, Neolithic communities built ash mounds and lived in organized settlements, raising cattle and farming millets. Though still small in scale, some Neolithic communities began to exhibit signs of social organization, including planned storage systems, community granaries, and burial practices that point to emerging beliefs and defined social roles.

The Neolithic age is the true beginning of settled human life in India. It is when people started shaping the land, organizing society, and planning for the future. Every village, every harvest, every home built today carries the legacy of those first Neolithic farmers. Their quiet revolution—based on seeds, soil, and tools—laid the foundation for everything that came after: towns, cities, writing, trade, and culture.

Chapter 2

Sarasvati: Myth or Reality?

For centuries, the Sarasvati has been considered a mythical river—a sacred flow described in the *Rigveda,* said to have nourished a luminous civilization long before the Ganges took central stage in Indian consciousness. Poets, priests, and pilgrims evoked its name as a symbol of purity, wisdom, and divine inspiration. But was the Sarasvati only a metaphor for knowledge, or did it once actually exist as a physical river that shaped the earliest chapters of Indian history? Recent archaeological and scientific research suggests that the answer might be far more complex —and far more exciting—than previously believed.

In the *Rigveda*—one of the oldest surviving texts of humanity, dated conservatively around 1500 BCE but possibly much earlier—the Sarasvati is described with unmatched reverence. She is praised as "the best of mothers, the best of rivers, the best of goddesses." Unlike other rivers which appear occasionally in the hymns, Sarasvati dominates the early 'Mandalas' (books) of the *Rigveda.* She is depicted as a mighty, flowing river between the Yamuna and the Sutlej, full of water, nurturing civilizations, and powerful enough to break through mountains. But here lies the paradox: by the time later Vedic texts like the *Brahmanas* and the *Upanishads* were composed, the Sarasvati seems to fade—first to a small seasonal stream, and later, a memory. This disappearance puzzled historians and became one of the central arguments used by Indologists to classify the Sarasvati as "mythical," akin to the symbolic Ganga of heaven or the river of knowledge within.

In the 20th century, a quiet revolution began. Satellite imagery, ground-penetrating radar, and geological surveys uncovered dry river beds in the northwestern part of India—running roughly along the modern-day Ghaggar-Hakra river system, stretching from Himachal Pradesh through Haryana, Rajasthan, and into Pakistan. Many scientists and archaeologists discovered that this dry riverbed matched the ancient descriptions of the Sarasvati. In particular, studies by the Indian Space Research Organisation (ISRO) and scholars like Dr. S.R. Rao and Prof. B.B. Lal (former director of the Archaeological Survey of India) found indeed that the Ghaggar-Hakra was the lost Sarasvati. These regions are also home to an extraordinary density of Harappan or Indus Valley sites—far more than those found along the Indus River itself. Sites like Kalibangan, Banawali, and Rakhigarhi (one of the largest Indus sites) lie along what would have been the banks of this ancient river. In other words, what we once called the Indus Valley Civilization may more accurately be the Sarasvati-Sindhu Civilization.

Why did this river disappear? Theories vary. Some suggest tectonic shifts diverted the tributaries that once fed the Sarasvati—namely, the Yamuna and Sutlej—toward the Ganges and Indus respectively. Others point to long-term climate changes and desertification that led to a drying up of the once-mighty flow. The drying of the Sarasvati explains the mysterious decline of the Harappan cities. As the river failed, agricultural surpluses diminished, trade weakened, and communities either dispersed or migrated eastward—toward the Ganges plain, laying the foundations of later Vedic civilization. This reinterpretation blurs the lines between what we thought was "prehistory" and what we considered "myth." It suggests that Vedic literature was not just symbolic poetry, but encoded memory—oral history of real landscapes, rivers, and shifts in civilization.

For much of colonial-era historiography, the Sarasvati was dismissed as "imaginary"—a classic example, they said, of how Indian texts relied on mystical allegory rather than empirical observation. The idea that an advanced civilization could have existed in the Indian subcontinent before 1500 BCE—before the so-called "Aryan migration"—was inconvenient for the colonial narrative of civilizational hierarchy. But today, that narrative is undergoing a deep reassessment. Western researchers, too, are beginning to understand that the Sarasvati once flowed and that its civilization predates the Indus. The work of French archaeologist Michel Danino, for instance, has helped bridge textual tradition and physical science, re-evaluating the Sarasvati not as legend, but as a geological and cultural reality.

Recent satellite imagery has revealed the existence of an ancient natural channel connecting the Indus and Sarasvati rivers, suggesting that these two river systems were once interdependent and hydraulically linked. This challenges the long-held view that they were entirely separate and reinforces the idea of a shared cultural and ecological network in northwestern India during antiquity. Meanwhile, geological and hydrological surveys—initially conducted to locate sources of drinking water in the arid regions of Bikaner, Ganganagar, and Jaisalmer—have brought to light the presence of underground riverbeds. These subterranean water channels are not fed by Himalayan glaciers, unlike the Ganga and Indus, but appear to be remnants of a once-mighty river system that no longer flows on the surface. The findings provide compelling evidence that these fossilized rivers are in fact vestiges of the ancient Sarasvati, long celebrated in the *Rigveda* as a vast and life-giving river flowing "from the mountains to the sea." Together, these studies offer strong geological and remote-sensing confirmation that the Sarasvati was not a myth, but a real and powerful river that once nourished one of the most extensive cultural landscapes of the ancient world.

Following the Pokharan nuclear tests conducted on May 11, 1998, scientists from the Bhabha Atomic Research Centre (BARC) undertook a series of studies to assess the environmental impact, particularly on the quality of groundwater in the surrounding desert region of Rajasthan. To their surprise, not only was the water found to be safe for human consumption, but radiocarbon and isotope analysis revealed something extraordinary: the underground water was between 8,000 and 14,000 years old! This meant that the aquifers tapped into paleo-hydrological reserves—ancient, untouched water systems dating back to the Late Stone Age, long before the rise of agriculture or civilization in the subcontinent. The implications were staggering. The presence of such prehistoric, fossil water supported geological theories about the existence of an ancient, active river system in the region—likely part of the now-vanished Sarasvati River, which once flowed through the Thar Desert. What began as a routine post-nuclear safety measure ended up providing one of the most compelling scientific clues yet to the antiquity of India's hidden rivers, buried beneath centuries of sand and silence.

In Indian culture, rivers are not merely water bodies—they are mothers, teachers, and symbols of inner awakening. Even if the physical Sarasvati ceased to flow thousands of years ago, her spiritual current continues. She is the goddess of learning, music, and eloquence. Schoolchildren across India pray to her before exams. Musicians invoke her before playing their first note. Artists and philosophers still call on Sarasvati for inspiration. Perhaps this is why the river, though invisible, has never truly disappeared. And now, science and tradition appear to converge, suggesting that the goddess of knowledge may indeed have once flowed as a real river, shaping one of the world's earliest urban civilizations—a reminder that what we often call "myth" may be memory misunderstood.

CHAPTER 3

The Forgotten Dawn: The Indus-Sarasvati Civilization (7000BCE-2600 BCE)

When we think of the great ancient civilizations, Mesopotamia, Egypt, and China often come to mind. Yet along the fertile river plains of the Indian subcontinent arose a civilization of comparable—if not greater—complexity, scale, and antiquity: the Indus–Sarasvati Civilization. For centuries, this civilization remained buried beneath layers of soil, colonial assumptions, and scholarly neglect. Today, it is being rediscovered not only through excavations but through a complete rethinking of Indian history itself. Traditionally, historians dated the so-called "Harappan Civilization" to around 2600-1900 BCE. But in the past few decades, archaeological evidence has radically revised this timeline. Excavations at Mehrgarh, located near the Bolan Pass in present-day Balochistan, show continuous human settlement as early as 7000 BCE—making it one of the oldest Neolithic cultures in the world. At Mehrgarh, people cultivated barley and wheat, herded sheep and goats, and lived in mud-brick houses. They practiced dentistry (as seen in drilled molars), made jewelry from lapis lazuli and turquoise, and created pottery decorated with geometric motifs. This was no primitive tribe—it was a society laying the foundations of urbanism long before the pyramids rose in Egypt.

The first recorded excavations at Harappa took place in 1853, under the supervision of Alexander Cunningham, a prominent British archaeologist and later founder of the Archaeological Survey of India (ASI). At the time, Cunningham believed he had found remnants of a relatively late historical site. His work was hampered by limited understanding, and the excavation was eventually abandoned. Over time, the monsoon rains reclaimed the trenches, covering the site once more and delaying the discovery of one of the world's oldest urban civilizations. It was not until 1919 that the first real breakthrough came. R.D. Banerji, an Indian archaeologist working with the ASI, was investigating a Buddhist stupa near Mohenjo Daro, located west of the Indus River. During the course of this excavation, he unearthed a flint scraper, a simple but unmistakable tool that hinted at a civilization far older than any Buddhist remains. Banerji's find raised immediate questions and led to further excavations which, within a few years, would bring to light the forgotten cities of the Indus-Sarasvati Civilization, revealing a lost chapter of human history buried beneath the sands and silts of the northwestern subcontinent.

What struck the first archaeologists who excavated Harappa and Mohenjo Daro was the extraordinary sophistication of these ancient cities. Unlike the chaotic sprawl typical of early urban centers elsewhere in the world, the Harappan settlements were laid out on a geometric grid, revealing a high degree of urban planning and civic organization. The cities were divided into distinct zones—some clearly residential, others dedicated to public functions. Large assembly halls, granaries, and the famous Great Bath of Mohenjo Daro pointed to the presence of communal spaces and complex social structures. In addition, entire industrial quarters were discovered, filled with workshops that had once produced copper tools, weapons, beads, bangles, finely crafted pottery, and intricate seals—used not only for trade but likely also for administrative and perhaps even ritual purposes. This combination of advanced infrastructure, craftsmanship, and organization, all dating back more than four thousand years, deeply impressed early excavators. It challenged 19th and early 20th century assumptions about the supposed primitiveness of India's past and revealed the Harappans as master urbanists, whose achievements in planning, hygiene, and craftsmanship rivaled those of Mesopotamia and Egypt.

Over the past two decades, more than 100 new Harappan sites have been uncovered by teams of Indian, American, and British archaeologists, dramatically expanding our knowledge of the Indus–Sarasvati Civilization. These discoveries have ushered in a new phase of research, moving beyond the initial focus on Harappa and Mohenjo Daro to reveal the vast geographic and cultural scope of this ancient urban world. A more concrete and detailed picture of Harappan society is now taking shape. For instance, American anthropologist Gregory L. Possehl has documented over 2,600 Harappan sites across the subcontinent. Of these, nearly 1,500 are agglomerations, villages, or towns—each covering an area of at least 50 acres, suggesting a high degree of urban density, planning, and sustained settlement over a large territorial expanse. This expanded archaeological map challenges earlier views that saw the Indus–Sarasvati Civilization as limited to a few major cities. Instead, it appears to have been a networked civilization, made up of thousands of interconnected communities—urban, rural, and industrial—thriving along rivers, trade routes, and ecological zones. The result is a civilization that was not only ancient and complex, but remarkably decentralized, resilient, and widespread.

But the Harappan Civilization did not emerge overnight. Today, historians and archaeologists speak of a pre-Harappan phase, a long formative period during which early villages and farming communities began to take shape along the Sarasvati and Indus river systems. These proto-urban cultures, slowly interconnected by ancient trade and migration routes, laid the foundation for what would later become one of the world's great Bronze Age civilizations. Archaeologist Jonathan Mark Kenoyer estimates that this pre-Harappan culture, flourishing between 5000 and 2600 BCE, was itself the outcome of an even earlier evolution beginning as far back as 7000 BCE. During this time, small farming settlements emerged, domesticating plants and animals, producing ceramics, and developing the foundations of social organization. One of the most important discoveries shedding light on this early period came from the work of French archaeologist Jean-François Jarrige, who excavated Mehrgarh, a remarkable site in present-day Balochistan, Pakistan. Dating to the 7th millennium BCE, Mehrgarh revealed one of the oldest known farming communities in South Asia, complete with mud-brick houses, granaries, and some of the earliest evidence of dental surgery and craft specialization. Thanks to these discoveries, it is now clear that the Indus–Sarasvati Civilization was not a sudden creation, but the culmination of millennia of cultural development—a deeply rooted tradition of settlement, innovation, and human adaptation to the riverine landscapes of the subcontinent.

As for the collapse of the Indus–Sarasvati Civilization, it is now widely accepted that it was not caused by an invasion, contrary to older colonial theories that will be discussed later in the chapter on the Aryans. Instead, recent research points to a combination of natural and environmental factors that gradually undermined the stability of this once-thriving civilization. Foremost among these was the drying up of the Sarasvati River, long considered a lifeline for many Harappan settlements. Geological studies suggest that a series of earthquakes triggered shifts in the tectonic plates, altering river courses and cutting off the Sarasvati's Himalayan sources. At the same time, a pattern of weakening monsoons led to a prolonged drought, causing widespread famine and the collapse of agricultural systems. These combined stresses—loss of water, failing crops, and the eventual abandonment of urban centers—contributed to a gradual decline, not a dramatic or sudden fall. Rather than disappearing entirely, many Harappan communities likely migrated eastward, integrating into later cultures and leaving behind a rich legacy of urban planning, craftsmanship, and social organization.

The civilization was extensively connected through trade, both within and beyond its borders. Goods flowed along the rivers and overland routes—from copper mined in Rajasthan, carnelian beads from Gujarat, lapis lazuli from Afghanistan, to shells from the Arabian Sea. Lothal in Gujarat even had what appears to be a dockyard, pointing to maritime trade links with Mesopotamia and Oman. Its artisans created finely crafted pottery, beads, seals, and figurines. Seals engraved with mysterious symbols—often called the Indus script—have been found throughout the region. Although still undeciphered, the remarkable consistency of these symbols over thousands of kilometers suggests a shared system of communication. Some scholars see links between this script and later Brahmi or Vedic symbolism. Culturally, the civilization seems to have revered animals like bulls, elephants, and possibly even early representations of Shiva-like figures in yogic postures. Terracotta figurines of women, possibly linked to fertility rites, are also widespread. The roots of later Indian religious iconography may well lie in this ancient matrix.

For centuries, Indian history was viewed through colonial lenses: static, myth-bound, and considered to begin only with the arrival of foreign influence. The rediscovery of the Indus–Sarasvati Civilization—and its profound antiquity—restores India's rightful place among the world's oldest continuous civilizations. More than that, it reveals a sophisticated society that thrived without empires, that achieved urban elegance without warlike conquest, and that may have laid the psychological and spiritual groundwork for the later flowering of Vedic thought, Jainism, Buddhism, and classical Hinduism. This is not a story of lost ruins—it is a story of deep continuity, of a civilization rooted in the rhythms of rivers, the geometry of cities, the logic of trade, and the subtle symbols of spiritual life. It is India's true beginning, no longer hidden beneath dust and dogma.

Chapter 4

The Copper, Bronze and Iron Ages of India

There is widespread misconception regarding India's technological achievements during the Sarasvati—Indus civilization. Western accounts suggested iron mastery came late to the Indian subcontinent. Yet the iron pillar at Delhi's Qutb Minar standing rust-free through centuries, reveals clearly that Indian blacksmiths could produce extremely complex alloys, long before anyone else. Here below, we set the record straight.

The Age of Copper in the Indus–Sarasvati Civilization (4500–3500 BCE)

This early phase of the Indus–Sarasvati Civilization is known as the Chalcolithic period, a term derived from the Greek *khalkos* (copper) and *lithos* (stone). It marks a transitional era, when human communities were beginning to experiment with metalworking, yet still relied heavily on stone tools for everyday life. Bronze metallurgy had not yet emerged, but the use of copper—hammered or smelted—signaled a major technological breakthrough. Dated roughly between 4500 and 3500 BCE, this period corresponds to the formative stage of Harappan society, laying the economic, social, and technological foundations upon which later urban centers like Harappa, Mohenjo Daro, and Rakhigarhi would rise. Along the fertile banks of the Sarasvati and Indus rivers, early farming communities began to thrive. They cultivated wheat, barley, pulses, and cotton; domesticated animals like cattle, goats, and sheep; and constructed mud-brick houses, sometimes with storage silos and rudimentary drainage.

These Chalcolithic villages—discovered at sites such as Mehrgarh, Bhirrana, Kunal, and Kot Diji—show increasing complexity in settlement design, economic specialization, and material culture. Pottery became more varied and decorated, reflecting both practical use and emerging aesthetic sensibilities. Tools made of bone, stone, and now copper coexisted, with copper used sparingly for items such as needles, small blades, or fishing hooks—suggesting cautious innovation and selective adoption of new technologies. Importantly, the Chalcolithic age was not just a period of technological progress, but one of cultural integration. There is evidence of long-distance trade, especially in semi-precious stones like lapis lazuli and carnelian, indicating that these early communities were well connected through networks of exchange that would later define the Mature Harappan economy.

Rather than being a primitive prelude to urbanism, the Copper Age now appears as a vital crucible of innovation and resilience. It was during this time that the Harappans began to articulate their distinctive identity—blending new technologies with ancient knowledge, adapting to changing environments, and building a sustainable way of life rooted in the rhythms of the rivers and the land.

THE BRONZE AGE IN THE HARAPPAN CIVILIZATION (3300–1200 BCE)

The Bronze Age marks a major turning point in the development of the Indus–Sarasvati Civilization. Bronze is an alloy of copper and tin, typically melted and combined in varying proportions to produce a metal that is stronger, more durable, and more workable than either of its components alone. Its introduction revolutionized tool-making, weaponry, and craft production across the ancient world. In the Indian subcontinent, the earliest evidence of bronze use dates as far back as 3300 BCE, placing it among the earliest Bronze Age cultures globally. During this period, the Harappans began producing a diverse array of bronze objects, including axes, chisels, knives, spearheads, mirrors, fish hooks, as well as elegant figurines—most notably the famous "Dancing Girl" of Mohenjo Daro, cast in bronze using the sophisticated lost-wax technique. The use of bronze enabled the creation of more precise tools and intricate ornaments, enhancing both agricultural productivity and urban craftsmanship. Artisans developed specialized techniques in metalworking, and bronze came to play a central role in trade networks, with copper likely sourced from Rajasthan and Baluchistan, and tin possibly imported from Afghanistan or Central Asia.

The Mature Harappan phase (2600–1900 BCE) marked the peak of bronze technology. Even after the decline of urban centers post-1900 BCE, bronze continued to be widely used in Late Harappan cultures and persisted into the early Iron Age, which began around 1200 BCE. Thus, the Bronze Age in India was not only a period of technological advancement, but also of cultural consolidation, where metallurgy, trade, and artistry came together to support one of the most sophisticated civilizations of the ancient world.

THE AGE OF IRON AND THE BIRTH OF NEW CIVILIZATIONS (1200–600 BCE)

In the *Vishnu Purana*, one of the oldest and most revered Indian texts, human history unfolds through great cosmic cycles. The final age, Kali Yuga, is also known as the Age of Iron—an era marked by moral decline, spiritual confusion, and material ambition. "In Kali Yuga, iron will be treated as gold; truth will be lost in illusion; and those who speak violently will pass for wise," says the *Purana*. This is not just allegory—it reflects a deep intuition about the nature of human progress, and its dangers. For decades, British archaeologists like R.E.M. Wheeler and D.H. Gordon dated the beginning of India's Iron Age to around 700 BCE, linking it to the arrival of Indo-Aryan groups. But archaeological discoveries now show that iron was smelted in India as early as 2000 BCE, particularly in the Ganga Valley, central India, and the Deccan plateau. These were not simple, borrowed techniques, but signs of an independent, indigenous metallurgical tradition. Indian smiths were among the first in the world to master the secrets of iron.

India was not alone in probing the mysteries of metal. In ancient Egypt, alchemists saw iron as the lowest metal in the cosmic ladder, linked to Mars and conflict, while gold represented the divine. Egyptian and

Greek thinkers connected metallurgy to the soul's journey—just as Indian rishis did, but with greater philosophical integration. In India, the transformation of matter was always linked to dharma—the right use of power, the ethical shaping of the world. By the time Alexander the Great arrived at India's frontiers in 326 BCE, he encountered a society already forged in iron: with warriors, elephants, cities, and iron weapons that rivaled his own. His encounter with King Porus showed that India was not a land of passive mystics, but a complex and sovereign civilization. His troops, weary and intimidated, refused to advance further east. The age of Indian iron had already arrived—not just as material, but as power, order, and resistance.

Yet in India, iron was never solely a material of war. Its most enduring symbol stands in Delhi, where the Iron Pillar of Mehrauli, dedicated to Vishnu, rises silently into the sky. Erected during the Gupta period, this seven-meter column has resisted rust for over 1600 years—a marvel of ancient metallurgy. Known as "Vishnu's column," it carries an inscription in Sanskrit that praises a just king and the preservation of dharma. In an age marked by iron, it offers a different legacy: not destruction, but continuity; not conquest, but cosmic alignment. It is known today as the Qutb Minar, which was conquered by Qutub-ud-Din Aibak in AD 1199, who razed all the Hindu, Jain, and Buddhist temples there (some of the columns with Sanskrit inscriptions can still be seen), but could not destroy the iron pillar, so strong it was.

In the Indian imagination, even the hardest metal could be turned into a pillar of truth. The age of iron, for all its shadows, remains a test of what we choose to forge—not only with our hands, but with our hearts.

CHAPTER 5

Indus or Hindus

As with the so-called mythical Sarasvati river, much misunderstanding surrounds the world of the 'Hindus'. Any attempt to write a new history of India must begin with the right foundations—and with setting the record straight. Thus, the first task is to demystify the word 'Hindu' about which there is so much misunderstanding.

Let's say it right away: there are no Hindus... This word was invented by European colonizers to designate a people which lived in the valley of the Indus. The exact appellation should be "*Indu*", a term which was actually used for centuries by outsiders, to name all India's inhabitants, be they Muslims, Christians, Buddhists or Hindus. But when *Indus* became *Hindus* at the hands of western colonizers, it grew to be a source of confusion and had catastrophic consequences for Indian history: it indirectly brought about the terrible partition of the subcontinent and is partly responsible today for the inter-religious strife in India.

Who are the Hindus then—or shall we say *Indus*? Western (and unfortunately also Indian) historians have often reduced Hinduism to a code of moral conduct and a set of rites and rituals, or have even negated Hinduism by associating it only with the hated system of castes, forgetting that Hinduism was not only a wonderful system of thought, which influenced many of the philosophical systems of our planet, but that it was—and hopefully still is today, even if it has lost some of its early purity—a unique spirituality, which went beyond all religions in the true spirit of "*Induity*". It may be necessary then—even for Indians, who often seem to have very little idea of the greatness of their culture—to remind the readers of a few of the lasting principles of Hinduism.

For the Hindus, in the beginning, the world was pure Being without duality: *Sat*. Certain sects of Hinduism even said that before man, before any living organism, there was only Non-Being: *a-sat*. But how could the Being emerge from Non-Being? In the beginning then, this world must have been Pure Being, unique, without past, present or future:

"*It was the hour before the Gods awakened.*
Across the path of the divine Event
The huge foreboding mind of Night, alone
In her unlit temple of eternity,
Lay stretched immobile upon Silence's marge..."

(Sri Aurobindo, Savitri, page 1)

And then, « something » happened:

"*Then Something in the inscrutable darkness stirred;*
A nameless movement, an unthought Idea,
Insistent, dissatisfied, without an aim,
Something that wished but knew not how to be,
Teased the Inconscient to wake Ignorance"... *(Idem, page 2)*

Human evolution had begun; the Non-Manifest had descended into Matter. And all the forms of life as we know them, were going to blossom during the millions of years which followed, until the *homo sapiens* of today.

And for the Hindus, the symbol, the unalterable proof of this descent of the Non-Manifest on our earth is *jiva*, the soul, a spark of the Infinite which is hidden in every thing. It is through *jiva* that the flower finds its infinite exquisiteness; it is because of *jiva* that the animal moves with such beauty, it is by the grace of *jiva* that man always aspires higher. "As tiny as an atom, as vast as the universe, *jiva* is unfathomable and cannot be seized; eternal, *jiva* cannot be destroyed; without attachments, free, nothing can touch it," says the *Taittirîya Upanishad*.

Hinduism has always maintained that *jiva* reincarnates itself from life to life, thus perfecting itself throughout the ages. Everything is valuable for *jiva* and there is nothing that it neglects, as each experience enriches the soul: sufferings and joys, honors and disgrace, king in this life, untouchable in the next, criminal yesterday, saint today.... When we die, the physical body goes back to the universal Earth, the intellect dissolves itself in the larger universal Mind, and the vital, or Life Force, which is the mass of the impulsions and desires which we have formed in the course of a lifetime, return to the universal Vital. And then *jiva* is reborn, again and again, until we become fully conscious of the Supreme Being from which we all emanate: "Old and feeble, he becomes young again and again," says the *Rigveda*.

This concept of reincarnation, without which it is difficult to understand the why of our often painful lives, or accept the inevitability (and immense cruelty) of death, has been lost in the West and most other parts of the world and religions, whereas it was prevalent nearly everywhere during Antiquity. "Which sadist God has decreed that we would have only one life to realize ourselves and through which colossal ignorance Islam and Christianity have decided that we shall go to Heaven, or to Hell, according to the deeds, bad or good, which we have committed in a single life?" asks French writer Satprem.

The ancient Hindus were intensely secular in spirit, as their spirituality was absolutely non-sectarian—and still is today in a lesser measure. Nine thousand years ago, Vedic sages, to define the Universal Law which they had experienced within themselves on an occult and supra-spiritual plane, had invented the word *dharma*. In a nutshell, *dharma* is all that which helps you to become more and more aware of *jiva* inside yourself. In fact, *dharma* defines good and bad: what helps you on the path of spiritual discovery can be considered good = *dharmic*; and what impedes you can be taken as bad = *a-dharmic*. And to help the seeker progress in his *sadhana*, the sages of ore had codified a series of systems called *yogas*. There is *hatha-yoga*, or the yoga of the body, the only Indian spiritual discipline which the West knows about and which has been copied by all the gymnastics and aerobics systems of the world; *karma-yoga*, or yoga of work; *jnana-yoga*, that of knowledge; *bhakti yoga*, the path of devotion, and so on. The Masters had also discovered that the personality of each human being is composed of three main "psychological" elements, or *gunas*: *tamas*, which is the principle of inertia, of heaviness and indolence; *rajas*, the more dynamic energy of our desires and impulsions; and *sattwa*, the most spiritualized and refined element in us. All yogas have thus attempted to promote *sattwa*, while taming *rajas* and uplifting *tamas*.

Karma is another very important tenet of Hinduism which has been perverted in modern times, not only because of its fashionable misuse in the West, but also in India itself where, because of influences during three centuries by missionaries and secular thought, it is often mixed up in varying degrees with the Christian concept of sin and virtue. Hindus (and Buddhists) have always maintained that all actions, good or bad, which we perform during a lifetime, carry automatic consequences for the next lives to come. But there is absolutely no moral implication, no notion of Good or Evil, as for Hinduism there is a mathematical and immutable logic in our actions: "Whatever the seed you planted, you will harvest its fruit sooner or later," says the Buddha. Consequently, there is never any absolute injustice: suffering in this life could be the consequence of a "bad" karma sown in another life; and today's happiness might result from a "good" karma performed in another body. With this knowledge, one can understand a little better the sufferings of humanity, even though many of them still look so unjust; but true compassion is always accompanied by right knowledge.

The concept of the *avatar* is also indispensable to the understanding of true *dharma*. Hindus have always believed that the Infinite, the Immanent, the Supreme, or whatever name you want to give to That which is beyond us, has manifested Himself throughout the ages in human bodies—particularly at crucial stages during the history of humanity. Christ, Krishna, Buddha, Confucius, Mohamed, are all *avatars* in the eyes of Hindus. Each of these "sons of God" explained and developed their messages in the terms and with the images of their times, which fitted into the understanding and culture of the country where they had incarnated themselves. None of them, except maybe Mohamed, ever said that he was "the only" son of God and that his religion was the only true one; it is their disciples and followers who later perverted their messages and converted what were essentially spiritual teachings into fixed religions with their intolerant and exclusive credos. It is these followers who today refuse to adapt their religions to modern times.

Finally, it is difficult to understand Hinduism if you fail to grasp the concept of *shakti*, the divine feminine energy. Because of the influence of British thought, it is nowadays fashionable in India to always highlight the downtrodden condition of Indian women and their underprivileged place in Indian society. As a result, Western correspondents are always keen to do stories on female infanticides in Bihar, child marriages, or *sati* cases in Rajasthan. But who knows that no country in the world has granted such an important place to women in its spirituality and social ethos ? "Without Him I exist not, without Her I am unmanifest," says a great Indian yogi. Thus in India—and it is true that it is often a paradox, as women, because of later Muslim influences, have often been relegated to the background—the feminine concept is a symbol of dynamic realization. She is the eternal Mother, who is all Wisdom, all Compassion, all Force, Beauty and Perfection. It is in this way that since the dawn of times, Hindus have venerated the feminine element under its different manifestations: *Makalaxmi, Mahakali, Mahasaraswati, Maheshwari*—and even India is feminine: "Mother India." She is the consciousness transcending all things, she is the emptiness beyond all emptiness, the smile beyond all smiles, the divine beauty beyond all earthly beauties. India has had many great female figures, whether warriors such as the Rani of Jhansi, or saints like Anandamai. And even today, behind all appearances—arranged marriages, submission to men, preference of male children in some rural areas (but girls are loved in India like nowhere in the world)—the role of women in India is essential and it can be safely said that very often, from the poorest to the richest classes, they control—even if behind the scenes—a lot of the family affairs: the education of their children (men in India are often "mama's boys"), monetary concerns, and men often turn to them for important decisions. Countries such as France or the United States, who are often preaching India on "women's rights," never had a woman as their top leader, whereas India had Indira Gandhi ruling with an iron hand for nearly twenty years; and proportionately they have less MPs than India, which is considering earmarking 33% of seats in Parliament for women, a revolution in human history! And finally this *shakti* concept is so rooted in the subcontinent that you have had women Prime Ministers, such as Benazir Bhutto or Kaleda Zia, in Islamic countries (Pakistan and Bangladesh), which are predominantly male-controlled in a much stricter way than India.

THE MYTH OF POLYTHEISM

The second great stumbling stock for western (and unfortunately many Indian) historians when they write Indian history is the myth of polytheism.

Throughout its long history, the concept of *dharma*, or the universal Law, gave such freedom to Indians that all kinds of branches and sects developed within Hinduism, which sometimes even went against each other. Indeed, Hinduism was never static, it never barred its followers from experimenting new techniques and spiritual paths : everything that helps you on the way is *dharmic*. It is this fundamental principle which allowed India to survive all over the ages with a prodigious continuity, whereas other civilizations saw their cultures and their religions systematically destroyed. Unfortunately, this enormous tolerance of Hinduism—or Induism, if you prefer—is not recognized in the world today, or even acknowledged by Indians themselves, for two reasons. The first one is the Muslim invasions and the second is European colonization. It is the immense shock between these two great monotheistic religions and Hindu polytheism, which has completely perverted our perception of India.

Yet, Hinduism—whether described as a religion or a spiritual system—is, its many ways, the most profoundly monotheist religion in the world. It has always affirmed that the Supreme can only be diverse and that he incarnates Himself in many forms—hence the countless gods and goddesses of the Hindu pantheon. Vedic sages had understood that man has to be given a multiplicity of different approaches, if you want him to fathom the Unfathomable. And truly, for the Hindus, the Divine cannot be "this" or "that", *neti, neti*; in its essence He cannot be several—or even one—and thus can never be perfectly seized by the human mind. Indeed, Hindus, who were once upon a time the best dialecticians in the world (and this is maybe why they are today the best software programmers of this planet), were able to come up with this kind of equation: (a) God is in the world; (b) the world is in God; (c) the world is God; (d) God and the world are distinct; (e) God is distinct from the world, but the world is not distinct from God; (f) it is impossible to discern if the world is distinct from God or not... Never has the unique nature of Hindu polytheism been better defined.

Hindus have also always recognized the divinity of other religions, as their concept of the *avatar* helped them to accept the reality of other prophets, masters or gurus. It is, for instance, perfectly acceptable for an ordinary Hindu to have on his wall the image of Krishna, alongside the one of Buddha, one of Christ, with a few photos of Mecca or even John Fitzgerald Kennedy! Hindus have always worshiped at non-Hindu places, such as Velankanni, the Christian place of pilgrimage of South India, or some Sufi shrine in Kashmir or Rajasthan. Not only that, but Hindus never tried to convert others to their own religion, not even by peaceful means, as the Buddhists did all over Asia; and their armies never set out to conquer other nations to impose their own culture and religion. Yet for the Muslims and later European invaders, who were both persuaded that their God was the only true one, Hinduism with its myriad of gods, represented the Infidel, the *Kafir* par excellence. Not only did they set upon, by violence, coercion, or devious means, to convert Hindus to their own "true" religion, but they also propagated in the world the image of the "Pagan" Hindus, which has survived even up to today in many ways, subtle—and not so subtle.

EUROPEAN CARTESIANISM AND HINDUISM

"Only believe what you experience on yourself," said the Buddha 2500 years ago. Indian philosophy and spiritual thought was thus always very down to earth and attempted to define scientifically and logically the different means and ways to reach the goal: "If you do this, this is what will happen; if you breathe in this way, this is what may result; if you practice this particular posture, these are the results you will gain"...

Yet the West is today wary of anything which has a Hindu flavor and is quick to label as "sects" everything that does not spring from the larger conventional family of Christianity. It is true that gurus teaching in the West can be a mixed lot, and some of them might have brought a bad name to Hinduism, but the ordinary Indian meditating every morning, or doing his *pujas*, practicing his *asanas*, chanting *bhajans*, or doing *pranayama*, does not feel he is doing anything out of the ordinary. There is no sectarianism here, no fake mysticism, no pagan obscure rites.

To understand India and Hinduism, one then has to go beyond the *clichés* of paganism and the accusations of sects that have been applied to Hindus, particularly after the coming of Christian missionaries to India who had a vested motive to show Hinduism in a bad light. It is true that Hindus adore gods made out of stone or cast in brass. But is it less rational or Cartesian to think, as the Catholics do, that Mary conceived a child while remaining a virgin, or that Christ came back from the dead and ascended physically to heaven (and not in his subtle body, which is more likely). Muslim invaders were also immensely shocked by this worshiping of images and gods and set upon destroying hundreds of thousands of temples and idols. But Alexandra David-Neel, the remarkable French explorer, writer and mystic, had remarked that the role that gods play in India is remarkable "because the images or statues are like a battery which is charged over the ages by the adoration of the devotees, who in turn can draw energy, inspiration, or grace from these statues." She goes on: "As a battery, the energy in the statue will not get discharged, as long as the faithful continue to worship it by their cult and adoration." And she concludes: "Gods are thus created by the energy given out by the faith in their existence."

At any rate, Hindus are great rationalists: they have discovered for instance that the sound *Aum*, "Amen" for the Christians, possesses very strong vibrations which take you to the deepest level and that the Creator is the Original Verb: *Shabda Brahman;* that the *ragas*, these few notes of music on which one can improve indefinitely, have also a strong inner power; or that the breath is the physical conduit to the Divine, which they have codified into *pranayama*, the Indian science of breathing. But nothing, without any doubt, is more scientific, more logical, more Cartesian, more noble and prophetic than the Vedas, the most ancient and sacred Scriptures of Hinduism, which are nearly totally ignored in the West and misunderstood in India.

CHAPTER 6

The Secret of the Vedas

A third 'wrong foundation' when writing Indian history is the interpretation of the Vedas by most western Indologists.

"One finds two theorems in modern science which have a profound spiritual echo," wrote Sri Aurobindo in 1926, regarded as India's avatar of the Modern Age. "First, that atoms are masses of swirling structures, like the solar system; and then that all the atoms are constituted of the same elements. If one considered these two theorems under their true light, they could lead science to new discoveries which are today unfathomable and in comparison of which the present realisations would look very primitive."

And Sri Aurobindo added: "Our ancient vedic rishis knew of a triple fire, which they had named agni: the ordinary fire—*jadaagni;* the electric fire—*vidyutagni*; and the solar fire—*sauraagni*. Modern science knows only these first two fires and the fact that the atom is like a solar system could lead them to the third discovery." This prophecy, of course, came to be fulfilled when the Americans exploded their first nuclear device in the Nevada desert in 1944. But how could Sri Aurobindo have guessed twenty years before this momentous event, that solar heat is the result of a nuclear fusion and that nuclear power is locked in the atoms?

Because nine thousand years ago, the Vedic rishis had experienced within themselves the different subtle properties of *agni*, the inner fire, which becomes solar, *saura agni* ,when one reaches the supra-mental levels of consciousness and of which nuclear energy is only the most material manifestation. "It is through *agni* that man can reach superior states of being and come into contact with the Gods: *agni* is the mouth of the Gods and it is through this mouth that they breathe," says the *Shatapâ-*

brâhmana. Who then were these "sages" who may have already pierced the secrets of our universe many thousands of years ago?

"I seek not science, not religion, not Theosophy, but Veda—the truth about Brahman, not only about His essentiality, but also about His manifestation, not a lamp on the way to the forest, but a light and a guide to joy and action in the world, the truth which is beyond opinion, the knowledge which all thought strives after—'yasminvijnatesarvamvijnatam' (which being known, all is known). I believe that Veda be the foundation of the Sanatana Dharma; I believe it to be the concealed divinity within Hinduism —but a veil has to be drawn aside, a curtain has to be lifted. I believe it to be knowable and discoverable. I believe the future of India and the world depends on its discovery and on its application, not to the renunciation of life, but to life in the world and among men." (*India's Rebirth*, p. 90)

Sri Aurobindo contended that Europeans have seen in the Vedas "only the rude chants of an antique and pastoral race sung in honor of the forces of nature and succeeded in imposing them on the Indian intellect." But he insisted that a time must come "when the Indian mind will shake off the darkness that has fallen upon it, cease to think or hold opinions at second and third hand and reassert its right to judge and enquire in perfect freedom into the meaning of its own scriptures." He argued that the Veda remains the foundation of Indian culture: "The Veda was the beginning of our spiritual knowledge, the Veda will remain its end. The recovery of the perfect truth of the Veda is therefore not merely a desideratum for our modern intellectual curiosity, but a practical necessity for the future of the human race. For I firmly believe that the secret concealed in the Veda, when entirely discovered, will be found to formulate perfectly that knowledge and practice of divine life to which the march of humanity, after long wanderings in the satisfaction of the intellect and senses, must inevitably return." (*India's Rebirth*, p. 94)

What is the secret of the Vedas? First, we have to discard the ridiculously early dates given by historians and bring it back to at least 7000 BC. Why did historians show such an eagerness in post-dating the Vedas and making them just a mumble-jumble of pagan superstition?

Because it would have destroyed the West's idea of its own supremacy: primitive barbarism could not possibly have risen to such high conceptions so early, particularly when the Westerners have started our era after the birth of Christ and decreed that the world began on 23rd October 4004 BC! Secondly, the Vedic seers, who had attained the ultimate truth, had clothed their oral findings in symbols and images, so that only the initiated would understand the true meaning of their aphorisms. For the more ordinary souls, "those who were not yet twice born," it meant only an outer worship which was fit for their level of spiritual evolution. The Vedic rituals have lost their profound meaning to us. Therefore, as Sri Aurobindo elucidates, when we read: "Sarama by the path of the Truth discovers the herds," the mind is stopped and baffled by an unfamiliar language. It has to be translated to us... into a planer and less figured thought: "Intuitions by the way of Truth arrive at the hidden illuminations." (*India's Rebirth,* p. 109) Lacking the clues, we only see in the Vedas a series of meaningless mouthings about the herds or the sun. Sri Aurobindo remarks that the Vedic rishis "may not have yoked the lighting to their chariots, nor weighed sun and star, nor materialized all the destructive forces of Nature to aid them in massacre and domination, but they had measured and fathomed all the heavens and earth within us, they had cast their plummet into the unconscious and the subconscient and the supraconscient; they had read the riddle of death and found the secret of immortality; they had sought for and discovered the One and known and worshipped Him in the glories of His light and purity and wisdom and power." (*India's Rebirth*, p. 116)

Ah, these are the two secrets of the Vedas, then, the reason why they have remained so obscure and lost their original meaning. Firstly, the Vedic rishis had realized that God is One, but He takes many faces in His manifestation; this is the very foundation of Hinduism. And secondly, the Vedic rishis had gone down in their minds and their bodies all the way to the roots of death, to that eternal question which haunts humanity since the beginning of times: why death? What is the purpose of living if one always has to die? Why the inevitable decay and oblivion? And there, in their own bodies, at the bottom rock of the Inconscient, they had discovered the secret of immortality, which Sri Aurobindo called later the Supramental and which he said was the next step in humanity's evolution... "Not some mysterious elixir of youth, but the point, the spring where All is One and death disappears in the face of the Supreme Knowledge and Ananda." (*India's Rebirth,* p. 95)

Is this then the work of a few uncivilized shepherds, who had colonized the poor Dravidians? No wonder the West cannot recognize the Vedas for what they are; the whole foundation of their moral domination would then collapse.

All the subsequent scriptures of Hinduism derive from the Vedas, even though some of them lost sight of the original Vedic sense. The Vedas are the foundations of Indian culture; the greatest power of the Vedic teaching, that which made it the source of all later Indian philosophies, religions, systems of yoga, lay in its application to the inner life of man. Man lives in the physical cosmos, subject to death and the falsehood of mortal existence. To rise beyond death, to become one of the immortals, he has to turn from the falsehood to the Truth; he has to turn onto the Light, to battle with and conquer the powers of darkness. This he does by communion with the Divine Powers and their aid; the way to call down these aids was the secret of the vedic mystics. "The symbols of the outer sacrifice are given for this purpose in the manner of the Mysteries all over the world an inner meaning; they represent a calling of the Gods into the human being, a connecting sacrifice, an intimate interchange, a mutual aid, a communion." (*Foundations of Indian Culture,* p. 145). Sri Aurobindo also emphasizes that the work that was done in this period became the firm bedrock of India's spirituality in later ages and from it "gush still the life-giving waters of perennial never failing inspiration."

David Frawley, born in 1950, today one of the best Vedic specialists in the West, could not agree more: "Ô Indians, your spiritual tradition, as it is encoded in the Vedas, represents the most precious treasure of the human race. Cherish it, support it, and above all share it with the entire world. For the Vedas are like a sun: in them you will find the key of all light, all life, all love and there is no individual or collective problem which cannot be solved by them." (*Arise Arjuna,* p. 221).

CHAPTER 7

The Influence of Indu India on the Western World

Once these foundations are properly understood, one can begin to see India a new, with fresh perception. For long it has been assumed that India was merely a melting pot of influences from the West— whether through trade or invasions— and that owed many of her achievements in science, philosophy and religion to external sources, whether it is by the way of the Aryan invasions for the Vedas, or via the Greek incursions, which are supposed to have influenced her architecture and philosophies. But more and more discoveries, both archaeological and linguistic, are pointing to exactly the opposite direction: In the millenniums before Christ, it is Indian civilization which went gradually westwards (we shall not speak of its march eastwards, as there is hardly any controversy about it) and influenced the religions, the sciences and the philosophies of many of the civilizations which are considered today by the West as the cradle of its culture and thought.

THE INFLUENCE OF THE HINDUS ON EGYPT, THE GREEKS AND PALESTINE

American mathematician A. Seidenberg has demonstrated that the *Sulbasutras*, the ancient Vedic mathematics, have inspired some of the mathematical sciences of the ancient world from Babylonia to Egypt and Greece. "Arithmetic equations from the *Sulbasutras* were used in the observation of the triangle by the Babylonians and the theory of contraries and of inexactitude in arithmetic methods, discovered by Hindus, inspired Pythagorean mathematics," writes Seindenberg. In astronomy too, Indus were precursors: Seventeenth century French astronomer Jean-Claude Bailly had already noticed that "the Hindu astronomic systems were much more ancient than those of the Greeks or even the Egyptians and the movement of stars which was calculated by the Hindus 4500 years ago, does not differ from those used today by even one minute." David Frawley has also demonstrated that the methods utilized in the building of Egyptian pyramids were also borrowed from the Hindus. "The funeral altars, for instance, he writes, which are also in the shape of pyramids, were known in the Vedic world under the name of *smasana-cit*."

What about philosophy? Hindu Shaivism appears to have had a tremendous influence in the Indo-Mediterranean world and reincarnated itself under different names, at different places, during Antiquity. French historian Alain Daniélou (1907-1994) noted as early as 1947 that "the Egyptian myth of Osiris seemed directly inspired from a Shivaïte story of the Puranas and that at any rate, Egyptians of those times considered that Osiris had originally come from India mounted on a bull (*nandi*), the traditional transport of Shiva." But it is mainly Greece that was most influenced by the myth of Shiva: many historians have noted that the cult of Dionysus (later known as Bacchus in the Roman world), definitely looks like an offshoot of Shaivism. Daniélou thus remarks that "the Greeks were always speaking of India as the sacred territory of Dionysus and historians working under Alexander the Great clearly mention chronicles of the Puranas as sources of the myth of Dionysus."

There is also no doubt that the impact of the Vedas and subsequent Hindu scriptures, such as the Vedanta and Upanishads, was tremendous on the different philosophical sects which flourished at different times in Greece, such as the eleatic, orphic, platonician, stoic, gnostic or neoplatonician movements. We know that the Greek Demetrios Galianos had translated the *Bhagavad-Gita* and French philosopher and historian Roger-Pol Droit writes in his classic *L'oubli de l'Inde* (*India Forgotten*) "that there is absolutely not a shadow of a doubt that the Greeks knew all about Indian philosophy." Alain Daniélou quotes Clement of Alexandria who admitted that "we the Greeks have stolen to the Barbarians their philosophy." And even William Jones, the 18th century linguist of British India, noted that "the analogies between Greek Pythagorean philosophy and the Sankhya school are very obvious." German philosopher Shroeder had also remarked in his book *Pythagoras und die Inder* that nearly all the philosophical and mathematical doctrines attributed to Pythagoras are derived from India, particularly the Sankhya school.

It also seems very clear that Hinduism played an important role in the making of Christianity, particularly the writings of the Gospel. Daniélou points out that "quite a few events surrounding the birth of Christ as they are related in the Gospels, are strangely similar to Buddhist and Krishnaite legends." And it is true that the resemblances existing between Buddhism and Christianity cannot be simple coincidences. Buddhism was flourishing in northern and north-east India during the times of Christ and there are many legends that he came to India to be enlightened (and supposedly died in Srinagar). Even if we discount these stories, there is no doubt that many Buddhist and Hindu teachers traveled to Palestine in the beginning of our era. Daniélou thus notes that the structure of the Christian church resembles that of the Buddhist Chaitya, that the rigorous asceticism of certain early Christian sects reminds one of Jaïna practices, that the veneration of relics, or the usage of rosaries are all Hindu customs." Sri Sri Ravi Shankar, the founder of the Art of Living, which is practiced in more than 140 countries, also remarks that Jesus sometimes wore an orange robe, the Hindu symbol of renunciation in the world, which was not a usual practice in Judaism. "In the same way, he continues, the worshipping of the Virgin Mary in Catholicism is probably borrowed from the Hindu cult of Devi." Bells too, which cannot be found today in synagogues, the temples of Judaism, are used in churches and we all know their importance in Buddhism and Hinduism for thousands of years. There are many other similarities between Hinduism and Christianity : incense, sacred bread (*prasadam*), the different altars around churches (which recall the manifold deities in their niches inside Hindu temples); reciting the rosary (*japamala*), the Christian Trinity (the ancient *Sanatana Dharma*: Brahma, Vishnu and Mahesh), Christian processions, the sign of the cross (*Anganyasa*), etc...

These Buddhist and Hindu influences started worrying later Christians: Saint Hippolytus is known to have called Brahmans "heretics" and later, Saint Gregory even destroyed some of the "pagan" gods of a colony of Hindus who had settled on the river Tigris.

THE SECRET LINKS BETWEEN HINDUS AND CELTS

India often exercises a fascination on French people, which is strange, as not only huge distances separate both countries, but also their cultures are utterly dissimilar. Yet, points out Guy Deleury (1922-2015), a French historian specialist on India, there is no doubt that quite a few Hindu tribes (the Gypsies being the remnants of one of them) emigrated westwards, about two millenniums before Christ, through Iran, Greece and Eastern Europe, to finally reach western Europe and the Celtic domains of Gaul and Ireland. "There was a time, which cannot be yet exactly determined with precision," writes Deleury, "when Celtic and Vedic tribes lived together and blended their customs."

And it is true that the similarities between the two cultures are striking: both Celts and ancient Indians utilized the same chariots and both described them in the same poetic terms, as the chariot to them was not only an instrument of war, but also an occult symbol of spiritual progress:

"The four directions of the earth are the four horses of the Gods
Earth and sky the two flanks of the horse;
The seasons, the reins; the intermediary space, the harness;
The year is the chariot; the cycle is the caisson of the chariot.
Indra is the warrior, the moon the charioteer"... (*Atharva Veda*)

Compare this to an old Celtic ballad:
"As the spokes of a chariot's wheel,
Everything is in the Breath:
Hymns and melodies, rituals,
The power of the priests and the force of the warrior"...

Deleury also notes that in Sanskrit the chariot of war is called *Ratha*, while the Gallic name is *Reda*, which is found in the name of a famous Gallic tribe, the *Redones*, and survives today in the name of *Rennes*, a

French town which used to be the capital of *Bretagne*, where Celtic culture flourished in the first millennium before Christ. The prefix *red* is also found in the Latin name for the horse: *paraveredus*, *palefroi* in French, *pferd* in German, or in the name of a famous Gallic chieftain who fought Cesar: Eporedorix. We also know that the name *Ann* is an ancient Shivaite name and that the Celtic legends of Saint Ann seem derived from Shivaite stories. British Professor Calvert Watkins has also shown that ancient Celtic versification, such as the one used in the Ballad of the four sons of *Cu'Shorbb*, has the same metric rhythm than Vedic poetry. "All French history books, concludes Deleury, should quote some of the Vedic chants of which we know many thousands and which bear an important part in the making of the Gallic ethos of today."

HINDU INFLUENCE ON WESTERN CIVILIZATION

Western philosophy and culture trace its sources to ancient Greece, which in turn was greatly influenced by Hinduism. Famous Indianist Jean Herbert (1897-1980) reminds us that "many many centuries before us, India had devised most of the philosophical systems which Europe experienced with later. They contained, at least in its essence, the philosophy of the Greeks, the Alexandrine mystique, the religious speculation of the Middle Ages, the rationalism of the XIXth century and even the most recent incarnations of modern pantheism." In 1782, already, French philosopher Pierre Sonnerat (1748-1814) had written: "Ancient India gave to the world its religions and philosophies: Egypt and Greece owe India their wisdom and it is known that Pythagoras went to India to study under Brahmins, who were the most enlightened of human beings."

But it is in 19th century Europe that an open admiration for ancient India's culture flourished best, particularly in Germany, where philosophers, such as Frederich Schlegel (1772-1829), said that "there is no language in the world, even Greek, which has the clarity and the philosophical precision of Sanskrit," adding "that India is not only at the origin of everything, she is superior in everything, intellectually, religiously or politically—and even the Greek heritage seems pale in comparison." The great Schopenhauer (1788-1860) agrees with him and writes in the preface of his *The World as a Will and as a Representation*: "According to me, the influence of Sanskrit literature on our time will not be lesser than what was in the XVIth century Greece's influence on Renaissance. One day, India's wisdom will flow again to Europe and will totally transform our knowledge and thought." And Nietzsche himself had read the Vedas, which he admired profoundly, could quote from the Law of Manu and thought that "Buddhism and Brahmanism are a hundred times deeper and more objective than Christianity."

France itself had in the 19th century a great India-tradition. Anquetil-Duperron (1731-1805) had translated the Upanishads in 1801, Eugene Burnouf published in 1844 an *Introduction to Indian Buddhism* and it is in Paris that was created the first Chair of Sanskrit in Europe. Schools and universities were teaching Indian philosophy and famous writers and philosophers, such as Edgar Quinet, Ernest Renan, Hippolyte Taine, or Charles Renouvier, were devoting pages and pages to India. One of the last great French Romantics, the remarkable historian Michelet (1798-1874), wrote: "From India comes to us a torrent of light, a river of Right and Reason."

THE FORGETTING OF INDIA

When Nietzsche (1844-1900) collapsed in January 1889, the India of philosophy, of the Vedas and spirituality, seemed to vanish with him from the consciousness of Europeans and the references to Indian culture gradually disappeared from all schools and universities. Since then, Europe (and the United States) practice what French philosopher and journalist Roger-Pol Droit (born in 1949) calls "helleno-centrism" (Greece-centered) education, which means that the West believes that all philosophical systems started with Greece and that there was nothing worth the name before them. In his remarkable book mentioned earlier, *L'oubli de l'Inde (The Forgetting of India)*, Droit explains the reasons for this "intellectual amnesia." Firstly, he says, the great responsible for this forgetting of India is German philosopher Hegel (1770-1831). "Hegel," he writes, "did not discover the Greeks, he *created* them and made up for them a destiny and thoughts which they did not always have." And it is true that it is Hegel who immortalized the myth that the Spirit of Europe, her philosophy and her history are eternally rooted in Greece. But Hegel had much more words for India: "As to the Indians, he wrote, their life and thoughts are solely an opium of foolish superstitions, which explain their utterly lethargic and dazed appearance"...

But the two main culprits for this forgetting of India in Europe are British colonizers and Christian missionaries. How could the English, who had come to civilize the Barbarians, admit that their very culture was derived from these very savages? And how could the missionaries, who had come to bring the True God to the Pagans, admit that their own religion was influenced by these very heathens? And it is this neo-colonialist spirit which makes Max Mueller (1823-1900), the so-called Sanskritist of the late 19th century say that "The Vedas are just a mixture of jumble-mumble," or Barthelemy de Saint Hilaire the Education Minister of the French Government of 1883, declare "that the Hindu system of thought is hideous, without any intellectual rigor and coherence and cannot be compared with those of ancient Greece or modern Europe." Thus, even today, one can hardly find a single reference to Indian philosophy in modern textbooks. "For instance, writes Roger-Pol Droit, one cannot come across a single mention, in the *Dictionary of Philosophers,* of the Buddhist philosopher Asanga, whose works are probably as important as those of Aristotle, nor his books can be found in libraries, while some letters that Nietzsche wrote to his mother when he was six years old are treated as intellectual marvels."

David Frawley considers that this breaking away between the West and the East is totally artificial and was created by Europe to prove its material and intellectual superiority. "Everything that then came from the East," he writes, "took an inferior, or pagan value." And yet, we know that the European scientific spirit found its roots in Greece, whose religion was also definitely pagan and was inspired by Hindu practices. Thus, he concludes: "If only the West knew that the philosophical and religious framework from which emerged later European science, partakes much more with eastern religions such as Hinduism and Buddhism, than with the Judeo-Christian tradition, they would look at India differently."

CHAPTER 8

The Wonder that Was India

Let us now have a fresh look at the foundations of Indian society which have been wrongly interpreted by most historians.

Most Westerners such as A.L. Basham (1914-1986), the author of the classic *The Wonder that Was India,* have often seen at best in India an exalted civilization of «religious» and artistic achievements. But India's greatness encompassed ALL aspects of life, from the highest to the most material, from the most mundane to the supremely spiritualized. As Sri Aurobindo emphasizes: "The tendency of the West is to live from below upward and from outwardly... The inner existence is thus formed and governed by external powers. India's constant aim has been, on the contrary, to find a basis of living in the higher spiritual truth and to live from the inner spirit outwards." (*India's Rebirth,* p. 109) The old Vedic seers said the same thing in a different form: "Their divine foundation was above even while they stood below. Let its rays be settled deep within us."

The foundations of Indian society were thus unique, because all the aspects of life were turned towards the spiritual. The original social system was divided in four *varnas*, or castes, which corresponded to each one's inner capacities. In turn, the life of a man was separated in four ashramas. That of the student, the householder, the recluse and the yogi. The elders taught the student that "the true aim of life is to find your soul." The teaching was always on the guru-*chela* principle, with the teacher regarded as a representative of God, earning profound respect and obedience from the pupils. Everything was taught to the students: art, literature, polity, the science of war, the development of the body— all this far away from the cities, in an environment of nature, conducive to inner growth, which was ecological, long before it became imperative and fashionable.

Indian society of that time was neither dry nor ascetic: it satisfied the urges, desires and needs of its ordinary people, particularly of the husband and wife—the beauty and comfort of Mohenjo-Daro is testimony to that fact. It taught them that perfection could be attained in all spheres of life, even in the art of physical love, where Indians excelled, as vouched so powerfully and artistically by Khajuraho and the *Kama-sutra*. And when man had satisfied his external being, when he had paid his debt to society and grown into wisdom, it was time to discover the spirit and roam the width and breadth of India, which at that period was covered by forests. In time he would become a yogi, young disciples would gather around him and he would begin imparting all the knowledge, worldly and inner, gathered in a lifetime—and the cycle would thus start again. That the great majority did not go beyond the first two stages is no matter; this is the very reason why Indian society provided the system of castes, so that each one fitted in the mold his inner development warranted.

"It is on this firm and noble basis that Indian civilisation grew to maturity and became rich and splendid and unique," writes Sri Aurobindo. It lived with a noble, ample and vigorous order and freedom; it developed a great literature, sciences, arts, crafts, industries; it rose to the highest possible ideals of knowledge and culture, of arduous greatness and heroism, of kindness, philanthropy and human sympathy and oneness. It laid the inspired basis of wonderful spiritual philosophies; it examined the secret of external nature and discovered and lived the boundless and miraculous truths of the inner being; it fathomed self and understood and possessed the world"... (*Foundations of Indian Culture*, pp.116-117) How far we are from A.L. Basham's vision of a militant Hinduism and evil Aryans, however brilliant the social and artistic civilization he describes! For not only did the Hindus (not the Indians, but the Hindus) demonstrate their greatness in all fields of life, social, artistic, spiritual, but they had also developed a wonderful political system.

THE GENIUS OF INDIAN POLITICS

Another of these great prejudices with which Indians had to battle for centuries is that whatever the spiritual, cultural, artistic, even social greatness of India, it always was disunited, except under Ashoka and some of the Mughal emperors—just a bunch of barbarian rulers, constantly fighting themselves—and that it was thanks to the Mughals and the British that India was finally politically united. This is again a grave injustice to India. The Vedic sages had devised a monarchical system, whereby the king was at the top, but could be constitutionally challenged. In fact, it even allowed for men's inclination to war, but made sure that it never went beyond a certain stage, for only professional armies fought and the majority of the population remained untouched. Indeed, at no time in ancient India were there great fratricidal wars, like those between the British and the French, or even the Protestants and the Catholics within France itself. Moreover, the system allowed for a great federalism: for instance, a long time after the Vedic fathers, the real power lay in the village panchayats. Sri Aurobindo refutes the charge (which Basham levels), that India has always shown an incompetence for any free and sound political organization and has been constantly a divided nation. «There always was a strong democratic element in pre-Muslim India, which certainly showed a certain similarity with Western parliamentary forms, but these institutions were **INDIAN**». The early Indian system was that of the clan, or tribal system, founded upon the equality of all members of the tribe. In the same way, the village community had its own assembly, the *visah*, with only the king above this democratic body. The priests, who acted as the sacrifice makers and were poets, occultists and yogis, had no other occupation in life and their positions were thus not hereditary but depended on their inner abilities. And it was the same thing with warriors, merchants, or lower class people. "Even when these classes became hereditary," remarks Sri Aurobindo, "from the king downwards to the Shudra, the predominance, say of the Brahmins, did not result in a theocracy, because the Brahmins in spite of their ever-increasing and finally predominant authority, did not and could not usurp in India the political power." (*Foundations of Indian Culture,* p. 326). The rishi had a peculiar place; he was the sage, born from any caste, who was often counsellor to the king, of whom he was also the religious preceptor.

Later, it seems that it was the Republican form of government which took over many parts of India. In some cases, these "Republics" appear to have been governed by a democratic assembly and some came out of a revolution; in other cases, they seem to have had an oligarchic senate. Throughout India, they enjoyed a solid reputation for the excellence of their civil administration and the formidable efficiency of their armies. It is worth noting that these Indian Republics existed long before the Greek ones, even the world often credits the Greeks with the creation of democracy. As is so often the case, history has been recorded through the prism of the Western world and remains highly selective indeed. One should also add that none of these Indian republics developed an aggressive colonizing spirit and that they were content to defend themselves and forge alliances amongst them.

But after the invasion of Alexander's armies, India felt for the first time the need to unify its forces. Thus, the monarchical system was raised up again; but once more, there was no despotism as happened in Europe until the French revolution: the Indian king did enjoy supreme power, but he was first the representative and guardian of Dharma, the sacred law; his power was not personal and there were safeguards against abuses so that he could be removed. Furthermore, although the king was a Hindu, Hinduism was never the state religion, and each cult enjoyed its liberties. Thus, Jews, Parsis, Jains, Buddhists, and even the early Christians (who at times abused that freedom) were able to practice their faith in peace. Which other religion in the world can claim such tolerance?

As in a human being, a nation has a soul, which is eternal; and if this soul, this idea-force, is strong enough, it will keep evolving new forms to reincarnate itself constantly. "And a people," maintains Sri Aurobindo, "who learns consciously to think always in terms of Dharma, of the eternal truth behind man, and learn to look beyond transient appearances, such as the people of India, always survives." (*Foundations of Indian Culture,* p.334)

In truth, Indians have always regarded life as a manifestation of the Self, and the guiding principle that shaped life, culture and social ideals in India has been the human quest for the inner self—everything was organized around this single goal. Thus, Indian politics, although very complex, always allowed a communal freedom for self-determination. In the last stages of the pre-Muslim period, the summit of the political structure was occupied by three governing bodies: the King in his Ministerial Council, the Metropolitan Assembly and the General Assembly of the kingdom. The members of the Ministerial Council were drawn from all castes. Indeed the whole Indian system was founded upon a close participation of all the classes; even the Shudra had his share in civic life. Thus, the Council had a fixed number of Brahmin, Kshatriya, Vaishya and Shudra representatives, with the Vaishya having a greater preponderance. And in turn, each town, each village, had its own Metropolitan Civic Assembly allowing a great amount of autonomy. Even the great Ashoka was defeated in his power tussle with his Council and he had practically to abdicate.

It is this system which allowed India to flourish in an unprecedented way, to excel perhaps as no other nation had done before her, in all fields, be it literature, architecture, sculpture, or painting and develop great civilizations, once upon the other and one upon the other, each one more sumptuous, more grandiose, more glittering than the previous one.

THE GREATEST LITERATURE?

Basham feels that "much of Sanskrit literature is dry and monotonous, or can only be appreciated after a considerable effort of the imagination" (The *Wonder that Was India,* p. 401), which shows a total misunderstanding of the greatness of the genius of that "Mother of all languages." Sri Aurobindo evidently disagrees with him: "The ancient and classical literature of the Sanskrit tongue shows both in quality and in body an abundance of excellence, in their potent originality and force and beauty, in their substance and art and structure, in grandeur and justice and charm of speech, and in the heightened width of the reach of their spirit which stands very evidently in the front rank among the world's great literatures." (*Foundations of Indian Culture*, p. 255)

Four masterpieces seem to embody India's genius in literature: the Vedas, the Upanishads, the *Ramayana,* and the *Mahabharata.* As seen earlier, the Vedas represent "a creation of an early and intuitive and symbolic mentality" (*Foundations of Indian Culture,* p. 260). It was only because the Vedic rishis were careful to clothe their spiritual experiences in symbols, so that only the initiated would grasp them, that their meaning has escaped us, particularly after they got translated in the last two centuries. "The Veda is the **WORD** discovering truth and clothing in image and symbol, the mystic significance of life," wrote Sri Aurobindo. (*India's Rebirth*, p.95)

As to the Upanishads, asserts the sage from Puducherry, "they are the supreme work of the Indian mind, that of the highest self-expression of genius, its sublime poetry, its greatest creation of thought and word... a large flood of spiritual revelation..." (*Foundations of Indian Culture*, p. 269). The Upanishads are Philosophy, Religion and Poetry blended together. They record high spiritual experiences, are a treaty of intuitive philosophy and show an extraordinary poetic rhythm. It is also a book of ecstasy: an ecstasy of luminous knowledge, of fulfilled experience, "a book to express the wonder and beauty of the rarest spiritual self-vision and the profoundest illumined truth of Self and God and the Universe ," writes Sri Aurobindo (*Foundation of Indian Culture*, p. 269). The problem is that the translations do not render the beauty of the original text, because these masterpieces have been misunderstood by foreign translators, who only strive to bring out the intellectual meaning without grasping the soul content of it and do not perceive the ecstasy of the seer "seeing" his experiences.

But without doubt, it is the *Mahabharata* and the *Ramayana*, which are dearest to all Indians, even today. Both the *Mahabharata* and the *Ramayana* are epical, in spirit as well as in purpose. The *Mahabharata* is on a vast scale, maybe unsurpassed even today, the epic of the soul and tells a story of the ethics of India of that time, its social, political and cultural life. "It is," notes Sri Aurobindo, "the expression of the mind of a nation, it is the poem of itself written by a whole nation... A vast temple unfolding slowly its immense and complex idea from chamber to chamber" (*Foundations of Indian Culture*, p. 287). More than that even, it is the **HISTORY OF DHARMA**, of *deva* against *asura*, the strife between divine and titanic forces. You find on one side a civilization founded on Dharma, and on the other, beings who are embodiment of *asuric* egoism and misuse of Dharma. It is cast in the mold of tales, legends, anecdotes, telling stories of philosophical, religious, social, spiritual values: "As in Indian architecture, there is the same power to embrace great spaces in a total view and the same tendency to fill them with an abundance of minute, effective, vivid and significant detail ." (*Foundations of Indian Culture,* p. 288)

The *Bhagavad Gita* must be the supreme work of spiritual revelation in the whole history of our human planet, for it is the most comprehensive, the most revealing, the highest in its intuitive reach. No religious book ever succeeded to say nearly everything that needs to be known on the mysteries of human life: why death, why life, why suffering? Why fight, why duty? Dharma, the supreme law, the duty to one's soul, the adherence to truth, the faithfulness to the one and only divine reality which pertains all things in matter and spirit. "Such then is the divine Teacher of the *Gita*, the eternal Avatar, the Divine who has descended into human consciousness, the Lord seated within the heart of all beings, He who guides from behind the veil all our thought and action." (Sri Aurobindo, *Essays on the* Gita, p. 17)

The *Ramayana's* inner genius does not differ from the *Mahabharata's*, except by a greater simplicity of plan, a finer glow of poetry maybe. It seems to have been written by a single hand, as there is no deviation from story to story... But it is, remarks Sri Aurobindo, "like a vastness of vision, an even more winged flight of epic in the conception and sustained richness of minute execution in the detail," (289). For Indians, the *Ramayana* embodies the highest and most cherished ideals of manhood, beauty, courage, purity, gentleness. The subject is the same as in the *Mahabharata:* the struggle between the forces of light and darkness; but the setting is more imaginative, supernatural and there is an intensification of the characters in both their goodness and evil. As in the *Mahabharata* too, we are shown the ideal man with his virtues of courage, selflessness, virtue and spiritualised mind. The *asuric* forces have a near cosmic dimension of super-human egoism and near divine violence, as the chased angels of the Bible possessed after them. "The poet makes us conscious of the immense forces that are behind our life and sets his action in a magnificent epic scenery, the great imperial city, the mountains and the ocean, the forest and wilderness, described with such largesse as to make us feel that the whole world were the scene of his poem and its subject the whole divine and titanic possibility of man, imagined in a few great or monstrous figures ." (*Foundation of Indian Culture,* p. 290)

Does India's literary genius end with the *Ramayana*? Not at all. It would take too long here to jot down all the great figures of Indian literature and this is not a literary treatise. But we may mention Kalidasa, whose poetry was imitated by all succeeding generations of poets, who tried to copy the perfect and harmoniously designed model of his poetry. The Puranas and the Tantras, "which contain in themselves," writes Sri Aurobindo, "the highest spiritual and philosophical truths, while embodying them in forms that are able to carry something of them to the popular imagination and feeling by way of legend, tale, symbols, miracles and parables." (*Foundation of Indian Culture,* p. 312). The Vaishnava poetry, which sings the cry of the soul for God, as incarnated by the love stories of Radha and Krishna, have struck forever Indian popular imagination, because they symbolize the nature in man seeking for the Divine soul through love. Valmiki also shaped the Indian imagination with his depiction of Rama and Sita, another classic example of India's idealized love couples— one that has endured through centuries of devotion, folklore and popular reverence, alongside the celebrated figures of Hanuman and Laksmana. "His diction," remarks Sri Aurobindo, "is shaped in the manner of the direct intuitive mind as earlier expressed in the Upanishads."

But Indian literature is not limited to Sanskrit or Pali. In Tamil, Tiruvalluvar wrote the highest ever gnomic poetry, perfect in its geometry, plan and force of execution. In Hindi, Tulsidas is a master of lyric intensity and the sublimity of epic imagination. In Marathi, Ramdas, poet, thinker, yogi, deals with the birth and awakening of a whole nation, with all the charm and the strength of true bhakti. In Bengal, there is Kashiram, who retold in simple manner the *Mahabharata* and the *Ramayana*, accompanied by Tulsidas who did the same thing in Hindi and who managed to combine lyric intensity and romantic flight of imagination, while retaining the original sublimity of the story. One cannot end this short retrospective without mentioning Chaitanya, Nanak, Kabir, Mirabai... All these remarkable writers have often baffled the Western mind, which could never understand the greatness of Indian literature, forgetting that in India everything was centered around the spiritual.

INDIAN ART: TURNED TOWARDS THE ESSENTIAL

"The highest business of Indian art has always been to describe something of the Self, of the soul, contrary to Western art, which either harps at the superficially beautiful or dwells at the vital-unconscious level." (Sri Aurobindo, *Foundations of Indian Culture*, p. 208)

This is indeed the great difference between Indian art and other art forms. For the Indian artist **first** visualizes in his inner being the truth of the element he wants to express and creates it in his intuitive mind, before externalizing it. Stories of how Indian sculptors of ancient times used to meditate for one year before starting on their particular work are common. Not the idea of the intellect or mental imagination, but the essence, the emotion, the spirit. Thus, for the Indian artist, material forms, colour, line and design are only physical means of expression, **NOT** his first preoccupation. So he will not attempt, as in Western art, which in its heydays continuously recreated scenes of Christ's life or that of saints, to reconstitute some scene of Buddha's life, but instead, he will endeavor to **REVEAL** the calm of Nirvana. And every accessory is an aid, a **MEANS** to do so. "For here spirit carries the form, while in western art, form carries whatever they think is spirit." (*Foundations of Indian Culture*, p. 211)

In effect, Indian art, its architecture for instance, demands an inner eye to be appreciated, otherwise its truth will not reveal itself. Great temples in India are an architectural expression of an ancient spiritual culture. Its many varied forms express the manifestation of the infinite multiplicity which fills the oneness of India. And indeed even the Muslim architecture was taken up by India's creative genius and transformed into something completely Indian.

Indian sculpture also springs from spiritual insight and it is unique by *its total absence of ego*. Very few of India's sculptural masterpieces are signed for instance; they are rather the work of a collective genius whose signature could be "INDIA." "Most ancient sculptures of India embody in visible form what the Upanishads threw out into inspired thought and the Mahabharata and the Ramayana portrayed by the word in life," observes Sri Aurobindo (*Foundations of Indian Culture*, p. 230). The Gods of Indian sculpture are cosmic beings, embodiment of some great spiritual power. And every movement, hands, eyes, posture, conveys an INNER meaning, as in the Natarajas for example. Sri Aurobindo admired particularly the Kalasanhara Shiva, about which he said: "It is supreme, not only by the majesty, power, calmly forceful controlled dignity and kinship of existence which the whole spirit and pose visibly incarnates ... but much more by the concentrated divine passion of the spiritual overcoming of time and existence which the artist has succeeded in putting into eye and brow and mouth. (*Foundations of Indian Culture*, p.233)

Indian painting has unfortunately been largely erased by time, as in the case of the Ajanta caves. It even went through an eclipse and was revived by the Mughal influence. But what remains of Indian paintings show the immensity of the work and the genius of it. The paintings that have mostly survived from ancient times are those of the Buddhist artists; but painting in India was certainly pre-Buddhist. Indeed, in ancient India, there were six "limbs," six essential elements "sadanga" to a great painting: The first is "rupabheda," distinction of forms; the second is "pramana," arrangement of lines; the third is "bhava," emotion of aesthetic feelings; the fourth is "lavanya," seeking for beauty; the fifth is "sadrsya," truth of the form; and the sixth is "varnikashanga," harmony of colors. Western art always flouts the first principle "rupabheda," the universal law of the right distinction of forms, for it constantly strays into intellectual or fantasy extravagances which belong to the intermediate world of sheer fantasia. On the other hand, in the Indian paintings, Sri Aurobindo remarks that: "The Indian artist sets out from the other end of the scale of values of experience which connect life and the spirit. The whole creative force here comes from a spiritual and psychic vision, the emphasis of the physical is secondary and always deliberately limited so as to give an overwhelmingly spiritual and psychic impression and everything is suppressed which does not serve this purpose." (*Foundations of Indian Culture*, p. 246). It is unfortunate that today most Indian painting imitates Western modern art, bare for a few exceptions. And it is hoped that Indian painters will soon come back to the essential, which is the vision of the inner eye, the transcription, not of the religious, but of the spiritual and the occult.

CHAPTER 9

The Invasion of Alexander the Great

In the grand chronicles of history, few figures are as mythologized as much as Alexander the Great (356-323 BC). Western historians have long celebrated his campaign in India as a final and glorious extension of his conquests, framing it as a successful incursion into the mysterious East. Greek texts narrate a tale of brilliance and valor: Alexander, with his disciplined phalanxes and indomitable will, triumphs over barbarian kings, extending the Hellenic light into the dark recesses of the Indian subcontinent. Yet, behind this shimmering narrative lies a different story—one marked not by victory, but by resistance, retreat, and myth-making. This episode in history, unfolding in 327 BCE, is notable for being the first recorded encounter between classical Europe and the Indian subcontinent. It is often presented as the collision of two worlds, but the collision was neither decisive nor glorious for the Greeks. It was, instead, a short-lived incursion that tested the limits of Alexander's army and his ambition.

Having conquered the Achaemenid Empire, Alexander's attention turned eastward. His dreams were no longer confined to Persia or Egypt; India, known to the Greeks as a land of exotic wealth and philosophical wisdom, beckoned as the next jewel in his imperial crown. But Alexander's understanding of India was fragmentary, pieced together from Greek geographers and Persian accounts. He imagined a disunited land of petty chieftains, seemingly ripe for conquest. What awaited him, however, was a civilization far older and more formidable than he had anticipated.

Alexander's army entered the northwestern frontier of the Indian subcontinent—what is today Pakistan—through the treacherous passes of the Hindu Kush. In the Swat Valley, near the city of Massaga, he encountered fierce resistance. The city was defended by the Aspasioi and Assakenoi, warrior tribes renowned for their martial prowess. The siege of Massaga proved far more difficult than expected. Alexander was wounded—perhaps gravely—and forced to retreat temporarily. On the fourth day, he proposed a truce. But that night, under cover of darkness, his forces launched a surprise attack, massacring the inhabitants, including women and children. The brutality of this act is glossed over in Greek sources, but it reveals a recurring pattern in Alexander's campaign: where diplomacy failed, ruthlessness prevailed.

The climax of Alexander's Indian campaign came in the spring of 326 BCE, on the banks of the Hydaspes River (modern-day Jhelum). Here he faced King Porus (or Puru), ruler of a powerful kingdom in the Punjab. Porus, unlike the fragmented hill tribes of the frontier, was an organized monarch commanding a trained army—and most significantly, war elephants. For the Macedonians, this was their first encounter with elephants in battle, and it left a lasting impression. According to Greek historians such as Arrian and Diodorus Siculus, Alexander employed a brilliant tactical maneuver. He led a select detachment 25 kilometers upstream under cover of darkness and crossed the river to flank Porus' army. As the main force of Porus confronted the diversion, Alexander struck from the side. Despite the elephants wreaking havoc on the Macedonian ranks, Greek accounts claim a decisive victory. However, not all historians agree. E. A. Wallis Budge, in *The Life and Exploits of Alexander the Great* (1896), offers a different version. He writes that during the battle, Porus' forces inflicted severe casualties on Alexander's cavalry, effectively neutralizing their mobility. Realizing that a prolonged engagement would risk annihilation, Alexander is said to have sought a truce. Remarkably, Porus, despite the heavy toll on his own troops, agreed. When asked how he wished to be treated, Porus famously replied, "Like a king." Alexander, impressed by his adversary's valor, allowed him to retain his kingdom—perhaps because he had little choice. Whether this magnanimity was genuine or merely expedient remains unclear. What is certain is that the battle did not open the gates of India to the Macedonians. It marked instead the beginning of their slow retreat.

Greek writers transformed Alexander's Indian expedition into an epic. In their narratives, it becomes a heroic journey into the unknown, a civilizing mission, even a quasi-divine venture. They likened Alexander to Dionysus and Heracles, who were believed to have reached the edge of the world. But this mythology obscures the sobering reality: Alexander's army, exhausted by years of campaigning and demoralized by the ferocity of Indian resistance, refused to advance further east. At the Beas River, only a few hundred kilometers from the heartland of the Ganges, his troops mutinied. No speech, no bribe, no promise of glory could persuade them. They wanted to go home. Alexander's withdrawal was ignoble. Although he left behind satraps (governors) and established cities, none endured. The Indian subcontinent swallowed his presence. Within a few years, all traces of Greek authority vanished from the region.

One curious artifact remains—a coin unearthed in Mir Zakah, Afghanistan. On one side, it depicts a bearded king riding an elephant and brandishing a spear—identified as Porus. On the other, Alexander is shown holding Zeus's thunderbolt and an imperial scepter, symbolizing divine power. This imagery has been interpreted by some historians as commemoration of a duel between the two kings, perhaps apocryphal, perhaps symbolic. Regardless, the fact that Alexander chose to strike a coin with Porus' image—not as a defeated enemy, but as a warrior-king—speaks volumes. It suggests not only respect but also the recognition that this battle had no true victor. In a land as ancient and complex as India, Alexander was not a conqueror, but a visitor.

The encounter between Alexander and India was brief but significant. It shattered the illusion of Western superiority that many Greek historians sought to propagate. Far from being a disordered land awaiting civilization, India proved to be a realm of proud rulers, rich cities, and formidable armies. Alexander's failure to penetrate deeper into the subcontinent laid bare the limitations of his campaign and, by extension, the limits of imperial ambition. In the centuries that followed, Western literature and theology absorbed the myth of Alexander in India, retelling it through the lens of European triumphalism. But Indian traditions remembered him differently—if at all. In their narratives, Porus was not a vanquished foe, but a symbol of resistance. The meeting of Alexander and Porus thus stands not as the beginning of European conquest, but as its pause—a moment when the tide of history momentarily turned back the spear. Meanwhile, great civilizations, one after the other, rose in India.

CHAPTER 10

The Great Civilizations

From the snows of the Himalayas to the palm-lined coasts of the South, India has been the cradle of some of the world's most enduring civilizations. Long before the emergence of modern nations, this subcontinent flourished with powerful kingdoms, radiant cities, and intricate spiritual traditions that not only shaped its own destiny but also influenced vast regions beyond. This chapter traces the grand mosaic of Indian history—from Gandhāra in the north, an artistic and intellectual crossroads, to Kashi, the eternal sacred city on the Ganges; from the imperial rise of Magadha, seedbed of empires, to the complex and debated legacy of Ashoka the Great. We then travel through the vibrant Dravidian South, discovering the maritime prowess of the Pandyas, the trading acumen of the Cheras, the architectural brilliance of the Pallavas, and the imperial ambition of the Cholas. Finally, we witness the last great Hindu bastion in the South—the Vijayanagar Empire—a dazzling kingdom of temples, poetry, and resistance. These civilizations did not merely coexist; they competed, enriched, and at times clashed with one another, leaving behind a legacy etched in stone, scripture, and collective memory. Together, they form the foundation of what we now call India.

GANDHĀRA: THE NORTHERN GATEKEEPER OF ANCIENT INDIA (1000 BCE TO 500 CE)

For centuries, the Indian subcontinent remained relatively insulated from large-scale invasions, not by geography alone, but by the strategic presence of powerful kingdoms in its northwestern frontier. Among these, none were more significant than Gandhāra, a kingdom whose location and cultural vitality made it not only a shield but a bridge—a threshold where

India met the world. Stretching across parts of present-day northern Pakistan and eastern Afghanistan, including Peshawar, the Swat Valley, Takṣaśilā (Taxila), and parts of Kashmir, Gandhāra stood at the crossroads of Central Asia, Iran, and the Indian heartland. More than a political buffer, it was a cultural conduit, absorbing and transforming influences from the West and East, long before Alexander's arrival or the Silk Road's rise.

Sri Aurobindo, in his writings on Indian history and civilization, made a prophetic observation:

> "The historic weakness of the Indian peninsula has always been until modern times its vulnerability through the North-western passes. This weakness did not exist as long as ancient India extended northward far beyond the Indus and the powerful kingdoms of Gandhara and Vahlika presented a firm bulwark against foreign invasion."

This observation captures a crucial truth. As long as India's frontier lay beyond the Indus, in the highlands of Gandhāra and Vahlika (Bactria), foreign invasions—from the Persians to the Greeks, Scythians, and later the Huns—were either reflected or absorbed before reaching the subcontinent's inner core. But as Gandhāra declined, and as the political unity of India fractured, the gates to the Indo-Gangetic plain stood dangerously exposed.

Gandhāra is first mentioned in the *Rigveda*, suggesting its early integration into the Vedic world. It was formally recognized as one of the sixteen Mahājanapadas around the 6th century BCE. Yet even earlier, it had forged a distinct identity—shaped by both Indo-Aryan and Iranian influences, owing to its proximity to Persia and the Central Asian steppes. Its capital cities—Takṣaśilā (Taxila) and Pushkalavatī—emerged as vibrant urban centers. Taxila, in particular, became a renowned center of learning, centuries before the founding of Nalanda or Vikramashila. Students from across the subcontinent and beyond came to study medicine, law, military science, astronomy, and philosophy under master teachers. It is here that Chanakya (Kautilya) (283-375 BC) is said to have trained and mentored Chandragupta Maurya, shaping the future of India's first great empire. In the 6th century BCE, Cyrus the Great and later Darius I of the Achaemenid Empire brought Gandhāra under Persian control, integrating it into the empire's eastern satrapies. The Behistun inscription of Darius lists Gandhāra (*Gadāra*) as one of the provinces paying tribute. The Persian administration introduced new models of taxation, coinage, and architecture—elements that would later be adapted by Indian politics. But Gandhāra was never merely a colony. It was a hybrid zone, absorbing and reinterpreting these influences in an Indianized framework. This ability to absorb without being overwhelmed would become its cultural hallmark.

As written above, in 327 BCE, Alexander the Great crossed the Hindu Kush and entered Gandhāra. Far from a smooth passage, he encountered fierce resistance from the Aspasioi and Assakenoi tribes in the Swat and Buner valleys. In the centuries following Alexander, Gandhāra fell under successive Indo-Greek, Indo-Scythian, and Kushan rulers. Each wave brought cultural fusion. Under the Kushans, especially Emperor Kanishka (2nd century CE), Gandhāra reached its zenith—not as a military power, but as the epicenter of Buddhist art, philosophy, and international exchange. This period saw the rise of the Gandhāra School of Art, a syncretic style that combined Greco-Roman realism with Indian spiritual themes. The earliest images of the Buddha in human form were sculpted here, portraying him with a Hellenistic toga, curly hair, and serene detachment. These were not mere cultural borrowings—they were innovations that helped spread Buddhism from India to Central Asia, China, and beyond. Gandhāra's monasteries and universities, including Taxila, became hubs for Mahayana Buddhism, which emphasized the universal compassion of the bodhisattva. Pilgrims and scholars like Faxian and Xuanzang visited Gandhāra, carrying its ideas across the Himalayas and along the Silk Road. By the 5th century CE, Gandhāra began to decline under pressure from White Hun (known as Hephthalites) invasions and the gradual erosion of Kushan authority. The rise of new kingdoms in the Indian heartland, such as the Guptas, further shifted power away from the northwest. Eventually, Gandhāra was absorbed into the emerging Islamic caliphates in later centuries, losing its Buddhist character and urban vitality. Yet its role as India's historical northern armor, as well as its spiritual and artistic legacy, never disappeared. The Bamiyan Buddhas of Afghanistan, the Ajanta caves, and even later Hindu and Jain temple iconography bear echoes of Gandhāra's synthesis.

Gandhāra stands today as one of the most underrated yet crucial players in Indian history. It was not only India's geopolitical shield, as Sri Aurobindo reminds us, but also a bridge of civilizations. It defended, absorbed, transformed, and transmitted ideas between India, Persia, Greece, and Central Asia. It resisted conquest, even as it welcomed exchange. To remember Gandhāra is to remember that India was never isolated. Its strength, in many periods, came precisely from its borderlands—where cultural frontiers met political vigilance, and where stone and spirit gave rise to enduring forms of knowledge and beauty. As modern India reclaims its past, Gandhāra deserves to be remembered not as a lost frontier, but as the first guardian of the Indian soul.

KASHI: THE ETERNAL CITY OF LIGHT

Long before the rise of Magadha or the conquest of Alexander, before even the birth of Gautama the Buddha, a city stood on the banks of the sacred Ganges—ancient, luminous, and deeply spiritual. That city was Kashi, later known as Varanasi or Benares, the oldest living city in the world. To call Kashi merely a kingdom or capital is to understate its significance. It was, and still remains, the beating heart of Indian civilization—a city of fire, of learning, of transcendence. The French Indologist Alain Daniélou, captivated by Kashi's enduring mystique, once wrote: "Kashi was a kind of Babylon, a sacred city, a centre of learning, of art and pleasures, the heart of Indian civilisation, whose origins were lost in prehistoric India." He was not alone in his reverence. Across the centuries, sages, kings, poets, and pilgrims have borne witness to Kashi's eternal flame—a city where death is believed to bring liberation, and where the sacred and the sensual have long mingled in intricate harmony. Archaeological evidence places the foundation of Kashi as early as 1200 BCE, though traditional accounts speak of it being much older—*anadi*, without beginning. Hindu cosmology holds that Kashi was founded by Shiva himself, who descended from his Himalayan abode to make the city his earthly residence. Even today, pilgrims refer to it as *Avimukta*, the "never forsaken" city of Shiva.

The earliest historical mentions of Kashi appear in the *Rigveda*, where it is referred to in hymns that describe its glory as a land of prosperity and knowledge. Later Vedic literature elevates Kashi to a major center of Brahmanical learning. By the time of the Upanishadic age (c. 800–500 BCE), Kashi had become a magnet for seekers, sages, and philosophers. It was not just a city—it was an ideal, a pilgrimage, a cosmic axis. Its ghats (steps leading to the river), its temples, and its schools of philosophy were not peripheral to Indian culture; they *defined* it.

Kashi's spiritual power lies above all in its intimate association with Lord Shiva, the god of destruction and regeneration, the archetypal yogi and patron of mystics. The city's pre-eminence as a Shaiva stronghold dates back at least to the 1st millennium BCE. Every stone in the city was believed to vibrate with the presence of the divine. At its heart stands the Kashi Vishwanath Temple, one of the twelve *jyotirlingas*—sacred pillars of light through which Shiva is said to manifest. Though destroyed and rebuilt many times, its sanctity has remained untouched. Unlike the rigid ritualism of Vedic orthodoxy, the Shaivism of Kashi was inclusive, experiential, and ecstatic—embracing renunciation as well as celebration, austerity alongside sensuality. It became the spiritual sanctuary for sadhus, *tantrikas*, yogis, and poets alike.

Historical records and literary testimonies consistently praise the refinement, beauty, and artistic vitality of Kashi. As early as the Ist millennium BCE, it was considered a kingdom of culture. It had well-planned urban layouts, ornate temples, music schools, and patronage of the fine arts. Unlike the purely political centers like Hastinapura or Taxila, Kashi cultivated a distinctly aesthetic urbanism—where architecture, sculpture, music, and philosophy coexisted. The kings of Kashi, many of whom claimed divine ancestry, ruled over a vast domain that at times extended into the Gangetic plains and even parts of the south. Though historical details are scarce, their legacy survives in the enduring cultural prestige of the city. Kashi was not an empire-builder in the conventional sense—it was a builder of civilization. Its influence is evident in the Mahajanapada period (c. 600 BCE), when it was counted among the sixteen most powerful states of northern India. Kashi's rulers engaged in both war and diplomacy, occasionally clashing with rival states such as Kosala and Magadha. Yet its true power was not military—it lay in cultural hegemony. Even its rivals sent students to study there, and rulers from distant lands sought the blessings of its priests.

One of the most transformative moments in Indian history occurred just a few kilometers outside Kashi, in Sarnath. It was here, in the Deer Park, that Gautama the Buddha delivered his first sermon, known as the *Dhammacakkappavattana Sutta*—"Turning the Wheel of Dharma." It was the birth of Buddhism as a religious tradition, and it happened in the shadow of Shiva's city. Buddha chose Sarnath, not by accident, but because it was near Kashi—then the most spiritually advanced city in the region. In doing so, he not only acknowledged its importance but symbolically placed his teachings within the Indian philosophical continuum. Later Buddhist kings like Ashoka would build stupas and monasteries in Sarnath, further enriching the spiritual landscape of Kashi. Thus, Kashi became a unique city where Hinduism, Buddhism, and later Jainism interwove, not in conflict but in dialog. It absorbed, adapted, and enriched each tradition.

Alain Daniélou's depiction of Kashi as a "city of pleasures" is not contradictory to its spiritual essence. Unlike the dualism of many other ancient civilizations, Indian culture saw no hard line between the sacred and the sensual. Kashi, with its dance schools, music halls, erotic sculpture, and public debates, embodied this holistic vision of life. It was the birthplace of classical music traditions, such as the Dhrupad and later Khayal. It housed legendary poets like Tulsidas, who composed the *Ramcharitmanas* in the vernacular, and mystics like Kabir, who challenged both orthodoxy and sectarianism with his piercing couplets. In time, Kashi became the spiritual center not just of Shaivism, but of bhakti itself.

Kashi has survived invasions, plagues, fires, and political decline. It was razed and rebuilt, desecrated and sanctified—but never abandoned.

Its eternity lies not in stone, but in continuity. It has been called "The City of Light" (*Kashi* literally means "to shine"), and many Hindus believe that to die in Kashi is to escape the cycle of birth and death—*moksha*. Even today, the flame of eternal knowledge (*jñāna*) and the sacred fire (*agni*) of cremation both burn ceaselessly in Kashi. The Manikarnika Ghat, where funeral pyres burn day and night, is not a place of sorrow but of release. Here, Shiva himself is said to whisper the *taraka mantra* into the ears of the dying, granting them final liberation. If India has a soul, it is Kashi. It predates dynasties, outlives empires, and transcends ideology. It is at once a sacred geography and a lived city, a repository of wisdom and a celebration of life. Its kings may have disappeared into the mists of time, but its legacy remains carved into the consciousness of a civilization. To understand Kashi is to understand the Indian genius for sacred continuity, where the divine resides not only in temples, but in streets, in music, in fire and water, in word and silence. And above all, in the belief that even the oldest city can always be reborn.

Narendra Modi has always shared a deep spiritual bond with Kashi, the ancient city of Lord Shiva and the eternal capital of India's soul. Long before he entering politics, as a young seeker, he spent time in Kashi—wandering along the ghats, meditating in its temples, and absorbing its timeless energy. This experience left a profound impression on him, binding him forever to the sacred city. Kashi, with its blend of tradition and resilience, became for him both a spiritual refuge and a symbol of India's civilizational strength. When Mr Modi became the Prime Minister in 2014, he chose to contest from Varanasi, reaffirming his lifelong connection with the city. Since then, he has worked tirelessly to restore Kashi's grandeur while modernizing it for the present. The transformative Kashi Vishwanath Corridor project has reconnected the temple with the ghats of the Ganga in a majestic way, opening the sacred space to millions with dignity and ease. His vision has heritage and progress—bringing better infrastructure, cleanliness, and global attention to the city. For Shri Narendra Modi, Kashi is not just a constituency. It is a sacred duty—a mission to honor India's spiritual heart while preparing it for the future.

THE RISE OF MAGADHA: FOUNDATIONS OF EMPIRE (600 BCE TO 321 BCE)

Before the emergence of the Mauryan dynasty and the towering figure of Chandragupta Maurya, there stood an older political and cultural power that shaped the early history of India: the kingdom of Magadha. Its story, stretching from around 684 BCE to 320 BCE, is one of gradual consolidation, strategic brilliance, and cultural vitality. Located in what is today southern Bihar, Magadha occupied a fertile and strategic region bounded by rivers and forested hills, and it would serve as the launching pad for the first true Indian empire. So central was Magadha to ancient Indian civilization that it finds mention in both the *Ramayana* and the *Mahabharata*, India's two great epic poems. In the *Mahabharata*, Magadha appears as a powerful kingdom with advanced urban centers, wealthy rulers, and a trained army. Jarasandha, one of its legendary kings, is portrayed as a formidable foe who had to be eliminated by Bhima, one of the five Pandava brothers. His capital, Rajagriha (later Gaya and then Pataliputra), was fortified and wealthy—suggesting that even in mythic memory, Magadha represented power and sophistication. In the *Ramayana*, too, references to Magadha indicate its prestige and influence. Though largely peripheral to Rama's personal journey, Magadha is shown as a kingdom of dharma and order, a land of temples and sages. These mentions, though literary in nature, reflect the respect and prominence Magadha held in the collective imagination of ancient India.

Magadha's dominance was no accident. Its geography was unusually favorable for state formation and expansion. Nestled between the Ganges to the north and the Vindhya mountains to the south, Magadha controlled major trade routes and had access to the rich iron ore deposits of the Chota Nagpur plateau. The rivers provided not only agricultural fertility but also military and economic mobility. Dense southern forests served as natural barriers, while its strategic location enabled it to challenge and eventually absorb rival kingdoms such as Kosala, Anga, and Kalinga. The Magadhan rulers also pioneered innovative statecraft and military organization. They developed a standing army, utilized war elephants long before they became standard in Indian warfare, and built fortifications that were considered impregnable at the time. Magadha was first ruled by the Haryanka dynasty, founded by King Bimbisara around 544 BCE. A contemporary of the Buddha, Bimbisara was a remarkable statesman who expanded the kingdom through diplomacy and military conquest. He married into several royal families of neighboring states—creating a web of alliances—and extended Magadha's boundaries to include Anga (modern-day Bengal), a vital economic region. His court at Rajagriha became a cosmopolitan center of learning, attracting scholars, ascetics and merchants.

His son Ajatashatru (reigned c. 492–460 BCE) continued his legacy, but with a more militaristic approach. He shifted the capital to Pataliputra, strategically located at the confluence of the Ganges and Son rivers, and fortified it into a mighty citadel. Pataliputra would later become the heart of the Mauryan Empire and one of the largest cities in the ancient world. After the Haryankas came the Shishunaga dynasty, followed by the brief rule of the Nandas. The Nanda dynasty, in particular, amassed great wealth and maintained a massive army said to include 200,000 infantry, 20,000 cavalry, 2,000 chariots and 3,000 war elephants. However, their rule was marked by centralization, excessive taxation, and unpopularity among the people and the nobility. By the end of the 4th century BCE, Magadha was ripe for revolution. Enter Chandragupta Maurya, a young man of modest origins, mentored and supported by the brilliant strategist Chanakya (also known as Kautilya). According to tradition, Chanakya (approx 375-283 BCE), a Brahmin scholar, had been insulted at the Nanda court and vowed to overthrow the dynasty. He recognized in Chandragupta the qualities of a future emperor and the timing could not have been more opportune. The political vacuum left in the northwest after Alexander's departure in 325 BCE, and the weakening of the Nandas, allowed Chandragupta to seize power in Pataliputra around 321 BCE, effectively ending the Nanda dynasty and founding the Mauryan Empire. This transition was more than a simple regime change. Under Chandragupta and his successors, Magadha transformed from a regional power into an empire that would, for the first time in Indian history, unify much of the subcontinent under a centralized administration. The governance model of the Mauryas—with its civil service, spies, regional governors, and codified laws—had its roots in the bureaucratic innovations of Magadha.

Magadha was also a spiritual center. It was in this region, during the 6th century BCE, that both Buddhism and Jainism emerged as reformist movements questioning the ritualism and social hierarchy of Vedic orthodoxy. Gautama Buddha spent much of his life in Magadha, delivering sermons, attracting followers, and receiving royal patronage—particularly from Bimbisara and later Ajatashatru. Similarly, Mahavira, the 24th Tirthankara of Jainism, lived and preached in the region. As such, Magadha was not just the political cradle of the Mauryan Empire; it was also the philosophical womb of India's spiritual renaissance. Magadha was the stage on which the curtain rose for India's first imperial drama. Its kings and strategists laid the political, economic, and military groundwork that Chandragupta Maurya would inherit and expand upon. By the time he ascended the throne, Magadha was already the most advanced kingdom in the subcontinent. Its roads, wealth, and institutions had turned it into a magnet for ambition—and a beacon of power. Though later overshadowed by the Mauryas and Guptas in historical memory, the Magadha Empire (684–320 BCE) was, in many ways, the real architect of India's first golden age. Without Magadha, there would have been no Maurya, no Ashoka, and perhaps no India as we know it.

ASHOKA THE GREAT: LEGEND AND REALITY (304-232 BCE)

In 274 BCE, Emperor Bindusara of the Maurya empire (297-273 BCE) fell gravely ill. His eldest son and heir, Sushima, was away on a military campaign in the northwest of the subcontinent. As soon as he heard the news, he rushed back to the capital, Pataliputra—but it was too late. His half-brother Ashoka had already seized the throne, with the help of Greek mercenaries.

Ashoka, born in Pataliputra, was the son of Bindusara and Maharani Dharma, one of his many wives. From an early age, Ashoka displayed a fierce temperament. Passionate about hunting and combat, legend has it that he once killed a lion with a spear. Fearless and ruthless, he was dispatched to suppress a rebellion in the Avanti region, of central India, quelling the uprising with remarkable brutality and earning appointment as its viceroy in 286 BCE. Later, he was recalled to assist his brother, Sushima, in putting down a revolt in Takshila. Once again, Ashoka employed extreme violence but was successful and became the region's viceroy. Upon Bindusara's death in 274 BCE, Ashoka took control of Pataliputra. According to Buddhist texts, he consolidated his rule by eliminating nearly all rivals—killing ninety-nine of his half-brothers, including Sushima, and sparing only his full brother, Tissa. He also purged the court, executing hundreds of officers loyal to his brothers. Ashoka officially ascended the Mauryan throne in 270 BCE. The early years of his reign were marked by widespread fear and violence. He was known as *Chand Ashoka*—Ashoka the Cruel.

The turning point in his story, at least according to popular legend, was the infamous Kalinga War. The kingdom of Kalinga (in modern-day Odisha) had once been under Nanda control before being conquered by Ashoka's grandfather, Chandragupta Maurya. After Ashoka's accession, Kalinga rebelled and declared independence—possibly in alliance with rival claimants to the Mauryan throne. In 262 BCE, Ashoka launched a massive campaign to bring the region back under control. The result was one of the bloodiest episodes in Indian history. By Ashoka's own account, a hundred thousand Kalingans were killed, 120,000 died from hunger or wounds, and 150,000 were taken as slaves. According to Buddhist chronicles, this horrific slaughter led to Ashoka's remorse and his conversion to Buddhism. However, this narrative is now questioned by historians. Stone edicts show that Ashoka had already embraced Buddhism two years before the war. Even Charles Allen, a well-known admirer of Ashoka, admits he had been in contact with Buddhist monks at least a decade before the Kalinga conflict.

So why did he become Buddhist? More recent research suggests dynastic politics may have played a bigger role than spiritual transformation. The Maurya dynasty, though ruling over a Vedic Hindu empire with Brahmin priests, had long harbored tensions with orthodox rituals. Chandragupta, Ashoka's grandfather, had allied with Jain monks in his later years. Bindusara, his father, leaned toward the Ajivikas, a now-extinct sect that flourished until the 14th century. Ashoka, a usurper with blood on his hands, likely faced internal resistance from Jain and Ajivika factions within the royal family. Buddhism, at the time, was a rising but still marginal faith, and politically, it served as a counterweight to the influence of both Jainism and Brahmanism. Ashoka's embrace of Buddhism may have been, in part, a strategic move to consolidate his power. The familiar image of Ashoka as a gentle and remorseful ruler—widely popularized in textbooks and public monuments—begins to unravel when other records are examined. His edicts, frequently cited as evidence of repentance, do not, in fact, convey personal sorrow. Nowhere does he ask forgiveness from the people of Kalinga. He did not free the Kalingan slaves. In fact, he continued to use inscriptions to threaten rebellious groups with harsh reprisals. These edicts may have served more as a political tool to soften his cruel image than as an expression of true transformation. Additional evidence from later Buddhist texts, such as the *Ashoka Bandara*, further complicates his legacy. According to this account, Ashoka's persecution of rival faiths continued well after his supposed conversion. It recounts how he executed 18,000 Ajivikas in Bengal in a single day—the first large-scale religious persecution in Indian history. In another incident, he reportedly had a Jain family burned alive for depicting the Buddha bowing to a Jain monk. He then promised a gold reward for every decapitated Jain head. This bloodbath ended only when his own brother, the Buddhist monk Tissa (or Vitashoka), was mistakenly killed in the chaos. Some scholars believe these stories are later Jain fabrications. Others note that such violence fits the pattern of Ashoka's reign and suggest that his cruelty continued under a new religious banner. While Ashoka did not antagonize Brahmins or Hindu rulers, he remained harsh toward sects he considered rivals to Buddhism.

Ashoka's rule also suffered in its later years. As he aged and became ill, the empire began to fragment. Rebellions flared up, revenue declined, and infighting weakened the administration. The Mauryas lost much of their western territories to the Seleucid Empire, and after Ashoka's death in 232 BCE, the Satavahanas took control of much of southern India.

Kalinga, once devastated, regained independence. This less flattering portrait—of a violent usurper who struggled to hold his empire together—stands in stark contrast to the legend of the enlightened emperor. In fact, Ashoka's veneration in India is relatively recent. Most of the glowing Buddhist texts about him come from Sri Lanka, Myanmar, and other countries that benefited from his missionary zeal but did not endure his rule. In India itself, Ashoka was mostly forgotten until the 19th century, when British scholar James Prinsep deciphered the Brahmi script on his edicts and revived his image.

Independent India later embraced this version of Ashoka. Prime Minister Jawaharlal Nehru saw in him an ideal symbol for a modern, peaceful and secular nation. He preferred Ashoka's Buddhist message to the more pragmatic, power-driven Arthashastra of Chanakya. Nehru highlighted Ashoka's edict, likening his care for his subjects to that of a wet nurse entrusted with a child, and promoted him as the prototype of a moral ruler. He even chose Ashoka's Dharma Chakra—the wheel of law—as the emblem on the Indian national flag.

Yet, history is rarely so simple. For all his brutality, Ashoka was undeniably a transformative figure. He ruled for nearly four decades and left a lasting mark on the Indian subcontinent. His patronage of Buddhism helped spread the faith across Asia. He sent his son Mahendra and daughter Sanghamitra to Sri Lanka, and missionaries to Myanmar, Thailand, and Sumatra. He convened the Third Buddhist Council in Pataliputra and helped formalize the Buddhist canon. Ironically, although Ashoka declared Buddhism the state religion, the faith eventually declined in India. While it survived and flourished abroad, it was nearly erased from its birthplace due to later invasions and shifts in royal patronage.

Some Buddhist legends claim that Ashoka became so detached from worldly affairs that he began gifting entire regions to monasteries. One story recounts that his ministers were so alarmed by his actions that they had him replaced by his grandson, Samprati. Ashoka, they say, died in obscurity, possibly in Takshila, far from the glory of Pataliputra. Whether a tyrant or visionary, Ashoka remains one of the most complex figures in

Indian history. His story, once flattened into legend, deserves to be revisited with nuance—revealing a man who was as ruthless as he was ambitious, and whose legacy was shaped as much by politics as by piety.

The Ājīvikas: The Lost Sect That Vanished into Silence

Among the many spiritual traditions that flourished in ancient India, one sect stood out for its determinism, teaching that all events and the soul's journey were preordained by fate (Niyati), leaving no role for free will or karma. This was the path of the Ājīvikas—now almost entirely forgotten, but once a powerful and controversial voice in the subcontinent's intellectual landscape. Founded in the 6th century BCE by the ascetic Makkhali Gosāla, the Ājīvikas rose alongside Jainism and Buddhism, drawing royal support and commanding public respect before eventually vanishing without a trace. Makkhali Gosāla was a contemporary of Mahāvīra, the founder of historical Jainism, and Gautama Buddha, the founder of Buddhism. Jain texts even describe Gosāla and Mahāvīra as early companions on the spiritual path, traveling together for years before parting ways due to philosophical disagreements. Gosāla then established his own sect, and the Ājīvikas emerged as an independent order of naked ascetics, with distinct doctrines and rigorous disciplines that set them apart from their rivals. At the core of Ājīvikas belief was *niyati*, the idea of absolute determinism. Unlike the Jainas, who believed in self-effort and the purification of karma through discipline, or the Buddhists, who taught that intentional actions shaped one's future, the Ājīvikas argued that everything in life was predestined. Joy and suffering, success and failure, even the final liberation of the soul—all were fixed by an impersonal cosmic force. Human effort, they claimed, had no power to alter the unfolding of fate. According to Gosāla, the soul wandered through innumerable lives like a ball of string unraveling, following a course already laid down since the beginning of time.

Their lifestyle was austere and uncompromising. Like the Digambara Jain monks, many Ājīvikas went naked, renounced all possessions, and wandered from village to village in silence. They avoided luxuries, practiced strict discipline, and inspired awe through their self-control. Their teachings found particular resonance in the Magadha empire, in the eastern Gangetic plain, where many unorthodox sects were competing for influence. It was in Magadha that the Ājīvikas gained powerful patrons. However, their fortunes changed dramatically under Ashoka. Although, as we mentioned earlier, history remembers Ashoka as a benevolent ruler who embraced nonviolence after the horrors of the Kalinga War, early Pali chronicles suggest a more complicated and darker side to his reign. One such text, the *Ashoka Bandāra*, records that Ashoka ordered the mass execution of 18,000 Ajīvikas in Bengal, all in a single day. The massacre was allegedly triggered by a blasphemous image circulated by an Ājīvikas teacher, depicting the Buddha bowing before a Jain figure. Enraged, Ashoka retaliated with unprecedented brutality.

After this persecution, the Ājīvikas went into decline. Over the following centuries, they gradually disappeared from Indian religious life. Unlike the Buddhists and Jainas, they left behind no sacred literature, no temples, and no lasting institutions. Their teachings survived only in scattered references, mostly preserved by their ideological enemies. The absence of a written canon meant their doctrines could not be systematically transmitted. By the time of the Gupta Empire, the Ājīvikas were remembered only as a strange and misguided sect, long eclipsed by the religious movements they once rivaled. And yet, their legacy deserves to be remembered. The Ājīvikas represent a vital thread in the intellectual history of ancient India—one that dared to question the optimism of karma and the moral architecture of dharma. They challenged the dominant belief that liberation must be earned through personal responsibility. Instead, they imagined a universe governed by inexorable fate, in which the soul's journey was fixed from the beginning, and no action could change its course. In doing so, they forced their contemporaries to defend the possibility of agency, transformation, and ethical life.

THE PANDYA DYNASTY (600 BCE-17TH CENTURY CE)

Among the oldest of the South Indian dynasties, the Pandya kingdom holds a unique place in the subcontinent's early history. Much of what we know about this ancient power comes from Tamil literary works such as the *Mathuraikkanci* and the *Silappatikaram*, key texts within the broader corpus of Sangam literature. These writings suggest that the earliest Pandya capital was located in Korkai, near the mouth of the Thamirabarani River, in what is today Thoothukudi. As the kingdom expanded, the capital eventually shifted inland to Koodal, known in modern times as Madurai.

The early Pandyas achieved wealth and influence primarily through maritime trade, particularly with the Greco-Roman world. Classical Western sources, including Pliny the Elder and Ptolemy, as well as the *Periplus of the Erythraean Sea*, describe ships from the Pandya coast exporting pearls, spices, ivory and conch shells, while importing goods such as wine, gold, glassware and horses. The Greek geographer Strabo even notes the presence of Pandyan envoys at the court of Augustus Caesar, attesting to their diplomatic reach.

The origin of the word "Pandya" has long intrigued historians. Some trace it to the Pandavas of the *Mahabharata*, who symbolized righteousness, in contrast to the Kauravas, associated with deception and injustice. Others propose a Dravidian root, linking it to the Tamil word *pandi*, meaning bull—a sacred animal in Hindu culture embodying both strength and intelligence. This etymology seems especially fitting when we consider the physical description of Kulasekara Pandyan I, one of the dynasty's most renowned kings, who was reputedly built like a bull.

According to *Purananuru,* a classical Tamil anthology of heroic poetry, the dynasty's founder was Nedunj Cheliyan I, whose reign began in Korkai. At that time, the region we now call Tamil Nadu was fragmented into smaller kingdoms, often at war with one another. Nedunj Cheliyan I began the work of consolidation by invading the kingdom of Kodal, slaying its ruler Akutai, and shifting the capital to Madurai, which remained the political center of the Pandyas for centuries. His son, Pudappandiyan, carried his father's legacy forward by defeating the Vaigai kingdom before launching a campaign westward to subdue Aayi, ruled by King Athiyan. In a gesture of statesmanship, the defeated rulers were appointed as military commanders, and the campaign extended further west into the Kongu region, pushing the frontiers of the Pandya realm from sea to sea. For these achievements, Nedunj Cheliyan II earned the title *Vidambalamba Ninra Pandyan*, which translates as "the sovereign of a land embraced by two oceans." As he continued to annex surrounding territories, he was also called *Pannadu Thantha Pandyan*, or "the ruler who unified many nations." One of his successors, Mudukummi Peruvaludhi, earned fame as a fierce and uncompromising warrior. Though he was ruthless on the battlefield, he remained deeply rooted in Vedic traditions and played a significant role in restoring Brahminical rituals to the royal court.

But the greatest of all Pandyan monarchs was Nedunj Cheliyan III, who expanded the kingdom to unprecedented heights. He confronted powerful enemies from northern and eastern India and triumphed, extending Pandyan control into parts of the Chola and Chera realms. A grand alliance of seven rival dynasties, including the Cheras and Cholas, rose to halt his advance, yet Nedunj Cheliyan III prevailed, further cementing his supremacy. Subsequent rulers, such as MusiriMutriya Cheliyan and Ukkirap Peruvaludi, continued this legacy, strengthening Pandyan rule and capturing key coastal cities such as Musiri, located on the Arabian Sea. These achievements transformed the kingdom into a true empire, with controlled over vast stretches of peninsular India. Nedunj Cheliyan III also established an administrative framework that would endure until the end of the dynasty. The monarch, though supreme, was advised by five major assemblies composed of ministers, Brahmins, healers, astrologers, and representatives of the populace. A secondary council, called the *Enberaayam,* consisted of eight bodies of officials. The highest dignitaries included the royal priest, chief astrologer, generals, and key ministers. The empire was divided into principalities or *kutrams,* which were subdivided into *mandalams*, and further into *nadus*—each *nadu* made up of several towns or *urs.* The individual homes within these towns were called *cheris,* a term that eventually evolved into names like Pondicherry (now Puducherry).

While the king ruled from the capital, he often delegated power to loyal family members or vassal kings who governed the outer provinces. Villages, the cornerstone of the Pandya administration, were managed by councils of elders who oversaw justice, land and local governance. Legal affairs were divided into civil and criminal categories. The former included disputes over loans, land and property, while the latter dealt with theft, treason, adultery and tax evasion. Penalties could be severe: false witnesses risked having their tongues cut off, and spies or thieves faced execution. These harsh measures ensured that crime remained rare. As commander-in-chief, the king led the army personally during major conflicts. The military was divided into four branches: elephants, infantry, cavalry, and chariots. Their arsenal included swords, spears, bows and arrows, tridents, clubs and shields. Revenue was collected through taxes on land, trade routes, customs duties, and tributes from subordinate rulers. A sixth of the agricultural yield was typically claimed by the state. These funds were used to support the army, build infrastructure such as roads and temples, develop irrigation systems, and maintain hospitals and schools. Whatever remained went toward maintaining the royal household.

Tamil society under the early Pandyas reflected a varna (caste) system similar to the north—Brahmins, Kshatriyas, Vaishyas and Shudras—but it was overlaid with numerous sub-castes. Interestingly, women enjoyed considerable freedom and access to education. This is reflected in the many female poets of the Sangam era, such as Auvaiyar (see box), Mudattamakkanniyar and Naachchellaiyaar, whose verses are admired to this day. Clothing varied by region and social status: women typically wore saris, while men donned a *lungi* tied at the waist. In the hills and forests, tribal communities fashioned garments from grass and flowers. Farmers usually wore a simple cloth around the waist, and village women often went bare-chested, covering their hips with short skirts known as *kachus*. Nobles wore more elaborate clothing, with fine silk cloths wrapped around their shoulders. Upper-class young girls often wore decorative half-saris, hand-embroidered with intricate patterns. Both men and women kept their hair long, darkening it with coconut oil.

The Pandyan diet was simple but nourishing. Rice was the staple, supplemented by millet, milk, butter, and honey. Villagers ate hunted game like deer, boar, or porcupine. The wealthy lived in well-constructed homes with brick walls, red-tiled roofs and mud floors. The poor built huts from thatch and bamboo. Floors were coated with dried cow dung, a natural antiseptic. Homes of the elite featured teak wood furniture, verandas, and murals of gods or floral motifs. Mattresses ranged from corn straw for the poor to luxurious feather-filled cushions for the rich.

In every sphere—politics, literature, trade, or urban planning—the Pandya dynasty left a legacy that shaped the destiny of South India. Theirs is a story of vision, conquest, and enduring civilization, spanning more than two millennia of history.

Auvaiyar is one of the most celebrated poetesses of Tamil literature, remembered both for her wisdom and for her simple yet profound teachings. She is believed to have lived during the Sangam age, around the 1st–2nd century CE, though tradition holds that there were actually several Auvaiyars over different periods, each contributing to Tamil poetry and moral literature. The very name "Auvaiyar" means "respected woman," reflecting the esteem she commanded in Tamil society.

According to legend, she was a saintly figure who renounced worldly life to devote herself to poetry, philosophy, and service to humanity. Though she enjoyed the patronage of Tamil kings such as the Cholas and the Cheras, she remained detached from power, choosing instead to share wisdom with children and common people. Her verses are marked by clarity, brevity, and deep moral insight. Works like *Aathichoodi* and *Kondrai Vendhan* are classics of didactic literature, teaching values such as honesty, kindness, humility and respect for elders in simple aphorisms that even young children can grasp.

Auvaiyar is also remembered for her devotional hymns to Lord Ganesha and Murugan, expressing both love and surrender. Her life and works continue to inspire Tamils across generations, making her not just a poet but a cultural icon whose wisdom remains timeless.

THE CHERA DYNASTY (3RD CENTURY BCE-10TH CENTURY CE)

Following the rise of the Pandyas, the Chera dynasty emerged as one of the earliest Tamil lineages to establish a hereditary monarchy in the vast landscape of South India. From around the 8th century CE, the Cheras ruled over large swathes of Tamil Nadu and extended their control into parts of Kerala as well. Their major cities included Pahalgat, Salem, Coimbatore, and the hill fortresses of Kollimalai.

Unlike the Cholas and the Pallavas, the Cheras did not seem to adopt a single dominant religion. Their society also appears to have operated without the rigid caste divisions that structured other parts of India at the time. The Cheras venerated their ancestors and worshiped a fierce goddess of war known as Kottavai. Rather than building temples, they placed divine images in open natural settings, often beneath trees—a tradition that still persists in Tamil Nadu today with the Aiyanar shrines, where clay horses and guardian deities stand vigil at village entrances. The Chera economy was primarily based on agriculture, but they also had an active maritime trade network. Roman texts from antiquity refer to the Cheras as capable seafarers who exported iron, cotton, silk, spices, gemstones and pearls. These goods departed from the bustling Kerala ports of Muziris, Tyndis, Bramagara and Nelcynda, and traveled westward to Rome and Greece, and eastward to Southeast Asia, including Malaysia and Indonesia. These trade links brought wealth to the Chera kingdom, and the kings collected revenue through war spoils and property taxation. Chera monarchs bore the titles *Ko* or *Kon,* both meaning "great king." Many rulers also acquired epithetical names, which were often based on their appearance, military conquests, or acts of valor. Over time, these epithets came to serve as historical markers in poetry and inscriptions. According to historian Stephen Barr, the Chera lineage was not a single, straightforward bloodline. It originated from two main dynastic branches: the Vanavaraman and the Irumporai. Intermarriages between these clans likely took place, making the Chera family tree complex and difficult to trace with absolute clarity.

The earliest recorded Chera ruler is Vanavaramban, who reigned around 430 BCE. He bestowed upon the dynasty its celestial prefix

"Vanavar," meaning "those who belong to the heavens." After his reign, the historical record refers to a sequence of nine unnamed kings—figures whose identities remain obscure but whose rule is echoed in fragments of early Tamil literature.

Later, a powerful monarch named Karuvur-Eriya-Ol-Val-Ko-Perruncheral Irumporai reigned until the close of the 1st century BCE. During this era, the Chera kingdom seems to have adopted a dual-kingship model, with a principal king overseeing the core territories and a subordinate ruler—possibly called a viceroy—administering newly acquired or distant regions. Throughout their history, the Cheras were frequently engaged in military conflict with the Pandyas and the Cholas, their two principal rivals in the Tamil south. Despite repeated hostilities, the Cheras managed to secure key victories. In 283 CE, they dealt a decisive blow to the combined forces of both the Cholas and the Pandyas, an achievement that elevated their status across southern India. They also faced incursions from other groups such as the Kandaba and the Yavana, terms often used to describe foreign or northwest Indian enemies.

However, by the end of the 2nd century CE, the flourishing maritime trade that had sustained the Chera economy began to decline, particularly the lucrative commerce with the Roman Empire. This economic downturn weakened their influence, and the Chera dynasty gradually lost ground to their more assertive neighbors. Still, the Cheras did not vanish entirely. A second wave of rulers rose to prominence in the 9th century CE, reasserting their control over parts of Kerala and Tamil Nadu. Among these later rulers, we find records of generals and military leaders such as Vanavar and Malayar, who helped consolidate Chera power during its final phase. The port city of Quilon, in southern Kerala, became a vital hub during this period, sending spices, pearls and textiles to distant markets in the Mediterranean world. The Cheras of this era maintained their diplomatic and trade relationships even as the political landscape of southern India continued to shift.

The Chera dynasty eventually disappeared from the historical stage, absorbed into the power struggles of later empires. But their legacy remains visible—in the cultural memory of Tamil Nadu and Kerala, in the old Sangam poems that preserve their names, and in the archaeological traces of a maritime civilization that once bridged East and West.

THE PALLAVA DYNASTY (2ND CENTURY BCE-9TH CENTURY CE)

The Pallavas hold a distinctive place in the history of South India. Though the exact origins of the dynasty remain uncertain, scholars agree that their political and cultural influence was profound. From their capital at the ancient and sacred city of Kanchipuram, they ruled a realm extending from northern Tamil Nadu to the southern regions of Andhra Pradesh. Some historians, notably V.A. Smith, have suggested that the Pallavas may have had mixed origins, perhaps incorporating tribal or non-Tamil elements from the north into their aristocracy. Despite these theories, what remains undisputed is the dynasty's enduring contribution to Tamil and Indian civilization.

One of the earliest known and most powerful Pallava rulers was Shivaskandavarman, who reigned in the early 4th century CE. Under his leadership, the Pallava kingdom expanded considerably, absorbing large portions of Andhra Pradesh and Karnataka. His reign marked the beginning of the Pallava ascendancy in peninsular India.

Another significant ruler emerged in the 6th century, Simhavarman, who took the throne around 575 CE. What made Simhavarman particularly noteworthy is that he was a Buddhist monarch, a rarity in southern India at the time. His reign extended into Sri Lanka and the central Indian territories, further consolidating Pallava influence. His embrace of Buddhism added a unique layer to the religious fabric of his court, which would later shift again with his successors.

Following Simhavarman came the legendary Mahendravarman I, who ruled from 600 to 630 CE. A polymath, Mahendravarman was not only a statesman but also a musician, poet and patron of the arts. Originally a follower of Jainism, he later embraced Shaivism, which deeply influenced his architectural and literary works. His most celebrated work, the *Vichitrachitram*, (see box below) remains a masterpiece of Tamil literature. He also composed a Sanskrit satirical play, *Mattavilasa Prahasana*, which offers valuable insight into the religious debates of his time. Yet Mahendravarman's greatest legacy may well lie in architecture. Under his patronage, the rock-cut temples of Mahabalipuram were begun, showcasing a unique style that blended artistic innovation with spiritual depth.

Mahendravarman's son and successor, Narasimhavarman I, also known as Mahamalla, took the throne in 630 CE and reigned until 668 CE. His reign is often regarded as the golden age of the Pallavas. A skilled warrior and an enlightened ruler, Narasimhavarman successfully repelled the Chalukya invasions, recapturing Kanchipuram and even sacking the Chalukya capital of Vatapi. His military accomplishments earned him the title Vatapikonda, meaning "conqueror of Vatapi."

It was during Narasimhavarman's reign that the famous Chinese monk Xuanzang (Hiuen Tsang) visited the Pallava kingdom in 640 CE. His travelogs provide us with a rare and vivid description of the Pallava domain. According to him, Shaivite temples and Buddhist monasteries coexisted peacefully, a testimony to the religious tolerance of the time. Agriculture remained the economic backbone of the state, yet the Pallavas were also prominent maritime traders, launching ships from the port of Mahabalipuram to distant shores in Sri Lanka and Southeast Asia. Despite these achievements, the Pallava dynasty began to experience gradual decline by the end of the 7th century. Kanchipuram was briefly occupied by the Chalukyas, and the Pallavas found themselves in continuous conflict with the rising powers of the Pandyas, who would eventually become their most formidable rivals.

One of the last significant Pallava rulers was Nandivarman II, who reigned from around 730 to 800 CE. A devout Vaishnavite, Nandivarman made substantial contributions to temple architecture in Kanchipuram, including the construction of some of the finest Vishnu temples still standing today. Despite his efforts, the dynasty's power continued to wane. By the 9th century, the Pallavas were no longer the dominant force in southern India. They gradually lost their royal status and became part of the lesser nobility in a land now controlled by other emerging powers.

Culturally, the Pallavas stand out for their deep connection to Vedic tradition, which they upheld with great reverence. More than any other

South Indian dynasty, the Pallavas closely followed orthodox Hindu practices as they were evolving in northern India at the time. Whether aligned with Shaivism or Vaishnavism, Pallava rulers upheld the *Dharmashastra* and other ancient texts as guiding principles of governance and moral conduct. This reverence for sacred tradition did not hinder intellectual or artistic creativity. On the contrary, the Pallava court became a vibrant center of literature and learning, producing distinguished works in both Sanskrit and Tamil. Their schools and universities attracted students from across India, offering instruction in both religious philosophy and secular subjects. Perhaps the most visible legacy of the Pallavas lies in their architecture, which remains among the most celebrated in Indian history. Their buildings combined elements of Buddhist, Jain, Shaivite and Vaishnavite design, resulting in a style that was both syncretic and sophisticated. The monolithic temples and intricately carved cave shrines of Mahabalipuram, now a UNESCO World Heritage site, are shining examples of their artistic vision and devotion.

Although their rule did not last as long as that of the Cholas or Pandyas, the Pallavas left behind a legacy of religious pluralism, intellectual excellence and architectural innovation. Their contribution to the spiritual and cultural heritage of South India remains profound, influencing not only their successors but also shaping the broader trajectory of Indian civilization.

Vichitrachitram by Mahendravarman I is generally dated to the early 7th century CE, during his reign (c. 600–630 CE). The play holds particular significant as it mirrors the cultural and religious debates of its era. Mahendravarman, once a follower Jain before embracing Shaivism under the influence of Saint Appar, often used his writings to critique the excesses of religious sects. In *Vichitrachitram*, he employed wit and irony to ridicule dogmatism, false asceticism, and hollow ritualism, while at the same time affirming the higher ideals of devotion and ethical living.

As a literary work, it stands out for its sharp dialogs, clever characterization, and lively humor, making it both entertaining and instructive. Along with his other play, *Mattavilasa Prahasana*, *Vichitrachitram* illustrates Mahendravarman's genius in blending satire with social commentary. It remains a window into Pallava society, showcasing how literature, politics and religion intersected in early medieval India.

THE CHOLA DYNASTY (300 BCE-1279 CE)

The Cholas stand as the longest-reigning dynasty in the history of South India. References to them appear as early as the 3rd century BCE in Ashokan edicts, and their rule ensured until the close of the 13th century. At the core of their empire lay the fertile crescent of the Kaveri River, though their influence reached far beyond this core region. The Cholas were also referred to as 'Choda' in the Sangam literature of the 2nd century BCE. Their power and reach are recorded in multiple historical texts, including the Greek *Periplus of the Erythraean Sea* and the Buddhist chronicle *Mahavamsa*, which recounts their conflicts with the kings of Sri Lanka.

Chola history is typically divided into four phases: the early Cholas mentioned in the Sangam texts; a period of relative obscurity; the rise of the Medieval Cholas beginning with Vijayalaya in the 9th century; and the final phase under rulers like Kulothunga Chola I.

The earliest known Chola king was Kantaman, a contemporary of the sage Agastya, followed by Karikala Chola and Kocengannan, who ruled from Urayur, now Tiruchirappalli. Later, the capital was moved to Kaveripattinam. Elara, another Chola ruler, conquered Sri Lanka in 235 BCE, explaining the presence of Tamil Hindus in a largely Buddhist island. The dynasty rose to unmatched prominence under rulers like Rajaraja Chola I, Rajendra Chola I, Virarajendra Chola and Kulothunga Chola I, transforming it into a dominant economic, military and cultural power across South and Southeast Asia.

Rajendra Chola I showcased this might through northern campaigns in the Gangetic plains and naval expeditions to the Maldives. He even sent an ambassador to China, a first for South India. However, the dynasty saw a decline beginning in the 3rd century CE due to the Kalabhra (rulers of some parts in Tamil Nadu, between the 3rd and the 6th Century CE) invasion, which disrupted existing political structures in Tamil Nadu. While the Cholas retained control of a small region around Urayur, alliances with the Pallavas and Pandyas enabled a revival. This resurgence was led by Vijayalaya, who recaptured Tanjore in 848 CE and expanded the empire to Andhra Pradesh.

Aditya I, his successor, defeated the Pandyas in Madurai and pushed into Karnataka, while Parantaka I reconquered Sri Lanka in 925 CE. The dynasty reached its zenith under Rajaraja Chola I and Rajendra Chola I, whose military exploits made the Chalukyas their vassals. Rajaraja Chola I was a brilliant administrator and strategist. In the year 1000 CE, he organized a comprehensive land survey of his empire and launched military campaigns that reached Orissa and Bengal. To commemorate these victories, he built the city of Gaṅgaikoṇḍa Chōḻapuram. Under Rajendra Chola I, the empire stretched from the Maldives to the Godavari and even into Malaysia and Indonesia. He conquered Pataliputra in Bihar and launched maritime expeditions that left a lasting imprint on Southeast Asia. The enduring cultural presence of the Tamil people in Malaysia today stands as one of the lasting legacies of this Chola expansion. Kulothunga Chola III formed strategic alliances, including with the Hoysalas, to suppress rivals like the Chalukyas. Despite persistent resistance from the Pandyas and military campaigns in eastern India against Kalinga, the Cholas retained their hold over Sri Lanka and re-consolidated their empire. His campaigns secured Chola dominance well into the 11th century.

Eventually, however, the dynasty began to decline. The Pandya king Sundara Pandya defeated the Cholas in 1215, triggering uprisings in Sri Lanka. Though Chola generals continued expeditions to places like Sumatra and the Philippines, their control weakened. Rajaraja III was captured by a vassal, and the Hoysala incursions added to the instability. The final blow came in 1299 when the Pandyas dethroned Rajendra, marking the end of the Chola Empire. Despite their fall, the Cholas left a deep legacy. They were great patrons of Tamil literature and prolific builders of temples, many of which still stand today. Temples were not only religious centers but also hubs of economic and social life. Like Chandragupta in the north, the Cholas established a centralized government supported by an efficient bureaucracy. Their territories included regions corresponding to modern-day Tiruchirappalli, Thanjavur, Tiruvarur, Nagapattinam and Kumbakonam. The Kaveri River played a vital role in their prosperity. Known as Ponni, or the Golden River, it was both an agricultural lifeline and an object of worship. The Cholas were skilled seafarers; ports like Kaveri Poompattinam and Nagapattinam were bustling trade hubs, where Roman ships once docked. Coins found in the Kaveri Delta testify to this vibrant exchange. Other important cities included Tanjore, Urayur and Kumbakonam.

For the first time in history, all of South India was unified under one rule. While monarchical, the Chola system allowed local autonomy through a network of vassal states and regional officers. The kingdom was divided into *mandalams, valanadus, nadus,* and *urs,* each with local assemblies responsible for tax collection and governance. The Vellalars, a dominant agricultural caste, filled many positions in the Chola administration.

Rajaraja Chola I used strategic marriages and military power to consolidate Tamil Nadu. His son Vikrama Chola solidified these conquests in 1133. Local governance structures like *ur, nadu, sabha,* and *nagaram* handled justice and taxation. Village courts dealt with petty crimes through fines or temple donations, while treason and serious offenses were punished by the king himself, often through confiscation or execution. The Chola military was highly organized, consisting of infantry, cavalry, war elephants and a formidable navy. Archers and swordsmen formed the core of the army. Elephants were prized assets, carefully trained and housed in large stables. They carried archers and spear-men into battle. Fortified cities were protected by stone and brick walls. According to the *Silappadikaram*, Tamil forts were defended with catapults and boiling liquids hurled on invaders. Weapons included swords, javelins, spear, and steel shields made from the famed wootz steel of South India. The navy was unmatched in its day. By the 12th century, it boasted over 100 ships and 10,000 sailors. Admirals often served as diplomats on missions to China and other parts of Asia. Martial arts were also encouraged, particularly **silambam**, a weapon-based fighting technique elevated to an art form by Tamil warriors. Masters of silambam were said to be capable of disarming even spear attacks with their bamboo staff.

The Chola Empire, while no longer extant, continues to shape the cultural and architectural landscape of South India. Their temples, literature and maritime ambitions laid the foundations of Tamil identity for centuries to come.

CHAPTER 11

Islam and the Muslim Invasions

WHY THE MUSLIM INVASIONS OF INDIA?

Nobody will ever be able to estimate the incredible damage done to Indian culture, civilization, human population and environment during the Muslim invasions which spanned nearly ten centuries. But it should be interesting to see why these invasions happened, for no civilization, if its inner core is strong and dynamic, can be trampled upon so mercilessly as the Arabs trampled India. What ever happened to that great Vedic culture, which gave birth to so many wonderful dynasties, which in turn devised illustrious democratic systems and whose Kshatriyas were supposed to protect the land of Bharat against barbarian invaders?

Since the beginning of human history, all civilizations have gone through the same cycle: birth-rise-peak maturity-decline-death. And so many great civilizations are no more but in the memories of our textbooks: Mesopotamia; Egypt; Rome; Great Africa; Greece... Yet, because of its extraordinary spirituality, because of the Dharma stored by its great rishis, India always had the extra impetus to renew itself, to spring forward again, when it seemed she was on the brink of collapsing. It blossomed thus for at least five millennia, more than any other civilization before or ever after. Then India started faltering and Alexander was able to invade her sacred soil and later the Arabs raped her beloved land. Why?

Buddhists believe that each nation, like the human soul, packs karma in each of its lives or cycles. Good karma or bad karma have one unique characteristic: they are like a tiny seed, bearing their fruits ages or cycles later, often giving the impression to the ignorant mind of total injustice done to innocent souls. Thus the individual who seems to suffer unfair circumstances in this life, may be paying for a bad karma done dozens of lives ago. In the same manner, a nation which appears to suffer inexplicable hardships—persecution, earthquakes, great natural catastrophes, dictatorships—may be amended for a karma accomplished centuries ago. The Tibetan people's plight seems to be a good example of this phenomenon. Here is one of the world's most harmless, peaceful, adorable and spiritually refined cultures—yet it has endured, and continues to endure, some of the worst atrocities at the hands of the Chinese communist regime. Their culture has been eradicated, hundreds of ancient and magnificent temples razed to the ground, and more than a million lives whether through direct violence, concentration camps, torture, or famine. Why? The Dalai-Lama (who just turned 90 years old in 2025), himself, one of the last great spiritual figures of this era, admits that it was because of an ancient "black karma," bad deeds. Was it feudalism? Was it not opening itself to the world for so long? Or misuse of Tantrism? Who knows and who can judge? It is reasonable to say that in truth there may be NO such thing as total injustice in this world. Everything springs from a *mathematical*, ultra-logical system, where one gets the *exact* reward one deserves, which bears NO moral connotation like in Christianity.

Thus, for India, the Muslim invasions and later the European ones, must be the result of a bad karma. But the difference with Tibet is that India's soul is so strong, so old, so vibrant, that she has managed so far to survive the terrible Muslim onslaughts and later the more devious British soul-stifling occupation.

There seemed to be two reasons for the decline of Indian civilization. The foremost is that in India Spirit failed Matter. At some point, India's yogis started withdrawing more and more in their caves, her gurus in their ashrams, her *sannyasins* in their forests. Thus slowly, a great *tamas* overtook matter, an immense negligence towards the material, an intense inertia set in, which allowed for the gradual degradation of the physical, a slackening of the down to earth values, an indifference towards the worldly, which in turn permitted successive invasions, from Alexander to the Muslim and finally the European, the rape of the land of the Vedas.

The second reason and the one which has been most commonly invoked, including by Muslim apologists—see beginning of this chapter—because it is so obvious, is the fossilization of the caste system and the gradual take-over of India by an arrogant Brahmin and Kshatriya society. What used to be a natural arrangement—a Kshatriya became a warrior to express heroic tendencies in him developed from countless births on earth—turned out to be an inherited legacy, which was not merited by chivalrous deeds. A Brahmin who used to deserve his status by his scholarship and piety, and was twice-born in the spiritual sense, just inherited the charge from his father. And the Shudras were relegated to a low status, doing the menial chores, when in their heyday, they fulfilled an indispensable role, which granted them recognition from the king himself. Thus, Hindu religion lost its immense plasticity, which allowed her to constantly renew herself—and India became ripe for invasions.

And finally, Buddhism and its creed of non-violence, however beautiful and noble, opened India's gates wide. Buddhists forgot the eternal principle of the *Gita*: "Protecting one's country from death, rape, mass slaughter, is 'dharma'; and the violence you then perform is not only absolved, karma-free, but it also elevates you."

THE MUSLIM INVASIONS OF INDIA

Let it be said right away: the massacres perpetrated by Muslims in India are unparalleled in history, bigger than the Holocaust of the Jews by the Nazis; or the massacre of the Armenians by the Turks; more extensive even than the slaughter of the South American native populations by the invading Spanish and Portuguese.

We shall quote from the French historian Alain Daniélou, as well as the Dutch scholar Koenraad Elst (born in 1959), who wrote thirty years ago a very interesting book titled *Negationism in India* (see next chapter), and finally from Sri Aurobindo, who was one of the very few amongst Indian revolutionaries who had the courage to say the truth about what was called then "the Mahomedan factor".

"From the time when Muslims started arriving, around 632 AD," remarks Alain Daniélou, "the history of India becomes a long monotonous series of murders, massacres, spoliations, destructions. It is, as usual, in the name of 'a holy war' of their faith, of their sole God, that the Barbarians have destroyed civilisations, wiped-out entire races." "Mahmud Ghazni," continues Daniélou, "was an early example of Muslim ruthlessness, burning in 1018 of the temples of Mathura, razing Kannauj to the ground and destroying the famous temple of Somnath, sacred to all Hindus. His successors were as ruthless as Ghazini: in 1030 the holy city of Benares was razed to the ground, its marvellous temples destroyed, its magnificent palaces wrecked." "Indeed, the Muslim policy 'vis à vis' India," concludes Daniélou, "seems to have been a conscious systematic destruction of everything that was beautiful, holy, refined." (*Histoire de l'Inde,* p. 222) In the words of another historian, American Will Durant (1885-1981): "The Islamic conquest of India is probably the bloodiest story in history. It is a discouraging tale, for its evident moral is that civilization is a precious good, whose delicate complex order and freedom can at any moment be overthrown by barbarians invading from without and multiplying within."

But more horror was to come, for without any doubt the bloodiest Muslim deeds in India were done from the 14th century onwards, thanks to the Mughals, who today have been nearly raised to the ranks of great art patrons and benevolent rulers, bringing to India such treasures as the art of miniature painting, *ghazals* and Sufism.

For instance, Daniélou points out that the sack of the magnificent city of Vijayanagar (see chapter below), which was like an island of civilization, chivalry and beauty, in the midst of a shattered and bleeding India, by Husain Nizam Shah, was an horror: "During nearly **FIVE** months," reminisces Daniélou, "the Muslims set themselves to the task of destroying everything, the temples, the palaces, the magnificent residences. The scenes of terror and massacre were unparalleled and mightier than the imagination can ever fathom. The victors grabbed so much richness in gold, jewels, precious furniture, camels, tents, girls, boys, slaves, weapons, armours, that there was not a single plain soldier who did not depart a rich man. And nothing remained after their departure from the most beautiful and prosperous city of that time, but smoking ruins." (*Histoire de l'Inde,* p.251)

Babur was another ferocious conqueror, indulging in unnecessary massacres, and his ultimate goal was the destruction and the enslaving of the Hindus. His successor, Sher Khan, was no better, ravaging Punjab, betraying his word to the Rajputs of Malwa, who were all massacred one by one after they had honorably surrendered. Women and children were killed by the Rajput themselves, fearing their fate if they fell in Muslims hands. As for Humayun, history has treated him well, forgetting that he too was a staunch Muslim. Under his reign, a terrible famine ravaged India, people were killed, erring miserably in their land. What happened to the beautiful land of Bharat, where once honey and wine flowed like a Himalayan delight?

Akbar was the exception in a sea of monsters, although he had his preceptor Bairam and the regent Adam Khan killed, and was responsible for the great massacre of Chittor. In his 40 years of conquests, he too must have slaughtered his fair share of Hindus. Nevertheless, he was better than the average lot, maybe because his mother was Persian and he married Hindu wives. His intelligence, his love of arts, his interest for his people, his religious liberalism, make him a unique emperor. Through his Rajput spouses, Akbar had a close contact with Hindu thought and he dreamed of a new religion that would be a synthesis of all creeds—and under him the Hindus were allowed some breathing space.

Unfortunately, his successors reverted to policies of massacre and persecution against the Hindus. His son, Jahangir, ordered the execution of Guru Arjun Singh. Jehangir was a warped personality, "he was moved by the shivering of elephants in winter," says Daniélou, "but had people he disliked whipped in front of him until they died. The story of how he had Husain Beg and Abdul Aziz, two enemies, sewn in the skins of a donkey and a cow and paraded in the city, has never been forgotten" (Daniélou, *Histoire de l'Inde,* p.269). But the worst of the Mughal emperors must be Aurangzeb.

CHAPTER 12

The Vijayanagar Kingdom (1336-1672)

While Islamic power had grown dominant in North India through successive invasions and the establishment of Sultanates, the South remained largely under the control of Hindu dynasties. However, by the early 14th century, Muslim incursions had begun to threaten the southern territories as well. In response, two noble brothers, Harihara and Bukka, were inspired and guided by the great sage Vidyaranya, the pontiff of the Sringeri Sharada Peetham, resolved to establish a strong and independent Hindu state capable of resisting these invasions. In 1336, they founded the Vijayanagar Kingdom between the rivers Krishna and Tungabhadra, with Hampi as its capital. In time, this kingdom would rise to become one of the greatest Hindu empires in Indian history.

The first king was Harihara, succeeded by his brother Bukka, who was then followed by his son, Harihara II, in 1379. Vijayanagar, based on the ancient Vedic principles of dharma, tolerance and martial strength, rose swiftly in stature and influence. The empire came to be admired for its military power, cultural richness, and devotion to the Hindu tradition. Under Krishnadevaraya (1509–1529), Vijayanagar reached its zenith. He was a remarkable king—a patron of literature and art, a temple-builder, a fair administrator, and a fearless military leader. Today, Vijayanagar's remains as Hampi stand as a UNESCO World Heritage Site, attracting visitors from around the world.

Krishnadevaraya's rule marked the golden age of the empire. He defeated the king of Orissa (now Odisha) and annexed important cities such as Vijayawada and Rajamahendri. In 1512, he captured Raichur from the Bijapur Sultanate. At its height, the Vijayanagar Empire stretched from Orissa in the east to Goa in the west, controlling vast areas of the Deccan plateau. Krishnadevaraya also cultivated strong diplomatic and commercial ties with European powers, especially the Portuguese, who left vivid accounts of the empire's magnificence.

He was himself a writer and encouraged the flowering of Telugu literature, sponsoring poets and scholars in his court. His administration was considered just and effective, and his subjects admired him for his generosity, charisma and fairness. After his death in 1529, however, the strength of the empire began to decline, and Muslim kingdoms of the Deccan saw an opportunity to strike.

In 1565, one of the most catastrophic moments in Indian history unfolded when the combined armies of the Deccan Sultanates—Ali Adil Shah of Bijapur, Hussain Nizam Shah of Ahmednagar, and Ibrahim Qutub Shah of Golconda—descended upon the mighty city of Vijayanagar. At the Battle of Talikota, the Hindu empire, which had stood as a bastion of art, knowledge, and dharma for over two centuries, suffered a brutal and unexpected defeat. What followed was not merely a conquest—it was a calculated annihilation.

The sack of Vijayanagar was not just bloody; it was apocalyptic. This was no ordinary war—but large-scale slaughter. The victorious Muslim armies, inflamed by triumph and a thirst for revenge, unleashed a wave of destruction so thorough, so vicious, it stands among the most barbaric acts in medieval history. For five long months, the once-glorious capital—home to towering *gopurams,* intricately carved temples, vast markets and universities, and teeming with scholars, dancers, priests, merchants and kings—was transformed into a field of fire, blood and ruin. Temples, which had stood as symbols of spiritual resilience, were torn down with fanatical fury. The sacred idols were shattered under the boots of zealots, their eyes gouged out, their ornaments looted, their sanctums defiled with filth and blood. Monuments that had taken decades to build were razed in hours. Flames consumed the palaces. The vast libraries were torched. Centuries of Hindu learning and culture vanished overnight. Entire neighborhoods were butchered, and cries of the dying mingled with the roar of collapsing domes and the crackle of burning wood.

The Muslim commanders had given no quarter. The massacre was systematic, deliberate and horrifying in its scale. Women of noble families were raped in public before being carted off as trophies of war. Children were impaled or thrown into rivers. Old men and sages were dragged from temples and beheaded in the streets. The Tungabhadra and Krishna rivers, it is said, ran red with blood, so thickly choked with corpses that the waters turned black. It was not conquest—it was extermination. The looting was equally monstrous. Eyewitnesses—European travelers, including Portuguese merchant Domingos Paes and chroniclers like Fernao Nunes—record that the Sultanate soldiers stripped the city down to its bones. Every home was broken into. Jewels, gold, silver, silks, ivory—all were seized. Horses, camels, palanquins, musicians, courtesans, cooks, scribes—nothing was spared. So thorough was the plunder that even the humblest soldier returned to his camp with gold, silk and slaves. The conquerors turned Vijayanagar into a ghost city, its greatness reduced to smoke and ash. The horror did not end with the sack. The very soul of South India was dealt a wound it would carry for centuries. Vijayanagar was not just a city—it was the last great fortress of Hindu civilization. It stood as a light in an era darkened by invasions and fanaticism. Its fall was more than a military defeat—it was a cultural genocide. The South had held out for two centuries against the tide of destruction that had already swept across the North—now it too had succumbed.

Alain Daniélou wrote: "The scenes of massacre and horror exceeded all that the mind can imagine. The Muslims made sure to destroy everything, from temples to palaces to magnificent residences. The rivers were choked with corpses, and the blood flowed for days." The victors looted so thoroughly that there was not a single soldier who did not return with wealth, women or slaves. When the smoke finally cleared, what had once been the most beautiful and prosperous capital of the Indian subcontinent was nothing more than scorched earth and ruins.

Vijayanagar's fall marked not only the end of an empire, but the collapse of the last grand defence of indigenous Hindu culture, architecture and religious freedom. Though a few princes of the royal line tried to rebuild what remained in parts of Tamil Nadu and Karnataka, the city itself—once home to half a million people, with temples that touched the heavens—was never inhabited again. Its ruins, remain mute witnesses to an era of unparalleled glory and unspeakable devastation. The cultural capital of the South, which had served as a bastion of Hindu art, architecture and administration, was reduced to ashes. The survivors, including the sons of Krishnadevaraya, retreated to southern parts of the empire, particularly in Tamil Nadu and Karnataka. They continued to rule from smaller courts, but the grandeur and unity of Vijayanagar was lost forever. When the last ruler, Sriranga, died in 1672, the empire came to an end.

Despite its fall, the impact of the Vijayanagar Kingdom endured. Alongside figures like Chhatrapati Shivaji Maharaj in the west, the empire had played a crucial role in preserving Hindu culture and social structures in the face of repeated invasions. The South remained a stronghold of temple architecture, Sanskrit and vernacular literature, traditional crafts, and a relatively higher status of women compared to the North, which bore the brunt of centuries of foreign rule. The legacy of Vijayanagar lives on in its monumental ruins, which continue to inspire awe. Hampi's stone chariots, towering *gopurams* and vast bazaars speak of a time when South India was not only a military power but also a vibrant center of civilization, wealth and spiritual devotion.

Chapter 13

Aurangzeb: The Hitler of India

If Vijayanagar was the worst of the collective massacre that Hindus had to endure, emperor Aurangzeb (1618-1707) was the single most cruel, intelligent and powerful emperor to rule over Hindus. He was the second son of emperor Shah Jahan, who built the Taj Mahal, and not even the favorite: his elder brother, Dara Shukoh (see next chapter), was loved and cherished by emperor Shah Jahan. Aurangzeb rose to power not through the peaceful order of succession, but through a ruthless path marked by fratricide, political cunning and unrelenting ambition. When Shah Jahan fell seriously ill in 1657, a succession crisis erupted between his sons. Dara Shukoh, the heir-apparent and favorite of Shah Jahan, was a philosopher and mystic known for his syncretic worldview. He translated the Upanishads into Persian, engaged with Hindu and Sufi thought, and was seen by many as a symbol of Mughal pluralism. Aurangzeb, by contrast, was a stern and puritanical Sunni Muslim, well-versed in Islamic law and guided by a sense of divine mission. The ensuing battle between brothers was brutal. Aurangzeb defeated Dara Shukoh in battle, paraded him through the streets in chains, and had him executed on charges of heresy. He then imprisoned his own father in the Agra Fort, where Shah Jahan spent the last eight years of his life, gazing at the Taj Mahal from a small window. Aurangzeb's other brothers, Shah Shuja and Murad, were likewise eliminated—executed or killed in captivity. By 1659, the throne was firmly his. Aurangzeb's reign, which stretched for nearly fifty years, transformed the Mughal Empire, though not in the spirit of his more illustrious predecessors like Akbar or Shah Jahan. While they had ruled with a degree of religious tolerance, artistic patronage and imperial grandeur, Aurangzeb's vision was starkly different. He saw himself as a defender of orthodox Islam, a warrior of faith whose task was not only to expand the empire but to purify it from within.

One of his first acts was to remove all court musicians and dancers. Music, which had flourished under his predecessors, was deemed un-Islamic and forbidden in the royal court. Poets and artists found no encouragement under his rule. The lavish patronage of Persian art, miniature painting and Indo-Islamic architecture came to an abrupt halt. Though he did commission a few mosques, such as the Badshahi Mosque in Lahore and the Moti Masjid in Delhi, the overall artistic vitality of the empire diminished. Aurangzeb also reversed the Mughal policy of religious accommodation. He reintroduced the *jizya,* a tax on non-Muslims that had been abolished by Akbar nearly a century earlier. All Hindu religious festivals were banned from courtly life. Temples were taxed heavily, and many were destroyed, including prominent shrines in Kashi and Mathura. While some of these actions were politically motivated—aimed at punishing rebellious Hindu rulers—the overall effect was to alienate the vast Hindu majority of the empire. This re-imposition of orthodoxy sparked resistance across the subcontinent.

In 1672, a group of peasants and artisans from Alwar—calling themselves the Satnamis—rose in rebellion. They were seen as heretics by Aurangzeb's scholars, and their defiance was met with terrible vengeance. According to the French traveler François Bernier (1620-1688) and later Indian chroniclers, Aurangzeb ordered the complete extermination of the Satnamis. Whole villages were razed, and thousands were slaughtered. Alain Daniélou, writing centuries later, called it "a massacre that emptied entire regions of human beings." Aurangzeb's religious bigotry also led to persecution of the Sikhs. Guru Tegh Bahadur, the ninth Sikh Guru, stood against the forced conversions in Kashmir and refused to embrace Islam. For this, he was arrested, tortured and executed publicly in Delhi in 1675. This act enraged the Sikhs, who from then on would militarize their movement under the leadership of Guru Gobind Singh. The Rajputs, too, who had enjoyed amicable relations with the Mughal court under Akbar and Jahangir, found themselves increasingly marginalized under Aurangzeb. The emperor's refusal to honor earlier treaties and his attempts to install his own candidates as rulers in Rajput territories led to a series of rebellions. The proud Rajput clans, notably the Sisodiyas and Rathores, fought fiercely to defend their independence and dignity. But the fiercest and most sustained resistance came from the south—from the Deccan plateau and the emerging Maratha power led by Shivaji Maharaj. Unlike Aurangzeb, Shivaji was charismatic, inclusive and deeply rooted in the land he sought to defend. While Aurangzeb saw himself as the guardian of Islamic law, Shivaji stood for a Hindu resurgence that sought to challenge Mughal dominance. After Shivaji's death, his son Shambhaji continued the struggle. In 1689, he was captured by Aurangzeb's forces along with his advisor, the poet Kavi Kalash.

What followed was an act of such cruelty that it darkened Aurangzeb's legacy irreparably. Shambhaji and Kavi Kalash were tortured for three long weeks. Their eyes were gouged, their limbs were broken and their bodies mutilated. Finally, on 11 March 1689, they were cut into pieces in public execution. The brutality shocked even some of Aurangzeb's generals. Despite his ruthlessness, Aurangzeb did succeed in expanding the Mughal Empire to its greatest geographical extent. By the end of his reign, it stretched from Kabul in the northwest to Tamil Nadu in the south. He spent over two decades campaigning in the Deccan, trying to crush the Marathas and annexing the sultanates of Bijapur and Golconda. But these conquests came at an enormous cost. The treasury, once overflowing with the spoils of war and trade, was nearly empty. The long wars had drained the empire's resources, and the over-extension of military power made it impossible to govern effectively. His policies of religious discrimination had alienated large segments of the population, and the administrative apparatus began to crack under pressure. Corruption spread. Famine and banditry became widespread in the countryside.

When Aurangzeb died in 1707 at the age of 88, he left behind an empire on the brink of collapse. In a letter to his son written shortly before his death, he confessed, "I came alone and I go as a stranger. I do not know who I am, nor what I have been doing." It was a stark admission from a man who had spent his life conquering and purifying, yet found no peace at the end.

The Mughal Empire would never recover from his reign. Within a few decades, it fragmented under the weight of its contradictions. The Marathas rose in the west, the Sikhs in the north, the British on the coast. What remained was a legacy of division and decline. Aurangzeb Alamgir, the last of the great Mughals, left behind an India wounded by religious intolerance and political decay. His life reminds us that the sword, however sharp, cannot hold an empire together when hearts and minds have turned away.

Fortunately, as we said, by then the Mughal empire was already crumbling; but the woes of Hindus were not finished. Nadir Shah, of Iran, attacked Delhi in 1739 and for one whole week his soldiers massacred everybody, ransacked everything and razed the entire countryside, so that the survivors would have nothing to eat. He went back to Iran taking with him precious furniture, works of arts, 10,000 horses, the Kohinoor diamond, the famous Peacock throne and 150 million rupees in gold, (Daniélou, p.290). After that blow, the Mughal dynasty was so enfeebled that India was ready for its next barbarians: the Europeans.

CHAPTER 14

Dara Shukoh: The Muslim Prince Who Dialogued with Other Religions

If Dara Shukoh (1615-1659), the legitimate heir to the Mughal empire, had become emperor, not only the history of India would have been different, but even the future of Islam would have had a totally more positive and peaceful outlook. Dara Shukoh remained a devout Muslim throughout his life but understood that the importance of fostering dialogue with other faiths, particularly Hinduism, the majority creed of India. Unfortunately, he was not such a great warrior as Aurangzeb, and was eventually defeated in battled. Branded a heretic for his openness to other religions, he was executed by beheading. Aurangzeb then imposed upon India a hard, rigid and violent Sunni type of Islam, which is still seen 500 years later in many Muslim countries of the world, and even espoused by educated Muslims.

History often pivots on a single moment, a single life, a single battle. The fate of India—and perhaps the evolution of Islam itself—was forever altered by the tragic downfall of Dara Shukoh, the rightful heir of Mughal Emperor Shah Jahan. If Dara had succeeded his father and ascended to the throne, the Mughal Empire—and the subcontinent as a whole—might have followed a radically different, more inclusive and more peaceful path. But fate chose otherwise. Dara was defeated by his younger brother Aurangzeb, a ruthless and devoutly orthodox Sunni, whose narrow interpretation of Islam and violent suppression of dissent cast a long shadow over India's future. Dara Shukoh was, by all accounts, a highly cultivated, humane and spiritually inclined man. He was born in 1615, into the heart of one of the most powerful empires in the world. Educated by the best scholars of the Mughal court, he was deeply immersed in Islamic theology and Sufi mysticism. Yet, unlike his brother Aurangzeb, Dara Shukoh did not view Islam as a fortress to be defended against all others. Instead, he saw it as a river, flowing in harmony with the great spiritual currents of other traditions. For Dara, the truth of Islam did not lie in dogma or conquest, but in inner realization and divine love. Dara Shukoh remained a Muslim his entire life—devoted to Allah, rooted in the *Qur'an*, and a follower of the liberal Qadiri Sufi order. But he also saw no contradiction in studying the *Bhagavad Gita*, the Upanishads, and the Vedas. In fact, he came to believe that the mystical core of Hinduism and the deepest teachings of Islam shared the same essence. In his eyes, the Upanishads were nothing less than the "hidden books" referred to in the *Qur'an,* and the rishis of ancient India were illuminated sages, much like the prophets of Semitic traditions. This led him to undertake one of the boldest intellectual projects of his time: the translation of fifty-two Upanishads from Sanskrit into Persian, a work he titled *Sirr-i-Akbar*, or *The Great Secret*. His aim was not only to understand Hindu thought, but to create a bridge between the Islamic world and the spiritual wisdom of India. He also translated the *Bhagavad Gita* and numerous other Sanskrit texts, working closely with Hindu scholars, Brahmins and yogis. Far from viewing these traditions as threats, Dara believed they offered a mirror through which Islam could better understand itself.

Dara's writings exude tolerance, compassion and a deep yearning for unity. In his treatise *Majma-ul-Bahrain* ("The Confluence of the Two Oceans"), he explored the spiritual parallels between Sufism and Vedanta, arguing that both traditions ultimately point to the same truth: the oneness of God and the divine essence present in every soul. He saw no merit in bigotry or in religious exclusivism. On the contrary, he condemned fanaticism and argued that the real enemy of religion was not the other, but ego, ignorance and violence in the name of God. But the brutal world of 17th-century Mughal politics, proved to be his undoing. When Shah Jahan fell ill in 1657, as we wrote, a fierce succession struggle broke out among his sons. Dara, as the eldest and most favored, had been named heir apparent. But his brothers, particularly Aurangzeb, resented his closeness to their father and despised his syncretic ideas. Aurangzeb, a rigid Sunni who viewed Sufism with suspicion and Hinduism with hostility, launched a military campaign to seize the throne. The two armies met in a series of battles. Dara, despite his superior position, was unprepared for the ruthlessness and military cunning of his younger brother. In 1659, he was defeated, captured and paraded through the streets of Delhi in chains. His dignified bearing, even in captivity, won him sympathy from many. But Aurangzeb would not risk having such a popular rival alive. He declared Dara an apostate for his supposed "heresies"—for his interest in Hindu philosophy, his rejection of strict Sharia, and his Sufi leanings—and ordered his execution. Dara was beheaded in the quiet of a prison courtyard. His severed head was sent to his father Shah Jahan, still imprisoned in Agra Fort, as a grotesque message.

With Dara's death, the dream of a pluralistic Mughal India died too. Aurangzeb ascended the throne and ruled for nearly 50 years. India, which had flourished under the cultural synthesis of Akbar, Jahangi, and in some measure Shah Jahan entered a period of repression and unrest. Aurangzeb's actions not only weakened the empire internally—leading to endless rebellions and bankrupting the treasury with constant wars—but they also left a deep scar on the collective memory of the subcontinent. Hindu-Muslim relations, which had evolved with complexity and occasional harmony for centuries, were now poisoned by suspicion and violence. The idea that Islam must dominate rather than coexist became institutionalized. This rigid and authoritarian interpretation of Islam, which Aurangzeb championed, still echoes in many parts of the Muslim world today—even among educated circles. The dream of a more inclusive, open-hearted Islam, rooted in love and unity, was smothered under a cloak of intolerance.

Dara Shukoh could have changed that. Had he become emperor, the Mughal Empire might have transformed into a genuine civilizational synthesis, where Hinduism and Islam enriched each other rather than clashed. India could have continued on a path of spiritual dialog, artistic brilliance and cultural coexistence. Islam, under Dara's leadership, might have offered the world a shining model of openness and tolerance. But history did not allow it. Dara's gentle soul was crushed by the brutal machinery of power, and his vision buried under the weight of orthodoxy and conquest. Yet, even today, centuries later, his legacy survives in the hearts of those who believe that India's true greatness lies not in uniformity, but in unity through diversity. Dara Shukoh remains a symbol of what could have been—and what might still be possible.

CHAPTER 15

Negationism and the Muslim Conquests

It is important to stop a moment and have a look at what Koenraad Elst has called "*negationism in India.*" In his foreword to the book of the same title, Elst explains that negationism, which means in this context "the denial of historical crimes against humanity," is not a new phenomenon. In modern history, the massacre by the Turks of 1,5 million Armenians, or that of the 6 million Jews by the Nazis, the several millions of Russians by Stalin, or again the 1 million Tibetans by the Chinese communists, are *historical* facts which have all been denied by their perpetrators.

But deny is not the exact word. They have been NEGATED in a thousand ways: gross, clever, outrageous, subtle, so that in the end, the minds of people are so confused and muddled that nobody knows anymore where the truth is.

Sometimes, it is the numbers that are negated or passed under silence: the Spanish conquest of South America has been one of the bloodiest and most ruthless episodes in history. Elst estimates that out of the population of native Continental South America of 1492, which stood at 90 million, only 32 million survived; terrible figures indeed but who talks about them today?

"But what of the conquest of India by Muslims," asks Elst?

In other parts of Asia and Europe, the conquered nations quickly opted for conversion to Islam rather than death. But in India, because of the staunch resistance of the 9000-year-old Hindu faith, the Muslim conquests were for the Hindus a pure struggle between life and death. Entire cities were burnt down and their populations massacred. Each successive campaign brought hundreds of thousands of victims and similar numbers were deported as slaves. Every new invader often literally made his hill of Hindu skulls. Thus the conquest of Afghanistan in the year 1000 was followed by the annihilation of the entire Hindu population there; indeed, the region is still called Hindu Kush, 'Hindu slaughter'. The Bahmani sultans in central India made it a rule to kill 100,000 Hindus a year. In 1399, Teimur killed 100,000 Hindus in a SINGLE DAY, and many more on other occasions. Elst quotes Professor K.S. Lal's *Growth of Muslim Population in Medieval India*, who writes that according to his calculations, the Hindu population decreased by 8O MILLION between the year 1000 and 1525. INDEED PROBABLY THE BIGGEST HOLOCAUST IN THE WHOLE WORLD HISTORY. (*Negatonismin India*, p.34)

But the "pagans" were far too numerous to kill them all; and Hinduism, too well entrenched in her people's soul, never really gave up, but quietly retreated in the hearts of the pious and was preserved by the Brahmins' amazing oral powers. Thus, realizing that they would never be able to annihilate the entire Indian population and that they could not convert all the people, the Muslims rulers, particularly under the Hanifite law, allowed the pagans to become *zimmis* (protected ones) under 20 humiliating conditions, with the heavy *jizya*, the toleration tax, collected from them.

"It is because of Hanifite law writes Elst, "that many Muslim rulers in India considered themselves exempted from the duty to continue the genocide of Hindus." The last *jihad* against the Hindus was waged by the much glorified Tipu Sultan, at the end of the 18th century. Thereafter, particularly following the crushing of the 1857 rebellion by the British, Indian Muslims fell into a state of depression and increasing backwardness, due to their mollahs' refusal of British education (whereas the elite Hindus gradually went for it) and their nostalgia for the "glorious past." It is only much later, when the British started drawing them into the political mainstream, so as to divide India, that they began regaining some predominance.

Negationism means that this whole aspect of Indian history has been totally erased, not only from history books, but also from memory, from the consciousness of Indian people. Whereas the Jews have constantly tried, since the Nazi genocide, to keep alive the remembrance of their six million martyrs, the early Indian leadership political and intellectual, made a wilful and conscious attempt to deny the genocide perpetrated by the Muslims. No one is crying for vengeance. Do the Jews of today want to retaliate upon contemporary Germany? NO. It is only a matter of making sure that history does not repeat its mistakes, as alas it is able to do today: witness the persecution of Hindus in Kashmir, whose 250,000 Pandits have fled their 5000-year-old homeland; or the 50,000 Hindus chased from Afghanistan; or the oppression of Hindus in Bangladesh and Pakistan. And most of all, to remember is to BE ABLE TO LOOK AT TODAY WITH THE WISDOM OF YESTERDAY. No collective memory should be erased for appeasing a particular community.

Yet, what has happened in India, at the hand of Hindus themselves, particularly Congress leaders and Marxist historians, is a constant denial and even a perversion of the genocide committed by Muslims in India. Hasn't the "radical humanist" M.N. Roy (1887-1954) written that "Islam has fulfilled a historic mission of equality and abolition of discrimination in India, and that for this, Islam has been welcomed in India by the lower castes. If AT ALL any violence occurred," he goes on to say, "it was a matter of justified class struggle by the progressive forces against the reactionary forces, meaning the feudal Hindu upper classes."

Want to listen to another such quote? This one deals with Mahmud Ghaznavi (971-1030), the destroyer of thousands of Hindu temples, who according to his chronicler Utbi, sang the praise of the Mathura temple complex, sacred above all to all Hindus... and promptly proceeded to raze it to the ground: "Building interested Mahmud and he was much impressed by the city of Mathura, where there are today a thousand edifices as firm as the faith of the faithful. Mahmud was not a religious man. He was a Mahomedan, but that was just by the way. He was in the first place a soldier and a brilliant soldier"... Amazing eulogy indeed of the man who was proud of desecrating hundreds of temples and made it a duty to terrorize and humiliate pagans. And guess from whom is that quote? From Jawaharlal Nehru himself, the first Prime Minister of India and one of the architects of independence!

M.N. Roy, and Nehru in a lesser degree, represented the foremost current of negationism in India, which is Marxist inspired. For strangely, it was the Russian communists who decided to cultivate the Arabs after the First World War, in the hope that they constituted a fertile ground for future indoctrination. One should also never forget that Communism has affected whole generations of ardent youth, who saw in Marxism a new ideology in a world corrupted by capitalism and class exploitation. Nothing wrong in that; but as far as indoctrination goes, the youth of the West, particularly of the early '60s and '70s, and today for the Palestinian cause, were all groomed in sympathizing with the good Arabs and the bad Jews. And similarly in India, two or three young generations since the early '20s were tutored on negating Muslim genocide on the Hindus. In *Communalism and the Writing of Indian history,* (1931), (1939) and (1928-2014) and Bipan Chandra, once professors at the JNU in New Delhi, the Mecca of secularism and negationism in India, denied the Muslim genocide by replacing it instead with a conflict of classes. The redoubtable Thapar in her *Penguin History of India,* co-authored with Percival Spear, writes: "Aurangzeb's supposed intolerance is little more than a hostile legend based on isolated acts such as the erection of a mosque on a temple site in Benares." How can one be so dishonest, or so blind? But it shows how negationism is perpetuated in India.

What are the facts? Aurangzeb did not just build an isolated mosque on a destroyed temple, he ordered ALL temples destroyed, among them the Kashi Vishwanath, one of the most sacred places of Hinduism, and had mosques built on a number of cleared temple sites. All other Hindu sacred places within his reach equally suffered destruction, with mosques built on them. A few examples: Krishna's birth temple in Mathura, the rebuilt Somnath temple on the coast of Gujarat, the Vishnu temple replaced with the Alamgir mosque now overlooking Benares and the Treta-ka-Thakur temple in Ayodhya. (*Negationismin India*, p 60). The number of temples destroyed by Aurangzeb is counted in 4, if not 5 figures; according to his own official court chronicles: "Aurangzeb ordered all provincial governors to destroy all schools and temples of the Pagans and to make a complete end to all pagan teachings and practices." The chronicle sums up the destruction like this: "Hasan Ali Khan came and said that 172 temples in the area had been destroyed... His majesty went to Chittor and 63 temples were destroyed. Abu Tarab, appointed to destroy the idol-temples of Amber, reported that 66 temples had been razed to the ground..." Aurangzeb did not stop at destroying temples, their users were also wiped out; even his own brother, Dara Shukoh, was executed for taking an interest in Hindu religion and the Sikh Guru Tegh Bahadur was beheaded because he objected to Aurangzeb's forced conversions. As we can see, Thapar, Spear or Audrey Truschke's (see box) today, statements of a benevolent Aurangzeb are a flagrant attempt at negationism. Even the respectable *Encyclopaedia Britannica* in its entry on India, does not mention in its chapter on the Sultanate period any persecutions of Hindus by Muslims, except "that Firuz Shah Tughlaq made largely unsuccessful attempts at converting his Hindu subjects and sometimes persecuted them."

The British, for their own selfish purpose, were of course greatly responsible for whitewashing the Muslims, whom they needed to counterbalance the influence of the Hindus and the majority – Hindu Congress. It is sad that Jawaharlal Nehru and the Congress perpetuated that brand of negationism. But that is another story.

The happiest in this matter must be the Muslims themselves. What fools these Hindus are, they must be telling themselves: we killed them by the millions, we wrested a whole nation out of them, we engineered riots against them, and they still defend us!

But don't the Hindus know that many orthodox Indian Muslims still cling to the Deoband school, which says that India was once "Dar-ul-Islam," the house of Islam, and should return to that status. (1888-1958), several times Congress President, and Education Minister in free India, was a spokesman for this school. The Aligarh school on the contrary, led by (1887-1938), propounded the creation of Pakistan. What particularly interests us in the Aligarh school is the attempt by Muslim historians, such as Mohammad Habib (1895-1971), to rewrite the chapter of Muslim invasions in India. In 1920, Habib started writing his magnum opus, which he based on four theories: (1) that the records (written by the

Muslims themselves) of slaughters of Hindus, the enslaving of their women and children and razing of temples were "mere exaggerations by court poets and zealous chroniclers to please their rulers;" (2) that they were indeed atrocities, but mainly committed by Turks, the savage riders from the Steppe; (3) that the destruction of the temples took place because Hindus stored their gold and jewels inside them and therefore Muslim armies plundered them; (4) that the conversion of millions of Hindus to Islam was not forced, "but what happened was there was a shift of opinion in the population, who on its own free will chose the Shariat against the Hindu law (smriti), as they were all oppressed by the bad Brahmins"...! (*Negationism in India,* p.42). In the 21st century, we have Audrey Truschke, who took on defending Aurangzeb and belittling Hindus (see box).

Audrey Truschke and the Denial of Aurangzeb's Cruelty

In recent years, american historian Audrey Truschke has sparked controversy with her attempt to reframe the legacy of Aurangzeb. In her writings, she portrays him not as a bigot or tyrant, but as a misunderstood ruler whose actions were driven more by politics than religion. Truschke argues that many claims about Aurangzeb's brutality stem from colonial-era narratives and Hindu nationalist reinterpretations. However, this view has been strongly challenged by many scholars and historians who point to overwhelming historical evidence of Aurangzeb's intolerance and oppression. His reign, as extensively mentioned above, was marked by religious persecution, particularly against Hindus, Sikhs, and even rival Muslims. Aurangzeb's cruelty was not limited to policy: the horrific torture and execution of Sambhaji, son of Chhatrapati Shivaji Maharaj (see previous chapter), is another example. These were not isolated acts, but part of a pattern of repression aimed at crushing dissent and imposing a rigid Sunni orthodoxy across India. Despite such facts—drawn from Mughal court records, Persian chroniclers, and foreign observers—Truschke's reinterpretation downplays these atrocities. Critics argue that she selectively quotes sources while ignoring the broader context of Aurangzeb's actions. By minimizing his crimes, they say, she engages in a form of historical negationism that disregards the suffering of millions.

The deeper concern is not simply academic. How we remember figures like Aurangzeb shapes how we understand India's past and its religious diversity. While historians should always question established narratives, revisionism must be grounded in honesty, balance, and respect for truth. To portray Aurangzeb as merely pragmatic is to erase the pain inflicted during his rule and to risk normalizing intolerance in the name of scholarship.

Unfortunately for Habib or Audrey Truschke, the Muslim invaders did record with glee their genocide on Hindus, because they felt all along that they were doing their duty; that killing, plundering, enslaving and razing temples was the work of God, Mohammed. Indeed, whether it was Mahmud of Ghazni (997-1030) no mere barbarian but a Turk, who patronized art and literature, and yet would recite a verse of the *Qu'ran* every night after razing temples and killing his quota of unbelievers—or Firuz Shah Tughlak (1351-1388), who openly confirmed that the destruction of Pagan temples was an act of piety and wrote: "On the day of a Hindu festival, I went there myself, ordered the executions of all the leaders AND PRACTITIONERS of his abomination; I destroyed their idols, temples and built mosques in their places." Finally, as Elst points out, "Muslim fanatics were merely faithful executors of Quranic injunctions. It is not the Muslims who are guilty but Islam." (*Negationism in India*, p. 44)

It is not only Indian historians who are negationists, but also western historians and India-specialists. We know that the first historians of Indian—the Britishers—twisted India's history to suit their theory that they had come to civilize a race which was not only inferior to them, but also was supposed to have been heavily influenced in its philosophies or arts by European invaders—read the Aryans or Alexander the Great. But what is less known is that today many western historians not only still cling to these old outdated theories, but also actually more or less willfully mislead the general European public, who is generally totally ignorant and takes these "knowledgeable" comments about India as the absolute truth. One example is France, which has a long tradition of Indianists, who devote their time and life to the study of India. The main school of historical research in France is called the National Center of Social Research (CNRS), which has a very important South Asia section, called Centre de Recherches Internationales (CERI), which has Christophe Jaffrelot as its director (see box). Many of these India-specialists, such as Jaffrelot, are not only Left-leaning, that is they are very close to the ideas of the JNU historians, with whom they are often in constant contact, but are also specialists of the Mughal period of India history, which is to say that they are sympathetic to Islam's point of view on India, while they often consider Hindus as fanatics...

Take for instance Christophe Jaffrelot's book (born in 1964) *L'Inde de Modi*, which is often seen as very biased because it frames Narendra Modi's India through a rigidly negative lens. The title itself labels the government as "ethnic democracy," a loaded term that suggests India is no longer a pluralistic nation. Throughout the book, Jaffrelot uses emotionally charged language and moral judgment rather than balanced political analysis. He selectively cites sources that confirm his viewpoint while ignoring evidence that might complicate his narrative—such as Modi's popularity among women, lower castes and rural voters. The book also simplifies India's complex society into a binary of secular liberals versus authoritarian Hindu nationalists. It offers little reflection on whether Western political frameworks are adequate for understanding India's civilizational uniqueness. Jaffrelot rarely engages seriously with Hindu thought or the reasons for the BJP's appeal. As a result, *L'Inde de Modi* reads more like a political indictment than an objective study, reinforcing pre-existing biases rather than offering new insight.

Or take *Histoire de l'Inde Moderne* (first published in 1994), by several authors, all French Indologists from the CNRS, do not only run down Hindus, they also glorify Muslims, particularly the Mughals. Babur, for instance, this monster who killed hundreds of thousands of Hindus and razed thousands of temples, becomes at their hands a gentle hero: " Babur did not like India and preferred to isolate himself in the exquisite gardens he had devised, with their geometrical design, their crossed canals, which evoked to him the rivers of paradise." Oh, God what a sensitive poet! And to make it sound even more glorious, the author adds: "There he translated a manual of Koranic law and a Sufi treaty of morals." Oh, what a saint and lover of humanity... Aurangzeb, the cruelest of the Mughal emperors, has also the full sympathies of the authors: "Aurangzeb seems to have concentrated on himself the hatred of militant Hindus, who attribute to him systematic destruction of temples and massive conversion drives. But this Manichean impression has to be seriously countered..." (p. 126) Unfortunately for the authors, as we have seen earlier, Aurangzeb was not only proud of what he was doing to the Hindus, but he had his scribes note each deed down for posterity... Later, the same authors published *L'Inde Contemporaine,* with the same prejudices and bias against Hindus and their political parties.

These French Indianists have also a tradition of speaking against the BJP, which they have always labeled as "fundamentalist" and dangerous for the "secular" fabric of India, although the BJP has been in power for nearly two decades and nothing dramatic has happened to the secular fabric of India. The problem is that these Indianists not only write lengthy and pompous articles in France's main newspapers, such as Left-leaning *Le Monde,* explaining to the ignorant reader why is India on the point of exploding, because of fanatic Hindus, or how Muslims in India, who had a descendants of the Arabs who raped and looted the sub-continent for centuries, are today "persecuted". But unfortunately they also advise the French government, who like its citizens, is often shamefully ignorant and uninterested by India. This is why the French government, which considers Corsica, an island, though it once belonged to Italy, as an integral part of France, is unable to recognize that Kashmir (see chapter below) has always been an integral part of India, once a Buddhist kingdom and the seat of Shaivism.

It would be nice to say that Indian journalists are not blind to this influence of French Indianists and the adverse impact it has on Indo-French relations, but when Jaffrelot, for instance who wrote many a nasty books on Hindu fundamentalism and is most responsible for the bad image the BJP in France, comes to India to release the English translation of his book, he is feted by the Press corps and all kind of laudatory reviews are printed in the Indian Press. So much for secularism in India.

Eventually, it is nothing short of a miracle that Hinduism survived the onslaught of centuries marked by violence, forced conversions and destruction of temples. This endurance is a testimony to the profound spiritual resilience of the Hindu people, to the depth of their faith, to the enduring force of their karma, and to how deeply ingrained dharma is in the soul of India. We do not write these words to provoke or to assign blame. History should be neither erased nor used as a weapon. But to deny what occurred, or to refuse to learn from it, is to invite repetition of the same tragedies.

The more pressing question today is not about vengeance or victimhood, but about coexistence. Can Islam, as it is practiced and preached in many parts of the world today, ever accept Hinduism as a valid spiritual path? This is not a question aimed at inciting conflict, but one that seeks clarity for the sake of future peace. For guidance, we may turn not to polemicists, but to sages—those who saw beyond hatred, who embraced the soul of India in all its contradictions. Among them was Sri Aurobindo, who internalized the *Gita's* message of karma and action, even when it called for necessary violence, yet whose words were softened by a vision of universal spiritual unity. "You can live with a religion whose principle is toleration," he once wrote. "But how is it possible to live peacefully with a religion whose principle is 'I will not tolerate you'? How are you going to have unity with these people? The Hindu is ready to tolerate. He is open to new ideas and to other cultures, and he has a wonderful capacity for assimilation—provided that India's central truth is recognised" (Sri Aurobindo, *India's Rebirth*, pp. 161, 173).

In another passage from September 1909, Sri Aurobindo foresaw with startling prescience the direction India was headed: "Every action, for instance, which may be objectionable to a number of Mahomedans, is now liable to be forbidden because it is likely to lead to a breach of peace. And one is dimly beginning to wonder whether worship in Hindu temples may be forbidden on that valid ground" (*India's Rebirth*, p. 55). More than a century later, this prophecy rings true: in many parts of India, Hindu processions are restricted or canceled for fear of triggering communal unrest! What Sri Aurobindo warned us about has now become a lived reality. To understand the deeper challenge at hand, we must say a word about monotheism. This is where the ideological chasm between the Abrahamic faiths and Hinduism becomes evident. Christianity, Islam and Judaism were born in reaction to what they saw as pagan polytheism—religions that honored many gods and goddesses. Monotheists proclaimed: "There is only one true God—ours. All others are false, mere idols." This fundamental conviction gave birth to centuries of religious conflict, and in the case of Islam, to an especially intense hostility toward religions like Hinduism, which it labels as idolatrous and impure. This animosity forged strange alliances, even between former enemies. In colonial India, the British, though Christian, often favored Muslims and Sikhs over the Hindu majority, whom they perceived as politically unreliable and spiritually backward. Or consider the words of the King of Morocco, a leader of moderate Islam, who declared in a recent interview: "We have no fight with Christianity. Our battle is against the infidel who adores many gods."

But what the monotheistic world has failed to understand is that Hinduism, as I wrote earlier, at its core, is perhaps the most monotheistic of all religions. It recognizes the Divine as One, infinite and formless, manifesting in countless forms to suit countless temperaments. It does not claim, "Only our God is real, and if you do not believe in Him, you must die." Instead, it says, "Yes, Mohammed was a messenger of the Divine. So too were Christ, Buddha, Krishna, and even Confucius." This inclusive view, far from being impious, offers the most evolved form of monotheism, for it sees unity in diversity. Yet this generosity of vision has often been met with violence. It is precisely this exclusivist mentality—this insistence that "if you do not accept Allah or Christ, you are an infidel to be eliminated"—that led to the slaughter of tens of millions of Hindus during the Islamic conquests of India, and the decimation of native populations in the Americas under the Christian conquest. The question that confronts us now is urgent: are the Muslims of today willing to accept Hinduism not as a political rival, but as a legitimate path to the Divine? Sadly, in most parts of the Muslim world, the answer remains no. Hinduism continues to be seen as the quintessential infidel religion. This rejection is embedded in theological dogma, reiterated in daily prayers, and reflected in attitudes that tolerate no alternative to the absolute supremacy of Allah. The events of 7 October 2023 offer us a stark reminder on our cruel and ruthless Islam can be with the 'Infidels'. On that day, Hamas militants executed a massacre of unspeakable cruelty—gunning down civilians, raping women and burning infants alive. This savagery was not random; it was rooted in the belief that such acts are sanctioned, even demanded, by divine scripture. In India, the armies of Babur are no longer at our gates. We do not wake to news of 100,000 Hindus being slain in a single day. Yet the danger has not disappeared; it has merely changed form. Yesterday, it might take the shape of bombs in Coimbatore or Varanasi, or of covert campaigns to sow division and hatred. Tomorrow, it might be the killing of Hindus in Kashmir, has it happened recently in Pahalgam. The goal remains the same: to weaken the fabric of India and, if possible, to annihilate her spiritual soul. And while the Indian Muslim may still feel a cultural kinship with his Hindu neighbor—after all, his ancestors were once Hindus—his religious teachings too often compel him to view the Hindu as an infidel. This, then, is the crux of the matter. If Islam is to survive and evolve in the modern world, it must confront this riddle. It must decide whether it wishes to coexist or to conquer. And Hindus, for their part, must reassert—not with hatred, but with clarity—the greatness and validity of their spiritual heritage. We may never fully measure the colossal physical damage inflicted upon India by the Muslim invasions. Even more elusive is the moral and spiritual trauma, the centuries of humiliation, loss and suppression of a vast civilization. But this is not a call for revenge, nor a summons to reignite old grievances. It is a plea not to repeat the mistakes of the past. The conquest, tragically, is not over. The seeds planted by Mahmud of Ghazni, by Babur, by Aurangzeb, have borne bitter fruit. Today, the descendants of forcibly converted Hindus—numbering more than 200 million in India (this number includes illegal Bangladeshis and Rohingyas)—often carry a rage and religious fanaticism that is alien to the Indian ethos. As Sri Aurobindo poignantly observed: "More than 90% of the Indian Muslims are descendants of converted Hindus and belong as much to the Indian nation as the Hindus themselves." (*India's Rebirth*, p. 237)

Yet the poison of secession that began with the first cries of religious conquest matured into Pakistan—a nation founded on the rejection of India's pluralism—and has returned again and again to haunt the subcontinent. Through the wars of 1947, 1965 and 1971, through Kargil, through Kashmir, and through the looming threat of nuclear conflict, this legacy endures. India must awaken. She must remember. And above all, she must reclaim the truth of her civilization—not in hatred, but in strength. Only then will peace, truepeace, be possible.

Christophe Jaffrelot and the Demonization of Hindu India

For over two decades, Christophe Jaffrelot has been one of the most prominent voices on Indian politics and society in French academic and media circles. Presented as a leading Indologist, he is often cited in international journals and think tanks as an authority on modern India. However, his work reveals a persistent and systematic tendency to portray Hinduism, Hindu nationalist movements, and particularly the Bharatiya Janata Party (BJP) in a negative, even hostile light. Jaffrelot's career has been largely devoted to analyzing the rise of what he calls "Hindu nationalism," which he associates with authoritarianism, religious intolerance, and the erosion of secularism. He draws a direct ideological lineage from early 20th-century figures like Vinayak Savarkar to contemporary leaders such as Narendra

Modi. In this view, the BJP is not a legitimate democratic party rooted in Indian traditions or responding to the aspirations of a majority, but rather a dangerous expression of majoritarian populism and ethnonationalism. Throughout his writings, Hinduism is rarely treated as a diverse or complex philosophical system. Instead, Jaffrelot often focuses on its supposed exclusivism, its caste hierarchies, or its alleged incompatibility with modern liberal democracy. While he rightly points out certain excesses and the dangers of politicizing religion, his approach often lacks nuance and appears to apply different standards when assessing other political or religious groups. For example, Islamist movements, separatist ideologies, or left-wing extremism rarely receive the same level of scrutiny or moral judgment in his work.

Jaffrelot frequently refers to the 2002 Gujarat riots—undoubtedly a tragic chapter in India's recent history—as the central defining event of Modi's political career, even though the courts have cleared Modi of direct responsibility. At the same time, he downplays Modi's later efforts in governance, including policies on development, sanitation, infrastructure, and digital inclusion, as either populist tactics or superficial gestures. This persistent demonetization has not gone unnoticed in India. Many Indian intellectuals, both Hindu and otherwise, have criticized Jaffrelot's work for its ideological bias and its failure to engage with the lived realities of ordinary Indians. Critics have noted that his framework tends to interpret all expressions of Hindu identity through a lens of extremism, without acknowledging the historical wounds inflicted on Hindu society—such as centuries of invasions, colonization, and missionary erasure. For such critics, Jaffrelot is not simply analyzing India; he is advancing a narrative that seeks to de-legitimize a civilization's natural cultural revival. Moreover, his disproportionate focus on Hindu nationalism as a threat to secularism tends to ignore the rise of aggressive religious identity politics among other communities. His silence on issues like Islamist radicalization, caste-based militancy, or religious conversions raises questions about the selective application of academic critique.

In the end, Jaffrelot represents a school of thought rooted in postcolonial theory and European liberalism, which struggles to understand the resurgence of cultural self-confidence in postcolonial nations like India. His writings have shaped how India is viewed in Western academia, especially in France, but they often miss the deeper spiritual and civilizational impulses that animate Indian society today. For many, his work is not so much a study of India as a political project—a project aimed at defining which voices are legitimate in India's national discourse, and which are not.

CHAPTER 16

The European Invasions

Among the early European colonists, the Portuguese perhaps best embodied the colonial disregard, hostility and destructive spirit of the West towards India. Despite the later folklore surrounding the "relaxed atmosphere" of Portuguese Goa—the good life, the wine, the sensuous women—the Portuguese were a ruthless lot. In 1498, Vasco da Gama, the Portuguese "hero," was generously received by Zamorin, the Hindu king of Calicut, who granted him the right to establish warehouses for commerce. But once again, Hindu tolerance was exploited and the Portuguese wanted more and more: in 1510, Alfonso de Albuquerque seized Goa, where he began a reign of terror, burning "heretics," crucifying Brahmins, using false theories to forcibly convert the lower castes and encouraging his soldiers to take Indian mistresses. Indeed, the Inquisition in Goa (see box) had nothing to envy the Muslims, except in sheer numbers. Ultimately, the Portuguese had to be kicked out of India, when all other colonists had already left.

There is no need to rewrite here the story of British India. From 1600, when the East India Company received its charter from Queen Elizabeth, to 1947, when Mountbatten packed up the Union Jack, the history of the British in India has been one of subtle treachery, crass commercial exploitation and sometimes of savagery. The English might have been totally ignorant of India's past greatness, when they set upon acquiring bit by bit their empire, but at least there was some early attempt at understanding each other between a few enlightened Britishers and some Indians. But after the mutiny of 1857, the English went into a frenzy of murder, revenge and atrocity and alienated themselves forever from the "natives." Henceforth they would live separately in their forts, or their cantonments, and would be totally segregated from Indians, ending once and for all any chance of bridging the gap between the two cultures. Indeed, Daniélou feels that the crushing of the revolt "was to trigger the slow and insidious destruction of one of the greatest civilisations of the world, of its philosophy, its arts, its sciences and its techniques now despised and discouraged. This was a disaster for universal culture," he concludes. (*Histoire de l'Inde*, p. 329)

Another question should also be asked: Was the European conquest a unifying factor in India? According to Western historians, such as A.L. Basham, yes. Prior to the British conquest, they label India as a nation of feudal kings, constantly infighting each other. But as seen earlier, when one discounts the theory of an Aryan invasion, when one understands the genius of Vedic India, the greatness of its institutions, the unparalleled tolerance and spiritual vision of Hinduism and how it had devised a remarkable political system adapted to its own needs and psychology, this theory does not stand under scrutiny.

In truth, the British divided India; they exploited the schism between Hindus and Muslims and aggravated a small discontentment in the Sikh community. Dividing India to them was only a practical need to further their imperial dream—it was not done out of sheer fanatical conviction. But does that make it more acceptable?

Nevertheless, when History will be rewritten, the British will have to share the blame for the harm that was done to India. And their share has four names: MISSIONARIES, SECULARISM, INDIAN ELITE, REPRESSION.

The Goan Inquisition: A Forgotten Holocaust

The Portuguese first arrived in India in 1498, opening the sea route via the Cape of Good Hope. While their initial mission was trade, they soon turned to conquest and religious conversion. In 1510, Afonso de Albuquerque captured Goa from the Sultan of Bijapur, and it became the capital of the Portuguese empire in the East. What followed was one of the darkest chapters in Indian history. The

Portuguese imposed brutal control over Goan society. Hindu temples were destroyed—more than 300 by some estimates—and churches were built atop the ruins. Mass conversions were carried out using violence, humiliation and coercion. Entire communities were threatened with exile or execution if they did not convert to Catholicism. Mixed-race marriages were encouraged to create a loyal colonial population. Orphans were kidnapped and baptized. Hindu names, clothing, rituals, festivals, even languages like Konkani were banned. In 1560, at the urging of Francis Xavier, the Portuguese crown established the Inquisition in Goa. The so-called "Holy Office" enforced religious conformity with brutal severity. Secret tribunals imprisoned thousands, while torture chambers operated within the notorious "Big House" of Old Goa. Prisoners—men, women, even children—were burned alive during public executions known as *auto da fé*. Eyewitnesses described mutilations, dismemberment and the torment of pregnant women. By the 18th century, British pressure finally curtailed the Inquisition. It was briefly halted in 1774, resumed in 1778, and permanently abolished in 1812. In its 250-year reign of terror, the Goan Inquisition destroyed not only lives but a vibrant spiritual and cultural heritage.

Though Goa today is celebrated for its beaches and churches, the ruins of the Inquisition remain buried in silence. Secular historians often ignore this painful past. Yet, as Mahatma Gandhi wrote, Christian missionaries in his time still insulted Hindu gods in the name of preaching. Francis Xavier himself encouraged children to destroy their own family idols, and wrote with satisfaction about demolishing temples. Goa, once celebrated as the "Kashi of the West," endured more than 400 uprisings during the four centuries of Portuguese rule. The story of its resistance and the martyrdom of its people deserves remembrance—not in a spirit of revenge, but as a safeguard to ensure that such atrocities are never repeated. The Shivaji Maharaj Museum of Indian History in Pune has probably the only exhibition in India (and in the world) on the Goa inquisition and what it did to Hindus. Please visit that Museum (factmuseum.com).

THE MISSIONARIES PRE-INDEPENDENCE

The missionaries arrived in India on the heels of the British. As mentioned earlier, their first prey were the Adivasis, the tribal people, which they promptly proceeded to name as the "original" inhabitants of India, who were colonized by the "bad" Brahmins, during the mythical Aryan invasion. "Was it not right," they said, "to free them from the grip of their masters, who had enslaved them both socially and religiously?" Thus they set the Adivasis against the mainstream of Hindu society and sowed the seeds of an explosive conflict which is ready to blow up today, particularly in Tamil Nadu and Maharashtra (see box). The missionaries in India were always supporters of colonialism; they encouraged it and their whole structure was based on "the good Western civilised world being brought to the Pagans." In the words of Charles Grant (1746-1823), Chairman of the East India Company: "We cannot avoid recognising in the people of Hindustan a race of men lamentably degenerate and base... governed by malevolent and licentious passions... and sunk in misery by their vices." (as quoted by Sitaram Goel, in his book *History of Hindu-Christian Encounters*, p. 32). Claudius Bucchanan, a chaplain attached to the East India Company, went even further: "...Neither truth, nor honesty, honour, gratitude, nor charity, is to be found in the breast of a Hindoo!" What a comment about a nation that gave the world the Vedas and the Upanishads, at a time when Europeans were still fornicating in their caves!

Lord Hastings, Governor General of India from 1813, could not agree more; he wrote in his diary on October 2nd of the same year: "The Hindoo appears to be nearly limited to mere animal functions... with no higher intellect than a dog or an elephant, or a monkey..." No wonder that the British opened the doors wide for missionaries! After the failed mutiny of 1857, the missionaries became even more militant, using the secular arm of the British Raj, who felt that the use of the sword at the service of the Gospel was now entirely justified. Remember how Swami Vivekananda cried in anguish at the Parliament of Religions in Chicago: "If we Hindus dig out all the dirt from the bottom of the Pacific Ocean and throw it in your faces, it will be but a speck compared to what the missionaries have done to our religion and culture." These missionaries indeed poisoned the minds of the people they converted, making them hate their own religion, their own country sometimes, cutting them from their own cultural roots. What better example of this than the Anglo-Indians, a race which became neither here nor there, disallowing their Indian-ness, but never being fully accepted as their own by their British masters. Hence, they had to slowly disappear, either reverting to their Indian-ness, or settling abroad: evolution does not tolerate a people that loses its soul. It is the same with the "Pondichériens," the French of Tamil origin from Pondicherry. Originated from lower castes, they were converted by the early French missionaries and in time assumed French names, French manners and considered themselves as French. But today the French have forgotten them, they cost too much to their government and apart from a few brilliant exceptions, they are also a race which is slowly dying and is gradually engulfed by the Indian Tamils. It is also true that the missionaries, such as "Saint" François Xavier, broke down many "idol" temples to build their churches, although it never had the ruthlessness and ferocity of the Muslims. Nevertheless, the missionaries in India were always a divisive force, which used the Adivasis for advocating covertly a breaking up of the country. Koenraad Elst writes that the missionaries were ultimately all set to trigger a Christian partition in India: "At the time of Independence, Christian mission centres had dreamed up a plan for a Christian partition in collaboration with the Muslim League. The far north-east, Chotanagur and parts of Kerala were to become Christian states, forming a non-Hindu chain with the Nizam's Hyderabad and with Pakistani Bengal. The secret agreement between the Muslim League and missionaries acting as "representatives of tribal interest," is sometimes used in Muslim propaganda, as proof that "Muslims and tribals are natural allies." Sadly for the Christians, Sardar Patel foiled their plans (*Indigenous Indian,* p. 229). Even after independence, the missionaries seem to have been involved in secessionist activities in India's north-east, as well as on the Burmese side of the border. Always pretending to act as mediators, they appear to have actually helped the separatists with vital information. Since then, they have been dictating policies in Nagaland,

Meghalaya and Mizoram, which recently celebrated with great fanfare its century of Christian rule.

What about today? Moderate Hindu leaders feel "that Christianity has often alienated Indian Christians from the mainstream. They are afraid for instance to participate in anything that has a Hindu connotation, or they are made to change their names. And since they get alienated, a certain fear psychosis sets in." And it is true that Christianity also introduced the feeling of guiltiness, of being a sinner, which is absent from Hinduism. Christians are also proud that they brought education to India, "but," counters Sri Sri Ravi Shankar, founder of the Art of Living movement, "it is not true: there were for instance 125,000 medical institutes in Madras before the British came. Indians never lacked education, the Christians only brought British education to India, which in fact caused more damage to India by westernising many of us."

Then of course, there is the subject of conversions by Christian missionaries, which has triggered a heated debate since the BJP Government first came to power in 1998. On this topic, Sri Sri Ravi Shankar, the Guru of Joy, feels "that when you honour and respect another religion, the culture of conversion is not needed. The Hindus honour the other religions, but unfortunately there is not yet any sanction to honour similarly other religions in Christianity. The problem with tribals in India is that if the missionaries had just done service there and left the tribals to their indigenous practices, there would not have been so many problems today."

Finally, no history of the missionary involvement in India can be complete without mentioning the health and education services they rendered. It is true that unparalleled selfless service was given and is still rendered all over the country, that Kerala got 100% literacy, thanks in greater part to Christianity, that some of the best schools in India are Catholic, that the medical care is unique and most advanced. Also that sometimes this service is rendered out of true Christian charity, without any ulterior motive. But nevertheless, there is no doubt about the ultimate purpose of that selfless service. The South Indian Missionary Conference of 1858 set forth very clearly the goals of education in India: "The object of all missionary labour should not be primarily the civilisation, BUT the evangelization of the heathen schools may be regarded as converting agencies and their value estimated by the number who are led to renounce idolatry and make an open profession of Christianity..." Has this policy really changed today? Not that much. The International School of Kodaikanal, under the guise of "religious studies," still tries to convert its students, many of whom are Indians. And nothing symbolizes better today the continuing spirit of the missionaries in India than the late Mother Teresa and other missionaries, who have been glorified by the book, *The City of Joy,* by Dominique Lapierre, a wonderfully written book, which unfortunately gives the impression that a small part of India (the slums of Calcutta, or Kolkata), represents the whole of the country.

The Language Wars in India: Hindi and the Struggle for Linguistic Identity

India is a land of extraordinary linguistic diversity. With 22 official languages recognized in the Constitution and hundreds of spoken tongues, language has always been central to India's cultural fabric. Yet in the years following independence, language also became a source of deep political conflict, especially around the imposition of Hindi. In 1949, the Constituent Assembly declared Hindi in the Devanagari script the official language of the Indian Union, with English to remain for only 15 years. This was seen as a natural choice by many in northern India, where Hindi is widely spoken. But in other parts of the country, this move was perceived as linguistic domination, triggering resistance movements that would reshape Indian federalism.

The fiercest opposition came from Tamil Nadu, where Tamil, one of the world's oldest living languages, is regarded not just as a means of communication, but as a civilizational identity. In 1965, as the deadline approached to make Hindi the sole official language, massive anti-Hindi agitations broke out in the state. Protests turned violent, students self-immolated, and dozens died. The agitation was led by the Dravida MunnetraKazhagam (DMK), which rode the wave of resentment to political power. The Centre was forced to amend its policy and allow English to continue indefinitely. Since then, Tamil Nadu has officially followed a two-language policy—Tamil and English—rejecting the Hindi-led three-language formula. Elsewhere, linguistic pride took different forms. In Maharashtra, the Samyukta Maharashtra Movement of the 1950s demanded a separate Marathi-speaking state. In 1960, Bombay State was divided, and Maharashtra was born. Though Marathi became the official language, concern remains over its marginalization in education, media and business. Political parties like the Shiv Sena and MNS continue to push for stronger enforcement of Marathi in public life.

In Karnataka, Kannada activists have demanded priority for Kannada in administration and education. In West Bengal, Bengali pride has frequently clashed with attempts to prioritize Hindi. Similar movements have emerged in Punjab, Assam, Odisha, and other regions, each asserting their linguistic uniqueness against the pull of central standardization.

At the heart of the issue lies a fundamental tension: how can a single nation speak with many tongues without silencing any? While Hindi is the most widely spoken language in India, it is not spoken by the majority. For many Indians, language is not just about literacy or governance—it is about dignity, memory, literature, and selfhood. The Indian state has since evolved a multi-lingual federal model, where the Centre uses Hindi and English, and states are free to operate in their official languages. But pressures remain. Periodic pushes to expand Hindi—through education policy or public signage—continue to provoke resistance. In India, language is identity. The language wars are not simply about opposing Hindi, but about resisting any attempt to erase or diminish other languages. In a land where unity rests upon diversity, linguistic respect is not optional—it is a necessity. Nevertheless, we agree to the fact that English is not India's natural language, but one imposed by colonial rule.

SECULARISM

Many post-independence Indians, particularly the Congress politicians, have always harped on the fact that "the British left no greater legacy in India than secularism." But in the name of secularism, how much irreparable harm has been done to India, how much damage, slander, stupidity has been heaped upon the land of Bharat!

The beauty and the genius of a truly secular India is indeed appealing. Who would not dream of an India where all would live in harmony: Muslims, Hindus, Christians, Parsis, Buddhists, Jains, Jews, North Indians, South Indians, Assamese, Kashmiris, Sikhs, Nepalese... Which country in the world can boast of such a diversity, such an incredible mosaic of races, religions and ethnic groups? There would be at the center a benevolent, non-religious, liberal, reform-oriented, secular government, which would allow for unlimited religious and regional autonomies, so that the soul of each culture, each religion, finds its right expression in the fold of a united India. Is this then the democratic inheritance left by India's erstwhile masters?

In reality, when the British arrived in India, they were only a handful, and realized that they could not govern such a huge country with so few of theirs. They then set upon dividing the nation, pitting each community against the other. In the Muslims they found a ready ear. It would be a total lie to say that the British engineered the Muslim-Hindu enmity and are to be held responsible for the creation of Pakistan. The Muslim-Hindu divide was a problem of religious incompatibility, on the parts of the Muslims, who saw in Hinduism an infidel religion, which had to be wiped out. Now the clash of swords was no more, and the British were there to pacify everybody; but they very quickly scented blood and felt they could use the ardent wish of Indian Muslims to be separate on their own, now that the bitter realization had downed upon them that they could not make of India a Dar-ul-Islam, a house of Islam. In the same way, the British were quick to seize upon the dissatisfaction of the Sikhs, who had fought them ferociously in war, but in times of peace, served them faithfully, forming—alongside the Gurkhas—their finest soldiers.

British 'equality' under the Raj often obscured Hindus, India's overwhelming majority status and its central civilizational role. At independence, Hindus constituted well over 300 million people, forming the core of India's cultural identity. Hinduism, far more than just a religion, represents for Hindus a living truth—Dharma—that has sustained and unified diverse Indian traditions across millennia. Yet, colonial policy deliberately cast Muslims and Christians as vulnerable "minority communities" deserving protection, implicitly placing them on the same institutional footing as the Hindu majority. This approach conveniently ignored India's historical truth: Hindu civilization is not a sectarian faith, but the foundation of India's ethos, arts, literature, and legal traditions—the very matrix from which minority cultures emerged. By equating all communities under the rubric of "minorities," the British flattened distinctions, framing Hindus as just another group needing "constraint," while minorities were entitled to special rights.This strategy served the colonial logic of "divide and rule." After the uprising of 1857, British officials such as Lord Ellenborough and Mountstuart Elphinstone openly strategized to placate Hindus at the expense of Muslims in order to maintain control. The introduction of the census system and separate electorates further institutionalized religious identities as political categories, deepening communal divisions and undermining the civilizational unity once symbolized by Dharma. Post-independence, India's farmers recognized this distortion. The Constitution granted universal franchise and refused special privileges to Hindus, relying instead on the democratic weight of their preponderance. Minority institutions were protected—but without undermining the majority. Still, the legacy of colonial minority-majority inversion remains visible. Political narratives often elevate minority grievances as equal to, or greater than, the historical experience of the majority. The central place of Dharma as India's unifying truth remains eclipsed in public memory—even as Hindus constitute roughly 80% of the population and sustain India's living spiritual continuity.

In short, British colonial "equality" smoothed over the reality that Hindu civilization is India's foundational bedrock, not one among many.

Recognizing this is essential—not to deny minority rights, but to restore the proper civilizational context in which India's unity through Dharma, can be re-embraced.

THE INDIAN ELITE

When they took over India, the British set upon establishing an intermediary race of Indians, whom they could entrust with their work at the middle level echelons and who could one day be convenient instruments to rule by proxy, or semi-proxy. The tool to shape these "British clones" was *education*. In the words of Macaulay, the "pope" of British schooling in India: "We must at present do our best to form a class, who may be interpreters between us and the millions we govern; a class of persons, Indians in blood and colour, but *English in taste*, in opinions, in morals and in intellects" Macaulay had very little regard for Hindu culture and education: "all the historical information which can be collected from all the books which have been written in the Sanskrit language, is less valuable than what may be found in the most paltry abridgement used at preparatory schools in England." Or: "Hindus have a literature of small intrinsic value, hardly reconcilable with morality, full of monstrous superstitions..."

It seems today that some of India's Marxist and Muslim intelligentsia could not agree more with Macaulay, for his dream has come true: nowadays, the greatest adversaries of an "Indianised and spiritualised education" are often the descendants of these "Brown Shahibs" : the "secular" politicians, the journalists, the top bureaucrats, in fact the whole westernized cream of India. And what is even more paradoxical is that most of them are Hindus! It is they, who upon getting independence, have denied India its true identity and borrowed blindly from the British education system, without trying to adapt it to the unique Indian mentality and psychology; and it is they who refuse to accept a change in India's education system, which remains entirely Western-oriented and continues to churn out machines that learn by heart dull statistics of little practical use in life. And what India is getting from this education is a youth that imitates the West without discernment. They crowd Starbucks and fast-food chains, spend hours on Instagram and Netflix, wear the latest Nike sneakers and designer labels, and often seem disconnected from the realities of their own country. Many become affluent but superficial consumers in a land where millions of gifted youngsters still struggle with poverty and lack of opportunity. They grow up like countless other globalized clones across the developing world, speaking in American accents, swearing by political correctness, and believing liberalism and imported secular narratives are the only path to salvation. In due course, they occupy influential positions, author books and articles that belittle India's traditions, and sit on international panels or human rights committees where they repeat fashionable rhetoric, rarely grounded in the lived truth of their own people. They also can become "secular" high bureaucrats who take the wrong decisions and generally do tremendous harm to India, because it has been programmed in their genes to always run down their own country. In short, they are the ones who continually look to the West for approval and persist in viewing India through a Western prism. It is said that a nation must be proud of itself to move forward—and unless there is a big change in this intellectual elite, unless it is more conscious of its heritage and of India's greatness, which has begun to happen in a small way, it is going to be very difficult for India to evolve in the 21st century as a real super power.

Indianising Education: A Civilizational Reawakening

Since Sri Narendra Modi's rise to power in 2014, there has been a clear shift toward reclaiming India's educational narrative. For decades, school and university curricula were shaped by colonial frameworks or Marxist historiography that often downplayed India's civilizational achievements and spiritual traditions. Under the Modi regime, a process of "Indianisation" has been initiated—an attempt to re-anchor education in India's own cultural and historical foundations.

This shift involves rewriting history textbooks to highlight ancient India's contributions in mathematics, astronomy, medicine and philosophy—achievements that long predated Western science. Emphasis is now placed on figures like Chanakya, Maharana Pratap, Rani Durgavati, Subhas Chandra Bose, and others who had been marginalized in earlier accounts focused heavily on Mughal rulers and the Gandhi–Nehru legacy. The goal is not merely to glorify the past, but to offer a more balanced and rooted understanding of Indian history. Hindu philosophical ideas—such as Dharma, Yoga and Vedanta—are being presented not as religious doctrine, but as civilizational values central to India's identity. Regional histories, tribal resistances, and forgotten heroes are also being woven into the national story, offering a more inclusive and pluralistic perspective. Supporters argue this is a long-overdue act of decolonization—a correction of the narrative imposed by British administrators and later perpetuated by Westernized Indian elites. Critics warn of "saffronization," claiming it promotes a Hindu nationalist view. Yet, for many Indians, it is a civilizational reawakening, a way to restore dignity and coherence to a past fragmented by centuries of foreign domination.

As India moves forward, this curriculum reform seeks to shape generations who know not just global history, but their own story, told through Indian eyes and anchored in the values of Dharma and cultural continuity. It is true that the BJP of Narendra Modi has been trying to Indianise school curriculum since coming to power (see box), but they have encountered significant resistance, not only on the part of the established intelligentsia establishment, but also historians such as Romila Thapar, and even from bureaucrats who cling to the old order.

REPRESSION, IMPOVERISHMENT

The British were certainly not the Muslims, whose ruthlessness and atrocities have never been equaled in India's history. Nevertheless, they did their fair share of harm to India, which has never fully recovered from two centuries of Raj. Their brutality, whether the hangings of Indian nationalists, or the incredible ferocity which followed the great Indian Mutiny, or the massacre of Jallianwala Bagh, are today part of history. They ruled for 250 years with the unshakable conviction of their own racial superiority which made Fitzjames Stephen, the philosopher of the Indian Civil Service, say: "Ours is essentially an absolute government, which has for base not the consent of the Indians, but their conquest. It does not want to represent the concept of the indigenous population of life and government and can never do so, because then it would represent idolatry and barbarism. It represents a belligerent civilisation and nothing could be more dangerous than to have in one's administration, at the head of a government founded on conquest—implying in all points the superiority of the conquering race, its institution, its principles, that men who hesitate to impose themselves openly." One of the most important aspects of British India was the development of the British system of education and of the English language as the sole base of university teaching. Only British diplomas were recognized and permitted to obtain a job. The ancient centers of Hindu culture were gradually bypassed and only the Brahmins kept the knowledge of Sanskrit alive.

Industrially, the British suffocated India, gradually strangling Indian industries, whose finished products, textiles in particular, were of a quality unique in the world, which had made them famous over the centuries. Instead, they oriented Indian industry towards jute, cotton, tea and oil seeds, which they needed as raw materials for their home industries. They employed cheap labor for their enterprises, while traditional artisans were perishing. India, which used to be a land of plenty, " where milk and honey flowed", started slowly dying. According to British records, one million Indians died of famine between 1800 and 1825; 4 million between 1825 and 1850; 5 million between 1850 and 1875; and 15 million between 1875 and 1900. **Thus, 25 million Indians died in one hundred years**! The British may be proud of their bloody record. It is probably more honorable and straightforward to kill in the name of Allah, than under the guise of petty commercial interest and total disregard for the ways of a 5000-year-old civilization. Thus, by the turn of the century, India was bled dry and had no resources left. Fortunately, visionaries like Jamshedji

Tata, established key industries so that there would be a structure at independence. He did so despite facing considerable resistance from the British. In textiles, for example, they imposed the free entry of Lancashire products and slapped a heavy tax on export of Indian textiles. Is it necessary to remind too, how the English "exported" Indian labor all over the world in their colonies, whether to Sri Lanka for the tea plantations, to Fiji, to South Africa, or to the West Indies?

Culturally, there is no need to recall the rape of India: the thousands of art treasures, the diamonds, the priceless statues stolen, which now adorn the houses of the rich in England, or the Queen's private collections (see box). That the British still do not feel the need to hand back these treasures to India is a shame. The ecological rape of India is also a fact: the tens of thousands of tigers needlessly shot, the great massacre of trees and forests for the voracious railways and the razing of old forts and houses.

Finally, the history of the British would be incomplete without mentioning the positive side. The unification of India by a single language, although it is hoped that it will be eventually replaced by India's true language of the future, acceptable to all. The vast railway system, which more than anything else unified India. The remarkable Postal system, whose structures have survived till today. The roads network of India. But all these were not really meant for the welfare of India, but for a better administration of their own colony.

And ultimately, the question should be asked: "Did the British leave India with any understanding, any inkling of the greatness of the country they had lived with for two centuries?" Except for a few souls like Annie Besant or Sister Nivedita, the answer seems to be **NO**. And today's British Prime Minister, Keir Starmer, probably does not understand one bit more about India than Lord Mountbatten did. But then Mountbatten ought to have known better.

Reclaiming India's Stolen Heritage

One of the lesser-known but powerful aspects of Narendra Modi's cultural policy has been the active repatriation of India's looted artifacts. For centuries, priceless sculptures, idols, manuscripts and art objects were taken from Indian temples, palaces and archaeological sites—especially during the British colonial period—and ended up in museums and private collections across the West, most notably in the British Museum and institutions in the U.S. and Europe.

Since coming to power in 2014, Modi's government has made the recovery of India's cultural treasures a diplomatic priority. Through international cooperation and legal efforts, more than 350 stolen artifacts have been successfully brought back to India—more than ten times the number repatriated since independence. These include iconic statues of Nataraja, Parvati, and Bodhisattvas, as well as objects dating back to the Chola and Gupta periods. Modi has personally thanked foreign governments for returning these symbols of India's ancient glory, asserting that "these are not just art, but living symbols of our civilization." This campaign reflects a broader civilizational revival—a reclaiming of cultural dignity that had long been ignored or suppressed. It signals a clear message: India will no longer remain silent about the theft of her soul.

Chapter 17

The Three Great Disinformations on India

A civilization is like the human soul: it has a childhood, where it struggles to learn; an adolescence where it discovers—sometimes painfully—the hard facts of life; an adulthood, where it enjoys the fruits of maturity; and an old age, which slowly leads to death and oblivion.

In this manner, since the dawn of human history, civilizations have risen, reached the top where they gravitate for some time, achieving their enduring excellence and then slowly begin their descent towards extinction. Usually, old age for these civilizations meant that they fell prey to barbarians, because they had lost the vitality and the inner obedience to their particular genius, which they had possessed at the time of their peak and which had protected them. This has been a natural process and barbarians have played an important role in the evolution of humanity, for they made sure, in the most ruthless manner, that civilizations did not stagnate; because like a human being, a civilization must die many times before it realizes the fullness of its soul and attains divine perfection.

There have been many such great civilizations that rose and fell throughout the ages: Mesopotamia, Egypt, India, Africa, China, Greece, or Rome. Human nature being what it is, most of these civilizations established their might by military conquest and thus imposed their order and their views upon others, a process which some have called civilization, others colonization.

The advent of Jesus Christ heralded the rise of the European-Western civilization, whose forerunners were the Greek and Roman cultures. For long, Europe was only a disunited lot of barbarian tribes fighting each other. The Crusades signaled the earliest attempt at unity, although the

French and the British, for instance, kept warring each other long after them. Some of these nations were great seafarers. Thus, Spain and Portugal, for instance, reached out to the far world and colonized huge chunks of territories in the Americas from the 14th century onwards. But it can be safely said that with the industrial revolution, European civilization started reaching its maturity at the beginning of the 19th century and that a great civilization, whose genius was consciousness in the material, developed henceforth. At the same time, of course, as all other civilizations had done before, Europe began expanding outwards, imposing its own culture on other societies that had lost vitality and were vulnerable to conquest. England, in particular, leveraged its mastery of the seas to move farther and faster than other European powers, such as France, who often had to settle for the crumbs. And certainly, Great Britain's prize possession, the jewel in its colonies, must have been India, whose mighty borders extended then from Afghanistan to Cape Comorin.

Western civilization must be intimately associated with Christianity, even though Christianity took different forms over the ages: Protestantism, Lutheranism, Russian Orthodoxy... According to the Hindus, Jesus Christ was an "avatar," a direct emanation from God. Christ was surely a great avatar of love. Christianity certainly had a softening influence on the Western world, where, let's face it, barbarism was the order of the day for many centuries. In the Middle Ages for instance, Christianity was the only island of sanity in a world of rape, black plague, murders and chaos; and as the Brahmins did in India, it was the Christians who preserved the oral and written word for posterity. There have been many great saints in Christianity, men of wisdom, who strove for divine vision in austerity. Such were Saint François of Assisi's, who reached high spiritual experience, Saint Vincent de Paul, who practised true Christian charity, or Saint Gregory, who attained authentic knowledge. Unfortunately, Christianity, became politicized and ossified under the influence of corrupt popes, often transforming into a rigid system of dogmas, rituals, and strict rules of conduct.

Generally, because Christians—like Muslims—believed that only their God was the true one, colonial powers sought to impose their version of the faith on the people they conquered, using the military authority of their armies to enforce it. It is true that this was done in good faith, that the "soldiers of Christ" thought that the civilizations they stumbled upon were barbarous, pagan and incomprehensible. True also that they sincerely believed that they brought upon these "savages" the virtues of Western civilization: medicine, education and spiritual salvation. But the harm done by Christian missionaries all over the earth will never be properly assessed. In South America, the Spanish soldiers and priests annihilated, in the name of Jesus, an entire civilization, one of the brightest ever, that of the Incas and the Aztecs. Everywhere the Christians went, they stamped mercilessly on cultures, eradicated centuries old ways of life, to replace them with totally inadequate systems, crude, Victorian, moralistic, which slowly killed the spontaneity of life of the people they conquered. They were thus able to radically alter civilizations and change their patterns of thinking. And three generations later, the children of those who had been conquered had forgotten their roots, adapted Christianity and often looked upon their conquerors as their benefactors.

Yet in 2006, more than two decades ago, the West was able to celebrate the 500 years anniversary of Columbus, discoverer of the "New World," with fanfare and pomp. But the New World was already quite old when it was discovered by the young Barbarians, much older in fact than the fledgling Western civilization. And Columbus, however courageous and adventurous, was a ruthless man, whose discovery of the New World triggered an unparalleled rape in human history.

However, not only the West still deifies Columbus, but no one in the Third World has been capable of challenging that undeserved status. The truth is that today, not only in the Western world, but also in the entire so-called developing world, we are constantly looking at things and events through a prism that has been fashioned by centuries of Western thinking. And as long as we do not get rid of that tainted glass, we will not understand the world in general and India in particular. For the stamp of Western civilization will still take some time to be eradicated. By military conquest or moral assertiveness, the West imposed upon the world its ways of thinking; and it created enduring patterns, subtle misinformation and immutable grooves, which play like a record that goes on turning, long after its owner has attained the age of decline. The barbarians who thought they had become "civilized", are being devoured by other barbarians. But today, the economy might have replaced the military killing machine.

THE 1ST DISINFORMATION: THE MYTH OF THE ARYAN INVASION

For over a century, one theory has cast a long shadow over the history of India: the notion that waves of fair-skinned "Aryan" invaders entered the subcontinent from the northwest around 1500 BCE, imposed their language—Sanskrit—on the indigenous peoples, and brought with them a rigid caste system that reshaped the cultural fabric of the region. This idea, deeply rooted in 19th-century European linguistics and colonial ideology, has influenced generations of scholarship, schoolbooks and even political discourse. But what if this theory was never supported by archaeology, literature, or science? What if the so-called "invasion" never happened?

The foundation of the Aryan Invasion Theory (AIT) lies in philology. In the 18th and 19th centuries, scholars began noticing that Sanskrit shared uncanny similarities with Latin, Greek and many European languages. This led to the idea of an "Indo-European" language family, supposedly spread by migrating—or invading—tribes of Indo-Europeans. Colonial scholars, operating at a time when Europe saw itself as the epicenter of civilization, readily imagined India's ancient heritage as a gift delivered by outsiders.

It was a convenient theory. If the Aryans had colonized India in antiquity, then modern European colonization could be seen as a mere continuation—or even completion—of that earlier mission. In 1858, H.H. Wilson, a Sanskritist of the British Empire, famously declared the British conquest of India as "the reunion of the Aryan family," with a duty to civilize and Christianize India.

But not everyone was convinced. Julian Huxley, one of Britain's leading biologists, dismissed the idea of a racial Aryan family as unscientific. Isaac Taylor, a 19th-century philologist, called the linguistic assumptions behind AIT "very dubious." Indian intellectuals and freedom fighters were quick to see through the political agenda. Swami Vivekananda thundered that no ancient Indian text ever mentioned an Aryan invasion. Sri Aurobindo and B.R. Ambedkar exposed how

European scholars had manipulated Sanskrit texts to fit their preconceptions.

As we have seen earlier, the unearthing of the cities of Mohenjo Daro and Harappa in the early 20th century and the discovery that Sarasvati and Harappa civilizations were one, radically challenged colonial narratives. These were not primitive tribal settlements, but advanced urban civilizations dating back to 3000 BCE, with paved streets, sanitation systems, metallurgy and standardized weights. Far from being invaded by more advanced outsiders, it now appeared that the so-called "pre-Aryan" people had been more sophisticated than the alleged Aryan conquerors. In fact, John Marshall, the director of the Archaeological Survey of India, marveled in 1931 at how "typically Indian" the Harappan civilization appeared, noting its resemblance to later Hinduism. V. Gordon Childe, a British archaeologist, observed that neither Harappa nor Mohenjo Daro showed signs of violent destruction—no burnt layers, no battle wounds on skeletons, no warrior graves. If there was an invasion, where was the evidence?

Skeptics of the AIT pointed to the absence of war imagery in Harappan art, the lack of breached fortifications, and healed wounds on skeletons allegedly linked to battles. American archaeologist George F. Dales, who directed excavations at Mohenjo Daro, concluded unequivocally: "There is not the slightest proof of armed conquest or even destruction by an alleged Aryan invasion." Faced with mounting archaeological contradictions, proponents of the AIT softened their stance, suggesting instead a peaceful "Aryan migration." But this new version, too, lacked material evidence. No tools, weapons, or objects associated with Indo-European pastoralists have been found in Indus Valley sites. French archaeologist Jean-Marie Casal stated clearly: "There is no Aryan archaeological definition." Furthermore, cultural continuity is undeniable. Symbols like the Shiva *lingam,* the *yoni*, and the reverence of Mother Goddess motifs persist across Harappan and Vedic sites. Rather than a cultural break, we see evolution and integration—suggesting that the Vedic culture emerged indigenously from within the subcontinent.

Genetics: Science Challenges the Colonial Narrative

The most formidable challenge to the Aryan invasion hypothesis comes from the field of genetics. Earlier anthropological theories, which categorized Indians into light-skinned Aryans and dark-skinned Dravidians, have now been thoroughly discredited. Multiple genetic studies over the past three decades have shown overwhelming continuity in the Indian gene pool from the time of the Indus Valley Civilization to the present day. Pioneering geneticist S.R. Walimbe demonstrated that skeletal remains from Mohenjo Daro matched those of modern populations in the region. Geneticist Partha Majumder found that despite India's linguistic and caste diversity, the Y-chromosome lineages are remarkably consistent across the subcontinent.

In 1999, Estonian population geneticist Toomas Kivisild, a Stanford University graduate, analyzed the genomes of Indians from Burma to Afghanistan and concluded: "The Aryan invasion, if it occurred, left no significant genetic trace." Later studies by Susanta Roy Choudhury and Sanghamitra Sengupta confirmed that both upper and lower castes, across language groups, share more than 80% of their DNA. Even tribes such as the Chenchus, long believed to be untouched by Aryan influence, show genetic affinities with high castes.

In 2019, a major breakthrough came from the genome sequencing of a 4,500-year-old woman buried at Rakhigarhi, a Harappan site in Haryana. An international team of scientists found no evidence of Steppe or Central Asian ancestry in her DNA, challenging the long-held theory of an Aryan migration or influx from the West. As Prof. Thangaraj from the Centre for Cellular and Molecular Biology noted: "The people of the Indus Valley Civilization had a distinct, indigenous genetic lineage."

TURNING THE ARROW AROUND: DID THE ARYANS GO WEST?

The term "Aryan" in ancient Indian texts refers not to race, but to nobility of character and conduct. Could the movement have been in the opposite direction—from India to the West? Some geneticists now propose that Indo-European languages may have spread from the Indian subcontinent toward Central Asia and Europe, rather than the reverse. As said earlier, French Indologist Guy Deleury mused that the ancestors of both Hindus and Celts once shared the same spiritual and poetic traditions. The war chariot—an important spiritual symbol in both the Vedas and Celtic mythology—is one such example. In Sanskrit, it is called *ratha*; in Gaulish, *reda*. The Vedic hymns, Deleury suggested, might shed light on the lost songs of the Druids.

> One of the central agruments of the Aryan invasion theory is the horse. Because the *Rig veda* contains frequent references to horses, while Harappan seals depict them only rarely, some historians concluded that the animal must have been introduced by invaders. However, archaeological discoveries from Surkotada, Lothal and Ropar have unearthed horse bones dated as early as 2400 BCE. Renowned Hungarian paleo-zoologist Sándor Bökönyi confirmed that domesticated horses existed in Harappan times. The absence of horses on Harappan seals may simply reflect cultural priorities. Indian society, until the medieval era, emphasized elephants and bulls far more than horses. Even during the 12th century CE, Rajput armies fought with elephants while Turkic invaders used swift cavalry. The Vedic glorification of horses, therefore, may have been symbolic rather than literal.

Today, the Aryan Invasion Theory is no longer taught as settled history in many academic circles. Yet its ghost lingers—in politics, identity debates and even skin cream advertisements. In Tamil Nadu, opposition to Hindi is sometimes framed as resistance to Aryan hegemony. Missionaries still tell tribal communities they are not "true Hindus" but the original inhabitants oppressed by invaders. But modern research tells a different story: of a deep, uninterrupted cultural and genetic continuity; of a civilization that rose indigenously; and of a people whose diversity cannot be explained by simplistic invasions or migrations. India's story, like its ancient epics, is vast, layered and complex—not a tale of conquest, but of integration.

Here below is an attempt at setting new dates for early Indian history.

	Period	Date
1.	End of Sarasvati River	2200-1900 BC
2.	Beg. of Great Drought	2200-2000 BC
3.	The Sulbasutras Period	3000-2000
4.	Beg of Drying of Sarasvati	3100 BC
5.	Peak of Sarasvati Civilization	Before 3200 BC
6.	Introduction of Silver (Kunal)	Appr. 3300 BC
	Period of 2d Vedas & brahmanas	3300 BC
7.	End of the Rig veda Age	3750 BC
8.	Beginning of Vedic Age	Appr. 7000 BC

THE 2ND DISINFORMATION: THE CASTE SYSTEM

Even more than the Aryan-Dravidian divide and the Vedas, the caste system has been the most misunderstood, the most vilified subject of Hindu society at the hands of Western scholars and even today by "secular" Indians. But ultimately, if one wants to understand the truth, the original purpose behind the caste system, one must go back to the Vedas. "Caste was originally an arrangement for the distribution of functions in society, just as much as class in Europe, but the principle on which this distribution was based was peculiar to India. A Brahmin was a Brahmin not by mere birth, but because he discharged the duty of preserving the spiritual and intellectual elevation of the race, and he had to cultivate the spiritual temperament and acquire the spiritual training which alone would qualify him for the task. The Kshatriya was Kshatriya not merely because he was the son of warriors and princes, but because he discharged the duty of protecting the country and preserving the high courage and manhood of action, and he had to cultivate the princely temperament and acquire the strong and lofty Samurai training which alone fitted him for his duties. So it was for the Vaishya whose function was to amass wealth for the race and the Shudra who discharged the humbler duties of service without which the other castes could not perform their share of labour for the common good." (Sri Aurobindo, in *India's Rebirth*, p. 26).

Many Indian sages have gone even further than Sri Aurobindo, arguing that in the occult relation India had with the Universal Force, each one was born in the caste corresponding to his or her spiritual evolution. There are accidents, misfits, errors, they say, but the system seems to have worked pretty well until modern times when it got perverted by the vagaries of materialism and western influence. Can one accept such a theory? Sri Aurobindo, while praising the original caste system, does not spare it in its later stages: "It is the nature of human institutions to degenerate; there is no doubt that the institution of caste degenerated. It ceased to be determined by spiritual qualifications which, once essential, have now come to be subordinate and even immaterial and is determined by the purely material tests of occupation and birth... By this change it has set itself against the fundamental tendency of Hinduism, which is *to insist on the spiritual and subordinate the material* and thus lost most of its meaning. The spirit of caste arrogance, exclusiveness and superiority came to dominate it instead of the spirit of duty, and the change weakened the nation and helped to reduce us to our present condition...(*India's Rebirth*, p. 27). And the Barbarians came!

But finally, have the people who dismiss caste as an Aryan imposition on the Dravidians, or as an inhuman and Nazi system, ever attempted to understand its original purpose and genius? Is it really worse than the huge class differences you can see nowadays in Europe? And can you really exclude it today off-hand, when it still survives so much in the villages—and even in more educated circles, where one is still married in matching castes, with the help of an astrologer? Does the caste system need to be transformed, to recapture its old meaning and once more incarnate a spiritual hierarchy of beings? Or, has it been recast in a different mold, taking into account the parameters of modern Indian society? Or else, will it finally disappear altogether from India, because it has become totally irrelevant today?

At any rate, Hindus should not allow it to be exploited shamelessly against them, as it has been in the last two centuries, by missionaries, "secular" historians, Muslims, and by pre- and post-independence Indian politicians—each for their own purpose.

Caste Reservations Under Shri Narendra Modi

Since coming to power in 2014, the Narendra Modi government has maintained the core structure of India's caste-based reservation system, which allocates quotas in education and government jobs for Scheduled Castes (SCs), Scheduled Tribes (STs), and Other Backward Classes (OBCs). However, Modi has introduced some important changes. In 2019, the BJP-led government passed a landmark bill creating a 10% reservation for the Economically Weaker Sections (EWS) of the upper castes—those who are not covered under existing quotas. This marked the first time economic criteria—rather than caste—were officially recognized in the reservation policy. While the move was praised by many as a step toward a more inclusive and merit-based system, critics argued it diluted the original intent of caste-based affirmative action. The Supreme Court upheld the EWS quota in 2022, calling it constitutional.

Despite ideological opposition from some quarters of the Sangh Parivar to caste-based politics, the BJP government has not dismantled the existing quotas, understanding their deep-rooted role in Indian electoral and social dynamics. Instead, it has focused on expanding access—opening up higher education and government jobs through schemes like "Sabka Saath, Sabka Vikas." Yet, caste tensions and demands for inclusion persist. Communities like the Jats, Patidars, and Marathas have staged large protests demanding OBC status. The Prime Minister had to carefully balance these aspirations with constitutional and legal frameworks, often deferring to the courts and state governments.

In sum, Modi's approach to reservations reflects pragmatism rather than radical reform—retaining the status quo while cautiously expanding its scope to include the economically disadvantaged across castes.

THE 3RD DISINFORMATION: THE VEDAS

The third piece of disinformation concerns the Vedic religion. Ah, the Vedas! So much misconception, so many prejudices, so much distortion have been spewed about this monument of a book, this unparalleled epic. Daniélou for instance, maintains that the original Vedas were an oral Dravidian tradition, which was reshaped by the Aryans and later put down in Sanskrit. He finds lineage between the Vedic religion and the Persian religion (Zarathustra), as well as the Greek gods; the problem is that he seems to imply that the Vedic religion may have sprung from the Zoroastrian creed! He also puts down all Vedic symbols as purely physical signs: for instance *Agni* is the fire that should always burn in the house's altar. Finally, he sees in the *Rig-veda* "only a remarkable document on the mode of life, society and history of the Aryans" (*Histoire de l'Inde*, p. 62).

But Daniélou must be the mildest of all critics. The real disinformation started again with the missionaries, who saw in the Vedas "the root of evil," the source of paganism and went systematically about belittling it. The Jesuits, in their dialectical cleverness, brought it down to a set of pagan offerings without great importance. Henceforth, this theory was perpetuated by most Western historians, who not only stripped the Vedas of any spiritual value, but actually post-dated them to approximately 1500 to 1000 years BC. It is rather unfortunate that these theories have been followed blindly and without trying to ascertain their truth, by many Indian historians and sociologists such as Romila Tharpar.

And even when more enlightened foreigners like Max Mueller, whose Sanskrit scholarship cannot be denied, took up the Vedas, they only saw "that it is full of childish, silly, even monstrous conceptions, that it is tedious, low, commonplace, that it represents human nature on a low level of selfishness and worldliness and that only here and there are a few rare sentiments that come from the depths of the soul". But, as we saw in the second chapter, as long as India will not realize what a treasure not only for herself, but also for the whole humanity it possesses in the Vedas, the seed of discord planted by the missionaries and the so-called Sanskritists will continue its work of ignorance.

The question must be asked: after 20 years of BJP influence at the national and state levels, are the Vedas taught to Indian children in mainstream schools or colleges? We find that in most government and private schools, the Vedas are only briefly mentioned in history or cultural studies, with no serious focus on their content, philosophy, or spiritual depth. Sanskrit, though offered as a subject in some schools, rarely includes direct exposure to Vedic hymns or chanting, and mainly emphasizes grammar and simple texts. In colleges, a few specialized departments in universities such as Banaras Hindu University or Sanskrit-focused institutions offer Vedic studies, but these are limited in scope and attract only a small number of students. They are treated as niche academic areas, not part of the core curriculum for the vast majority. Some traditional *gurukuls* and *pathshalas* continue to teach the Vedas in the oral tradition, often with deep devotion and scholarly rigor, but these remain marginal and lack mainstream recognition or support. While the BJP government has promoted Indian knowledge systems through initiatives like the National Education Policy 2020 and shown rhetorical support for Vedic heritage, the actual integration of Vedic learning into the national education framework has been minimal. The Vedas, as living texts of wisdom, are still largely excluded from the modern Indian educational experience. Sad, but true.

Thus, once these three disinformations, that of the Aryans, the caste system and the Vedas, have been set right, one can begin to perceive in its proper perspective the Wonder that IS India.

Chapter 18

The Independence Movement

It is hoped that one day the history of India's independence movement will be rewritten in full. What is taught today— both in the West and in India—often reflects only the superficial, the convenient, or even the distorted. Figures who contributed little to India's independence, or worse who were partially responsible for its most terrible traumas, are celebrated as heroes. Meanwhile, those with a deeper vision, who worked with dedication for a true, wholesome independence, remain in the shadows, sidelined or misrepresented by historians.

History wants us to believe that the independence movement started with the Indian National Congress. But originally, the Congress was a tool fashioned by the British for their own use. Witness the fact that it all began in December 1885, with an Englishman, A.O. Hume (1829-1912), with the avowed aim to: "Allow all those who work for the national (read British) good to meet each other personally, to discuss and decide on the political operations to start during the year."

And certainly, till the end of the 19th century, the Congress, who regarded British rule in India as a "divine dispensation," was happy with criticizing moderately the government, while reaffirming its loyalty to the Crown and its faith in "liberalism" and the British innate "sense of justice"!

Thus, for a long time, the Britishers considered the Congress favorably and sought to use it to justify their continuing occupation of India. But soon, of course, it changed into suspicion and downright hostility, as the Congress, realizing its folly, turned towards constitutional agitation to obtain from the British Parliament a few laws favorable to India. And the Englishmen did hand over a few crumbs here and there, such as giving

Lord Sinha (Lord Sinha indeed!) the honour of becoming the first Indian to be part of the Governor's Executive Council... So what?

What must be understood to grasp the whole history of the Congress is that its pre-independence leaders were anglicized, western educated Indians, whose idealism was at best a dose of liberalism peppered with a bit of socialism "British Labour style." They were the outcrop of an old British policy of forming a small westernized elite, cut off from its Indian roots, which will serve in the intermediary hierarchies of the British Raj and act as go-between the master and the slaves. Thus, not only were these Congress leaders "moderate" (as they came to be called), partially cut off from the reality of India, from the greatness that Was India, the soul-glory of its simple people, but because their mind worked on the pattern of their masters, they turned to be the greatest Hindu-baiters and haters of them all—as verily their descendants, even until today, still are.

But these westernized moderate Congress leaders struggled to connect with the vast mass of India, who remained deeply rooted in their religious traditions. Thus, they encouraged the start of "reformed" Hindu movements, such as the Arya Samaj or the Brahmo Samaj, through which they could attack the old Hindu system, under the guise of transforming it, which is perfectly acceptable to all Hindus, as Hinduism has always tolerated in its fold divergent movements. It is these early Congress leaders who began the slow but insidious crushing of the Hindu society. For instance, the Congress governments, which were installed after July 1937 in most of the provinces, encouraged everywhere the development of education modeled on the British system. And comments Daniélou: "The teaching of philosophy, arts, sciences, which constituted the prestigious Indian cultural tradition, became more and more ignored and could only survive thanks to the Brahmins, without any help whatsoever from the State." When the first true cultural, social and political movements, which had at heart the defence of India's true heritage started taking shape, such as the much decreed Hindu Mahasabha, which attempted to counterbalance the Muslim League's influence, or the even more maligned Rama Rajya Parishad, initiated by the remarkable Hindu monk Swami Karpatri, they were ridiculed by the Congress, which used to amplify the problems of untouchability, castes, or cow worshiping to belittle these movements. Which, after all, were only trying to change India from a greatness that was to a greatness to be.

"The Congress," writes Daniélou, "utilised to the hilt its English speaking press to present these Hindu parties as barbaric, fanatical, ridiculous; and the British media in turn, took-up, as parrots, the cry of their Indian counterparts." (*Histoire de l'Inde*, p. 345) To this day, nothing has changed in India: the English-speaking press still indulges in Hindu-bashing and it is faithfully copied by the western correspondents, most of whom are totally ignorant of India and turn towards Indian intellectuals to fashion their opinions.

But this strategy was good enough to convince the British that when they left, they would have to hand over power to the "respectable" Congress (after all, we are all gentlemen), even though it constituted a tiny westernized minority, whereas India's true Hindu majority would be deprived of their right.

The Congress did turn radical finally in 1942, when because of Mahatma Gandhi's rigorous non-violence policy, it adopted a non-co-operation attitude towards the war effort. Thus, the British declared the Congress illegal, jailed most of its leaders and embarked on a policy of heavy repression. But the truth is that those of the Congress who were imprisoned and are deified today for that fact, went there not directly for India's independence, but because Mahatma Gandhi refused to cooperate in the second world war.

So, ultimately, what was true nationalism? Who were the real revolutionaries, those who had an inner vision of what the British really represented, those who knew what was the genius of India and how it was destined to be great again? Once more, we have a wrong understanding of nationalism, because we are induced in error by the West's opinions about it. In Europe, nationalism means external revolutionary movements, revolutionaries and materialism. But India's greatness has always lain in her spirituality; her strength has always flowed from the power of the Spirit. Not only the Brahmins, but also the Kshatriyas, Vaishyas and Shudras drew their heroism from this wellspring. It was therefore natural that India's nationalist movement, the true REAWAKENING of her soul, began at the source: in her Spirit.

Sometimes a nation's soul is more predominant in one region, in one particular culture. In India's early independence movement, it was Bengal which held high the light of reawakening. This has often been forgotten and justice should be done again. Thus, in Bengal, there was born a man who could not read and write a single word. A man without intellectual training, a man who would be considered totally useless by Britishers, or westernized Indians. But this man's inner strength was so great, his truth so radiating, that from all over India, educated and uneducated, rich and poor, they came to the temple of Dakshineswar in Calcutta and bowed at the feet of Shri Ramakrishna. The work of salvation, the work of raising India out of her lethargic sleep HAD BEGUN. Narendranath Dutta, later known as Swami Vivekananda, was the brightest disciple of Ramakrishna, and a true son of India. He was the first spiritualized Indian political leader, an ardent Hindu, who was not afraid to call for Hinduism's adaptation to the modern world. He was also the first to inspire in the Western world a certain respect towards Hinduism, because of his education and his forceful personality.

But the man who was the true visionary of an independent India, the man who worked most of all for her liberation, the man who was a yogi, a saint, an avatar, has been mostly ignored by history. Others, who played only a superficial role and did not have a millionth of his vision, took the forefront. That man of course was Sri Aurobindo. Born on 15 August 1872 in Calcutta, he spent his first years at Rangpur (now in Bangladesh) and at the age of 5 was sent to Loreto Convent School in Darjeeling. His father, who wanted him to have a thorough Western education, packed him off to England, where he entered St Paul's School in London in 1884 and King's College, Cambridge in 1890. Sri Aurobindo was a brilliant student and passed the I.C.S., but "failed" to appear for the riding test and was disqualified. After spending 13 years in England, Sri Aurobindo returned to India on 6 February 1893 at the age of 20. He joined the Baroda State Service from 1897 to early 1906 and taught French and English at the Baroda college, before eventually becoming its principal. It was at that time that he started writing a series of articles, "New Lamps for Old" in the *Indu Prakash*, a Marathi-English daily from Bombay. A sample of his early writing includes: "I say of the Congress that its aims are mistaken, that the spirit in which it is proceeding is not a spirit of sincerity and whole-heartedness and that the methods it has chosen are not the right methods, and their leaders in whom it trusts, not the right sort of men to be leaders. In brief, we are at present the blind led, if not by the blind, at least by the one-eyed. (*Rebirth of India,* p. 10). From 1900 onwards, Sri Aurobindo realized that passive resistance, constitutional agitation, "A La Congress," was not the right path to achieve an independent India. In the true spirit of a yogi, he re-enacted the *Bhagavad Gita's* great message: that violence is sometimes necessary, if it flows from Dharma—and today's Dharma is the liberation of India. Thus, he began contacting revolutionary groups in Maharashtra and Bengal and tried to coordinate their action. One should remember that at that time, and indeed until independence, violence against the oppressive British was not organized; it was the work of a few individuals or a sudden outburst of uncontrolled anger and that the famous freedom fighters of the Congress only went to jail because they were passive resisters. At Sri Aurobindo's initiative, P. Mitter, Surendranath Tagore and Sister Nivedita formed the first Secret Council for revolutionary activities in Bengal. But action was accompanied by inner vision: "While others look upon their country as an inert piece of matter, forests, hills and rivers, I look upon my country as the Mother. What would a son do if a demon sat on her mother's breast and started sucking her blood?... I know I have the strength to deliver this fallen race. It is not physical strength—I am not going to fight with sword or gun, but with the strength of knowledge" (*India's Rebirth*, p. 16)

In 1905, the terrible Lord Curzon partitioned Bengal. This divide-and-rule move was meant to break the back of Bengali political agitation and use the East Bengal Muslim community to drive a wedge between Hindus and Muslims, a policy that was to culminate in India's partition in 1947. Bengal responded to its partition with massive and unanimous protests in which many personalities took part, such as Rabindranath Tagore, Surendranath Banerjee, Bepin Chandra Pal... The ideal of Swadeshi, which called for the boycott of British goods, spread widely. It was at this time that B.C. Pal launched the famous English daily, *Bande Mataram*; Sri Aurobindo joined it and soon became its editor. Day after day, he jotted down his vision and tried to instil fire and courage in the nation through the pages of *Bande Mataram*. What was true nationalism for Sri Aurobindo? "Nationalism is not a mere political programme; nationalism is a religion that has come from God; Nationalism is a creed which you shall have to live. If you are going to be a nationalist, if you are going to assent to this religion of Nationalism, you must do it in the religious spirit. You must remember that you are the instruments of God... "Then there will be a blessing on our work and this great nation will rise again and become once more what it was in the days of spiritual greatness. You are the instruments of God to save the light, to save the spirit of India from lasting obscuration and abasement..." (*Vande Mataram*, p. 655)

But Sri Aurobindo had to fight against the Congress Moderates (who, it must be remembered, came out openly for complete independence only in 1929), of whom he said: "There is a certain section of India which regards Nationalism as madness and they say Nationalism will ruin the country. They are men who live in the pure intellect and they look at things purely from the intellectual point of view. What does the intellect think? Here is a work that you have undertaken, a work so gigantic, so stupendous, the means of which are so poor, the resistance to which will be so strong, so organised, so disciplined, so well equipped with all the weapons science can supply, with all the strength that human power and authority can give... (*Vande Mataram*, p. 656)

Sri Aurobindo was very clear in what was demanded of a leader of India: "Politics is the work of the Kshatriya and it is the virtues of the Kshatriya we must develop if we are to be morally fit for freedom." *(India's Rebirth,* p. 19) Or: "What India needs at the moment is the aggressive virtues, the spirit of soaring idealism, bold creation, fearless resistance, courageous attack." (*India's Rebirth,* p. 22) But if the Moderates dismissed Sri Aurobindo as a "mystic," Lord Minto, then Viceroy of India, made no such mistake, calling him, "the most dangerous man we have to deal with at present." Thus, Sri Aurobindo was arrested on 2 May 1908, following a failed assassination attempt on a British judge by a nationalist belonging to his brother's secret society. Sri Aurobindo spent a year in jail, which proved to be the turning point of his life as he went through the whole gamut of spiritual realizations. When he came out, the nationalist movement had nearly collapsed and he set about giving it a fresh impetus, launching a new English weekly, the *Karmayogin,* as well as a Bengali weekly, *Dharma.* The following is an extract from his famous Uttarpara speech, where he speaks of his spiritual experiences in jail: "Something has been shown to you in this year of seclusion, something about which you had your doubts and it is the truth of the Hindu religion. It is this religion that I am raising up before the world, it is this that I have perfected and developed through the rishis, saints and avatars, and now it is going forth to do my work among the nations. I am raising this nation to send forth my word... When therefore it is said that India shall rise, it is the Sanatana Dharma that shall rise. When it is said that India shall be great, it is the Sanatana Dharma that shall be great. But what is the Hindu religion? It is the Hindu religion only, because the Hindu nation has kept it, because in this peninsula it grew up in the seclusion of the sea and the Himalayas, because in this sacred and ancient land it was given as a charge to the Aryan race to preserve through the ages. That which we call the Hindu religion is really the eternal religion, because it is the universal religion which embraces all others. If a religion is not universal, it cannot be eternal. A narrow religion, a sectarian religion, an exclusive religion can live only for a limited time and limited purpose... I say no longer that Sanatana Dharma is for us nationalism... Sanatana Dharma IS nationalism." (*India's Rebirth,* p.46)

In mid-February 1910, news reached that the British had again decided to arrest Sri Aurobindo and close down the offices of the Karmayogin. By that time Sri Aurobindo had the vision that India was free; for the external events are always preceded by an occult happening, sometimes long before they become "fait accompli." Sri Aurobindo then received an "Adesh," an inspiration that he must go to Pondicherry, then under French rule. He settled there, with a few disciples, the number of whom slowly swelled, until it became known as the Sri Aurobindo Ashram. He wrote all his masterpieces and devoted the remainder of his life to bringing down what he called the "supramental manifestation on the earth." The great Sage passed away on 5 December 1950.

For Sri Aurobindo, true Hinduism was not only the foundation of India's past greatness, but also the very essence of her nationalism—the MEANS of her liberation, and the bedrock upon which the future of India must be built. Unfortunately, the leaders of the Indian National Congress did not share the same vision. Of these leaders, history has mostly remembered two, the most famous of all: Jawaharlal Nehru and Mahatma Gandhi.

JAWAHARLAL NEHRU

"Nehru," writes Daniélou, "was the perfect replica of a certain type of Englishman. He often used the expression 'continental people,' with an amused and sarcastic manner, to designate French or Italians. He despised non-anglicised Indians and had a very superficial and partial knowledge of India. His ideal was the romantic socialism of 19th century Britain. But this type of socialism was totally unfit to India, where there was no class struggle and where the conditions were totally different from 19th century Europe." (*Histoire de l'Inde,* p. 349) It should be noted that Nehru was not a fiery leader—perhaps due to his innate "gentlemanship." He often yielded not only to Gandhi's views, with which he sometimes disagreed, but also to the pressure of Jinnah and the fanatical Indian Muslim minority, as well as to the British—particularly Lord Mountbatten. Though history often portrays Mountbatten as the benevolent last Viceroy of India, he was in fact one of the chief architects of Partition, whatever despite what *Freedom at Midnight*—a highly romanticized book—would have us believe. (Remember Churchill's statement upon learning of Partition: "At last we had the last word.") It may be added that the British had a habit of leaving a total mess when they had to surrender a colony, witness Palestine, Ireland, or India.

Nehru has also been made into a myth by foreign writers, such as French Catherine Clement (born in 1939), who wrote a ridiculous and pompous novel depicting the love between Nehru and Lady Mountbatten. The problem is not whether they had sex or not together, the problem rather is that this "affair" only symbolizes the fatal attraction which Nehru had for the White Skin—for Edwina Mountbatten was certainly not a beauty, but was in fact renowned for her nymphomania and inconsequence—an attraction for the White Skin which the Congress perpetuated faithfully and still incarnated today by Sonia Gandhi, who was able to woo the masses, when she had absolutely no qualifications to lead India through a proxy PM. The problem is not whether Mountbatten was made a cuckold or not—but that it was India which was cuckolded, for Nehru was unfaithful to India by letting his weaknesses influence him in accepting partition and the terms dictated by the British.

The Congress has today made an icon out of Nehru, which nobody has yet dared to touch, but as we will see in the next chapter and as history will show more and more, Nehru did tremendous harm to India by initiating movements and patterns, which not only did vast damage in their times, but continue to survive and weigh down the Indian nation, long after their uselessness has been realized.

MAHATMA GANDHI

Mahatma Gandhi was indeed a great soul, an extraordinary human being, a man with a tremendous appeal to the people. But, unfortunately, he was a misfit in India. Karma or fate, or God, or whatever you want to call it, made a mistake when they sent him down to the land of Bharat. For at heart, Gandhi was a European, his ideals were a blend of Christianity raised to an exalted moral standard and a dose of liberalism "à la Tolstoy." The patterns and goals he put forward for India not only came to naught, but sometimes did great harm to a country, which unquestionably he loved immensely. Furthermore, even after his death, Gandhism, although it does not really have any relevance to Modern India, is still used shamelessly by all politicians and intellectuals, to smoke-screen their ineffectiveness and to perpetuate their power. To understand Gandhi properly, one has to put in perspective his aims, his goals, and the results today.

One has to start at the beginning. There is no doubt that after his bitter experiences with racism in South Africa, he took to heart the plight of fellow Indians there. But what did he achieve for them? Second class citizenship! Worse, he dissociated them from their black African brothers, who share the same color and are the majority. And today the Indians in South Africa are in a difficult position, sandwiched between the Whites who prefer them to the Blacks, but do not accept them fully as their own and the Blacks who often despise them for their superior attitudes. Ultimately, they sided with the Moderate Whites led by De Klerk and this was a mistake as Mandela was elected and the Blacks wrested total power in South Africa.

The Mahatma did a lot for India. But the question again is: What remains today in India of Gandhi's heritage? Spinning was a joke. "He made Charkha a religious article of faith and excluded all people from Congress membership who would not spin. How many, even among his own followers, believe in the gospel of Charkha? Such a tremendous waste of energy, just for the sake of a few *annas,* is most unreasonable," wrote Sri Aurobindo in 1938 (*India's Rebirth* p. 207). Does any Congress leader today still weave cotton? And has Gandhi's khadi policy of village handicrafts for India survived him? Nehru was the first to embark upon a massive "Soviet type" heavy industrialization, resolutely turning his back on Gandhi's policy, although handicrafts in India do have their place.

Then, nowhere does Gandhi's great Christian morality find more expression than in his attitude towards sex. All his life he felt guilty about having made love to his wife while his father was dying. But guilt is truly a Western prerogative. In India sex has (was at least) always been put in its proper place, neither suppressed, as in Victorian times, nor brought to its extreme perversion, like in the West today. Gandhi's attitude towards sex was to remain ambivalent all his life, sleeping with his beautiful nieces "to test his brahmacharya," while advocating abstinence for India's population control. But why impose on others what he practised for himself? Again, this is a very Christian attitude: the popes, today, enjoin all Christians to do the same. But did Gandhi think for a minute how millions of Indian women would be able to persuade their husbands to abstain from sex when they are fertile? And who will suffer abortions, pregnancy and other ignominies? And again, India has totally turned its back on Gandhi's policy: today its birth control program must be the most elaborate in the world—and does not even utilize force (except for a short period during the Emergency), as the Chinese have done.

For all the world, Gandhi is synonymous with non-violence. But once more, a very Christian notion. Gandhi loved the *Mahabharata.* But did he understand that sometimes non-violence does more harm than violence itself? That violence sometimes is "Dharma," if it is done for defending one's country, or oneself, or one's mother, or sisters? Take the Cripps' proposals for instance. In 1942, the Japanese were at the doors of India. England was weakened, vulnerable and desperately needed support. Churchill sent Sir Stafford Cripps to India to propose that if India participated in the war effort, Great Britain would grant her Dominion status (as in Australia or Canada) at the end of the war. Sri Aurobindo sent a personal letter to the Congress, urging it to accept. Nehru wavered, but ultimately, Gandhi in the name of non-violence put his foot down and the Cripps proposal was rejected. Had it been accepted, history might have been changed, Partition and its terrible bloodshed would have been avoided.

Gandhi also never seemed to have realized the great danger that Nazism represented for humanity. A great *Asuric* wave had risen in Europe and threatened to engulf the world, and it had to be fought with violence. Calling Hitler "my beloved brother," a man who murdered six million Jews in cold blood just to prove the purity of his own race, is more than just innocence; it borders on criminal credulity. And did not Gandhi also advise the Jews to let themselves be butchered?

Ultimately, it must be said that whatever his saintliness, his extreme and somehow rigid asceticism, Gandhi did enormous harm to India and this harm has two names: Muslims and Untouchables.

The British must have rubbed their hands in glee: here was a man who was perfecting their policy of rule-and-divide, for ultimately nobody more than Gandhi contributed to the partition of India, by his obsession to always give in to the Muslims, by his obstinate refusal to see that the Muslims always started rioting—Hindus only retaliated; by his indulgence of Jinnah, going as far as proposing to make him the Prime Minister of India. Sri Aurobindo was very clear about Hindu-Muslim unity: "I am sorry they are making a fetish of Hindu-Muslim unity. It is no use ignoring facts; someday, the Hindus may have to fight the Muslims and they must prepare for it. Hindu-Muslim unity should not mean the subjection of the Hindus. Every time the mildness of the Hindu has given way. The best solution would be to allow the Hindus to organise themselves and the Hindu-Muslim unity would take care of itself, it would automatically solve the problem. Otherwise we are lulled into a false sense of satisfaction that we have solved a difficult problem, when in fact we have only shelved it." (*India's Rebirth,* p. 159)

Gandhi's love of the Harijans, as he called them, was certainly very touching and sprang from the highest motivations, but it had also as its base a Christian notion that would have found a truer meaning in Europe, where there are no castes, only classes. Glorifying the scavenger as a man of God makes good poetry, but little social meaning. In the words of Sri Aurobindo: "The idea that it needs a special "punya" to be born a Bhangi is, of course, one of these forceful exaggerations which are common to the Mahatma and greatly impress the mind of his hearers. The idea behind is that his function is an indispensable service to society, quite as much as the Brahmin's, but that being disagreeable, it would need a special moral heroism to choose it voluntarily and he thinks as if the soul freely chose it as such a heroic service to the society and as reward of righteous acts—but that is hardly likely. In any case, it is not true that the Bhangi life is superior to the Brahmin life and the reward of special righteousness, no more that it is true that a man is superior because he is born a Brahmin. A spiritual man of pariah birth is superior in the divine values to an unspiritual and worldly-minded Brahmin. Birth counts but the basic value is in the soul behind the man and the degree to which it manifests itself in nature." (*India's Rebirth,* p. 201)

Once more Gandhi took the European element in the decrying of the caste system, forgetting the divine element behind. And, unfortunately, he sowed the seeds of future disorders and of a caste war in India, of which we see the effects only today.

Non-violence, you say? But Gandhi did the greatest violence to his body, in true Christian fashion, punishing it, to blackmail others in doing his will, even if he thought it was for the greater good. And ultimately, it may be asked, what remains of Gandhi's non-violence today? India has fought four wars with Pakistan, if you included Kargil had to combat the Chinese, has the second biggest army in the world and has to fight counter-insurgency movements in Punjab, Assam and Kashmir. Gandhi must have died a broken man indeed. He saw India partitioned, Hindus and Muslims fighting each other and his ideals of Charkha, non-violence and Brahmacharya being flouted by the very men he brought up as his disciples.

However, his heritage is not dead, for it survives where it should have been in the first instance: in the West. His ideals have inspired countless great figures, from Martin Luther King, to Albert Einstein, to Nelson Mandela, the Dalai Lama or David Attenborough (the British writer and environmentalist), and continue to inspire many others. Gandhi's birth in India was an accident, for here there is nothing left of him, except millions of statues and streets and saintly mouthings by politicians, who don't apply the least bit what Gandhi had taught so ardently.

History will judge. But with Nehru on one side and his westernized concept of India and Gandhi on the other, who tried to impose upon India a non-violence which was not hers, India was destined to be partitioned. Thus when the time came, India was bled into two, in three even, and Muslims took their pound of flesh while leaving. India never recovered from that trauma and today she is still suffering from its consequences. Yet has anybody really understood the lessons of history?

Sister Nivedita: A Rare Exception to Western Imperialism

The history of India's independence movement would be incomplete without acknowledging the West's complex but notable contribution. Amid the overarching insensitivity and exploitation of colonial rule, a few Western voices stood out in admiration and defence of India's spiritual and cultural heritage. Among them, Sister Nivedita—an Irish disciple of Swami Vivekananda—remains a luminous figure. She not only recognized India's innate greatness, but also immersed herself completely in its service, dedicating her life to the upliftment of Indian women, education, and ultimately, the cause of India's freedom. Her devotion was not superficial but deeply rooted in an understanding of India's spiritual soul. Similarly, the Theosophical Society, founded in 1875 by Madame Blavatsky and Colonel Olcott, played an important role in bringing the philosophical depth of Hinduism to the Western world. Under Annie Besant's dynamic leadership, the Society inspired many Indians to rediscover the pride of their ancient civilization. Besant herself became a powerful voice in the freedom movement and served as president of the Indian

National Congress in 1917. Her vision was clear: "The action to pursue is to revitalise ancient India to bring back a renewal of patriotism, the beginning of the reconstruction of the nation."

However, the Theosophical Society also, at times, drifted too far into a romanticized vision of the "mystical Orient," losing touch with the more grounded, pragmatic needs of a country in bondage. Nonetheless, these Western allies of Indian civilization left behind a valuable legacy: they reminded colonized Indians that their culture was not primitive or backward, but among the deepest and most refined humanity has known. Their efforts helped rekindle a sense of self-worth and pride that ultimately nourished India's quest for independence.

CHAPTER 19

1947, Independence

India was free—but at what price? Was this the independence for which countless nationalists had struggled and laid down their lives? Was this truncated, diminished, partitioned land truly the Bharat of old, whose vast frontiers had once extended from Cape Comorin to Afghanistan?

Moreover, who was responsible for the Partition of India? Yes, the British used to the hilt the existing divide between Hindus and Muslims. Yes, the Congress was weak; it accepted what was forced down its throat by Jinnah and Mountbatten, even though many of its leaders, including Nehru, and a few moderate Muslims, disagreed with the principle of partition. It was also Gandhi's policy of non-violence and gratifying the fanatical Muslim minority, in the hope that it would see the light, which did tremendous harm to India and encouraged Jinnah to harden his demands.

Ultimately, to understand Partition, one must return to the roots—to the very beginning. Only by journeying back through history can we grasp the overall picture. That is why memory matters, and why Holocausts—of any people must never be forgotten.

For the Jinnahs, the Zia ul-Haqs, the Musharrafs or today's Asif Ali Zardari (born in 1955, the present President of Pakistan) are only the vehicles, the instruments, the avatars, the latest reincarnations of the medieval Muslims coming down to rape and loot and plunder the land of Bharat. They are the true sons of Mahmud Ghaznavi, of Muhammed Ghazi, of Aurangzeb. They took up again the work left unfinished by the last Mughal two centuries earlier: 'Dar-ul-Islam', the House of Islam. The Hindu-Muslim question is an old one—but is it really a Muslim-Hindu question, or just plainly a Muslim obsession, their hatred of the Hindu pagans, their contempt for this polytheistic religion? This obsession, this hate, is as old as the first invasion of India by the original Arabs in 650. After independence, nothing has changed: the sword of Allah is still as much ready to strike the *Kafirs,* the idolaters of many gods. The Muslims invaded this country, conquered it, looted it, razed its temples, humiliated its Hindu leaders, killed its Brahmins and converted its weaker sections. True, it was all done in the name of Allah and many of its chiefs were sincere in thinking they were doing their duty by hunting down the Infidel. So how could they accept on 15 August 1947 to share power on an equal basis with those who were their slaves for thirteen centuries? "*Either the sole power for ourselves, and our rule over the Hindus as it is our sovereign right, we the adorers of the one and only true God—Or we quit India and found our own nation, a Muslim nation, of the true faith, where we will live amongst ourselves.*"

Thus, there is no place for idolaters in this country, this great nation of Pakistan; they can at best be "tolerated" as second-class citizens. Hence the near total exodus of Hindus from Pakistan, whereas more than half the Muslim population in India chose to stay, knowing full well that they would get the freedom to be and to practice their own religion. In passing, the Muslims took revenge on the Hindus—once more—and indulged in terrible massacres, which were followed by retaliations from Sikhs and hard core Hindus, the ultimate horror.

The Partition triggered one of the most terrible exodus in the history of humanity. And this exodus has not ended: they still come by the lakhs every year from Bangladesh (it is estimated that there are today *twenty million* illegal Bangladeshis in India, some of them Rohingyas, see box), fleeing poverty, flooding India with problems, when the country already has so many of its own. Some even say that they bring with them more fundamentalism, a Third Column, which one day could organize itself in a political, social and militant body.

The Rohingya Menace

The presence of Rohingya refugees (a Muslim ethnic minority primarily from the western region of Rakhine in Myanmar) in India has raised several concerns, especially in regions where they have settled in significant numbers such as Jammu, Hyderabad, Delhi, and parts of West Bengal. While many came fleeing ethnic persecution from Myanmar, their arrival and settlement have not been without controversy. One of the primary issues cited is the illegal nature of their entry. India does not have a national refugee law, and since it is not a signatory to the 1951 UN Refugee Convention, most Rohingyas are classified as illegal immigrants. Despite this, some state and local authorities have been accused of providing them with ration cards, Aadhaar IDs, and even voter IDs, allegedly to secure their political loyalty in elections. This raises serious concerns about the integrity of India's electoral process and the potential misuse of identity documentation systems.

There have also been allegations that some Rohingya settlements have caused friction with local Hindu populations. These include disputes over land encroachment, economic competition, and, in rare instances, accusations of criminal activity. In areas like Jammu, local Hindus have expressed fear of demographic imbalance and cultural disruption due to the growing presence of a largely Muslim refugee population. More troubling are the security concerns. Intelligence agencies have reported instances where radical Islamist groups may have tried to influence or recruit vulnerable Rohingya youth. While such cases are limited, the potential for radicalization in a stateless, impoverished population is taken seriously by Indian authorities.

In summary, while many Rohingyas in India are simply trying to survive after fleeing violence, their presence has also been politicized. Some politicians allegedly use them for vote banks, while others warn of the long-term security and demographic implications. The situation remains complex, with humanitarian, political and national security dimensions all interwoven.

For Daniélou, the division of India was on the human level as well as on the political one, a great mistake. "It added," he says, "to the Middle East an unstable state (Pakistan) and burdened India which already had serious problems." And he adds: "India, whose ancient borders stretched until Afghanistan, lost with the country of seven rivers (the Indus Valley), the historical centre of her civilisation. At a time when the Muslim invaders seemed to have lost some of their extremism and were ready to assimilate themselves to other populations of India, the European conquerors, before returning home, surrendered once more to Muslim fanaticism, the cradle of Hindu civilization ." (*Histoire de l'Inde,* p.355)

For Sri Aurobindo also, the division of India was a monstrosity: "India is free, but she has not achieved unity, only a fissured and broken freedom... The whole communal division into Hindu and Muslim seems to have hardened into the figure of a permanent political division of the country. It is to be hoped that the Congress and the Nation will not accept the settled fact as forever settled, or as anything more than a temporary expedient. For if it lasts, India may be seriously weakened, even crippled; civil strife may remain always possible, possibly even a new invasion and foreign conquest. **The partition of the country must go... For without it the destiny** of India might be seriously impaired and frustrated. That must not be." (Message of Sri Aurobindo on the 15 August 1947)

Sri Aurobindo had long seen through the British and Jinnah's games and had warned the nation as early as the beginning of the century. His answer to a disciple on 7 October 1940 is very illustrative of the point: "Q. But now that our national consciousness is more developed, there is more chance of unity if the British don't bolster Jinnah and his Muslim claims.

A. Does Jinnah want unity?...What he wants is independence for Muslims and if possible rule over India. THAT IS THE OLD SPIRIT... But why is it expected that Muslims will be so accommodating?"

Nevertheless, Sri Aurobindo thought that although the old spirit of the real warriors of Islam, the Muslim invaders, was still present, the majority of Indian Muslims were unconcerned: "The idea of two nationalities in India is only a new-fanged notion invented by Jinnah for his purposes and contrary to the facts. More than 90% of the Indian Muslims are descendants of converted Hindus and belong as much to the Indian nation as the Hindu themselves. Jinnah is himself a descendant of a Hindu named Jinnahbhai... (*India's Rebirth,* p. 237)

Sri Aurobindo also sought to dispel the widespread notion that the Muslims brought so much to India: "The Islamic culture hardly gave anything to the world which may be said of fundamental importance and typically its own Islamic culture was mainly borrowed from the others. Their mathematics, astronomy and other subjects were derived from India and Greece. It is true they gave some of these things a new turn, but they have not created much. Their philosophy and their religion are very simple and what they call Sufism is largely the result of Gnostics who lived in Persia and it is the logical outcome of that school of thought largely touched by the Vedanta... Islamic culture contributed the Indo-Saracenic architecture to Indian culture. I do not think it has done anything more in India of cultural value. It gave some new forms to art and poetry. Its political institutions were always semi-barbaric." (*India's Rebirth,* p.189)

How could Partition have been avoided? Sri Aurobindo had advocated firmness: "As for the Hindu-Muslim affair, I saw no reason why the greatness of India's past or her spirituality should be thrown into the waste paper basket in order to conciliate the Muslims who would not be conciliated at all by such a policy. What has created the Hindu-Moslem split was not Swadeshi, but the acceptance of a communal principle by the Congress." (*India's Rebirth,* p. 189) History was going to show the accuracy of Sri Aurobindo's predictions: the Congress' obstinate pandering to Jinnah and his terms proved to be disastrous and the partition of India was a blow from which the nation has not yet recovered.

All right, Nehru got his 'tryst with destiny,' although a truncated tryst. India was free and everything was anew, the sky was the limit and a new glory was awaiting the land of Bharat. But what did Nehru and the Congress proceed to do with this new India? Writes Daniélou: "The Hindus who had mostly supported the Congress in its fight for independence, had thought that the modernist ideology of an Anglo-Saxon inspiration of its leaders was only a political weapon destined to justify independence in the eyes of Westerners. They thought that once independence was acquired, the Congress would revise its policies and would re-establish proper respect towards Sanskrit culture, Hindu religious and social institutions, which form the basis of Indian civilisation. But doing nothing, the minority formed by the Congress leaders was too anglicised, to reconsider the value of what they had learnt. Few things changed in Indian administration, only the colour of the skin of the new rulers, who were most of the time lower ranked officials of the old regime." (*Histoire de l'Inde,* p. 348)

And indeed, atop the tragedy of Partition lies another calamity for modern India: under Nehru's leadership, the nation largely turned its back on its ancient social and political institutions, adapted blindly and completely the British system—constitutional, social, political, judicial, and bureaucratic. In doing so, not only was the greatness that was India neglected, but, perhaps unconsciously, steps were taken to ensure that the greatness that is India could never fully emerge.

Democracy was then the new name of the game for India. But Sri Aurobindo had very clear ideas on western democracy: "I believe in something which might be called social democracy, but not in any of the forms now, and I am not altogether in love with the European kind, however great it may be an improvement upon the past. **I hold that India, having a spirit of her own and a governing temperament proper to her own civilisation, should in politics as in everything else, strike out her original path and not stumble in the wake of Europe. But this is precisely what she will be obliged to do if she has to start on the road in her present chaotic and unprepared condition of mind.**" This was written, mind you, on 5 January 1920 (*India's Rebirth,* p. 143)—and it was exactly what happened. Sri Aurobindo also felt: "The old Indian system *grew out of life;* it had room for everything and every interest. There was monarchy, aristocracy, and democracy; every interest was represented in the government. While in Europe the Western system *grew out of the mind*: they are led by reason and want to make everything cut and dried without any chance for freedom or variation. India is now trying to imitate the West. The parliamentary government is not suited to India..."

Socialism certainly has its values, as Sri Aurobindo observed in 1914. "The communistic principle of society is intrinsically as superior to the individualistic as is brotherhood to jealousy and mutual slaughter; but all the practical schemes of Socialism invented in Europe are a yoke, a tyranny and a prison." (*India's Rebirth,* p. 99). At India's independence, Nehru opted for what Daniélou calls "romantic socialism." Was socialism best suited for India? It was maybe a matter for the best in the worst, to forestall a complete take-over by communism,(*) which would have, as in China, entirely killed the soul of India and damaged for ever its Dharma. But if Nehru and the Congress leaders had not been so anglicized and had known a little more of the exalted past of their country, they would have opted for a more Indianized system of socialism, such as the ancient panchayat system (which Rajiv Gandhi would attempt to revive later). Their socialism, although it was full of great and noble intentions, created great evils in India. Writes Daniélou: "But this socialism was empty of meaning, for there existed no class struggle in India, nor social conditions similar to those in Europe. The controls established by an incapable and corrupted bureaucracy, the ruin of private property, the incredible taxes slapped on capital, the confiscations, the dictatorial exchange controls, and the heavy custom duties, plunged India in a terrible misery. The lands of the zamindars were distributed to the poor peasants, without any institution of agricultural financing, and farmers, depending 100% on the loan shark, got completely ruined and agricultural production went into a slump. The prohibition to export profits as well as the excessive taxes, forced all capitalists to flee the country." (*Histoire de l'Inde,* p. 349)

One of the worst legacies of Nehru and the Congress is political. Like the British, Nehru centralized all the power at the Centrel the states were formed in an arbitrary manner and very little political autonomy was left to them. This created a land of *babus* and bred corruption. In turn, it triggered in certain states such as Tamil Nadu, whose culture has been preserved much more than in North Indian states (maybe because it was more sheltered from Muslim incursions by the Deccan plateau), a resentment against the Centre, who is trying to impose Hindi on them, for instance, and fostered a seed of separatism.

Nehru also initiated the entire bureaucratization of India, which was a terrible mistake, if only because it was a system established by the British who wanted to centralize and control everything from the top. It was all right when the English were there, they were the masters, they made their riches out of plundering the country and had no need to be corrupt. But how do you give so much power to an insensitive *babu,* who is now very well paid, thanks to Narendra Modi? Hence, corruption and bureaucracy flourished together in India under Nehru. The Soviet-type industrialization, such as massive state industries, big steel, mills and mega dams, have already proved a failure in the West; yet Nehru and his successors all went for it. India became a state-owned country which produced sub-standard quality goods. The only merit it had was to shelter her from a take-over by multinationals and allow her to develop her own products, however deficient.

Nehru's foreign policy was often misguided. Nothing exemplifies this better than his attitude vis a vis Red China. He made the mistake of applying to the letter his famous "Hindi Chini bhai-bhai" slogan, when he should have known that China could not be trusted. And indeed the Chinese attacked India treacherously in 1962, humiliated the Indian army and took away 20,000 square kilometers of her territory, which they have not yet vacated. Nehru was generous enough to offer India's hospitality to the Dalai Lama and his followers (see box) when they fled the Chinese occupation of their sovereign country in 1959. But in order not to offend the Chinese, Nehru and all the successive Prime Ministers, let down Tibet, not only by not helping them to regain their independence, but also by stopping the Dalai Lama from any political activity in India, including protesting against China. Do the Chinese show any gratitude? Not at all! They are still claiming Indian territory, particularly the beautiful Arunachal Pradesh. More than that, India could never see that Tibet was the ideal buffer between her and China, if denuclearized and demilitarized, as the Dalai Lama has proposed in the European Parliament of Strasbourg. And India's betrayal of Tibet will come back to haunt her, as it did recently, when the Indian occupation of Kashmir was equaled with the Chinese occupation of Tibet. The Chinese killed 1,2 million Tibetans and wiped out in 66 years a wonderful 2000-year-old civilization. On the other hand, in Kashmir, there has been no genocide, only war casualties and India is fighting to retain what has been hers for 5000 years.

The Dalai Lama's 90th Birthday

As written above, the Dalai Lama recently celebrated his 90th birthday, with major celebrations in Bodh Gaya and Dharamshala. Prime Minister Narendra Modi publicly greeted him, calling him a symbol of compassion and moral leadership. Several Indian ministers, including Kiren Rijiju (the Union Parliamentary Minister Affairs), were present at the events, emphasizing India's respect for the Tibetan spiritual leader. However, India handled the occasion carefully. While it expressed warmth and admiration for the Dalai Lama, it avoided making strong political statements that could further provoke China. Beijing reacted angrily to Modi's birthday wishes and reiterated that the Dalai Lama is a separatist. China also insisted that only Beijing has the authority to approve the Tibetan leader's successor.

India maintained that the issue of succession is purely a religious matter and that the Dalai Lama himself has the final say. Though India has supported the Tibetan cause on moral and humanitarian grounds, it continues to walk a diplomatic tightrope, balancing its strategic interests with China. Thus, while the Dalai Lama was honored with reverence and dignity, India avoided direct political confrontation with China, staying true to its principle of religious freedom but mindful of its complex relationship with its northern neighbor.

Indians take great pride in their judicial system—but is it not essentially it a carbon copy of the British model, carrying with it a host of problems? Political interference in judicial appointments, an astonishing backlog of pending cases, and overcrowded prisons are just a few of its enduring consequences. Again, the Indian judiciary relies for his judgments on western values, on European jurisprudence, which are totally unfit for India. Once more, it is proud of its "secular" values and often comes down heavily on the fanatical bigots, meaning the Hindus.

In education, Nehru carried on with the British policy of imposing a westernized English system: more and more the universities and schools of India, many of them run by Christians missions, produced a generation of English-speaking diploma holders, who did not belong any more to Hindu society, but only to a fake bureaucratic society with westernized manners.

Finally, Hindu-bashing became a popular pastime under Nehru's rule. Jawaharlal had a great sympathy for communism (*), like many men of his generation and indeed of the generations thereafter till today. We have all been duped by communism, whose ideal is so appealing in this world of inequalities, but whose practice was taken over by *Asuric* forces, whether in Stalin's Russia, or in Maoist China. Nehru encouraged Marxist think-tanks, such as the famous JNU in Delhi, which in turn bred a lot of distinguished "Hindu-hating scholars" like the venomous Romila Thapar, who is an adept at negating Muslim atrocities and running to the ground the greatness of Hinduism and its institutions. Today even, most of the intellectuals, journalists and many of India's elite have been influenced by that school of thinking and regularly ape its theories.

(*) And so has Sonia Gandhi whose Manmohan Singh government (2004-2014) was propped up by communists who did great damage to India's interests, such as helping a Maoist government come to power in Nepal, the only Hindu state in the world.

CHAPTER 20

21st Century India: Still a Partial Self-denial

Why is it that Indians, particularly its elite—the intelligentsia, the journalists, the writers, the top bureaucrats, the diplomats—hold an image of themselves which is often negative, and have a tendency to run down their own country?

The self-perception that Indians have of themselves is often *detrimental* to their self-confidence. This is particularly striking among Indian journalists, who always seem to look at India through a *western* prism and constantly appear to worry how the foreign press views India, how the foreign countries—particularly the United States of America—perceive India, what the human rights agencies say about India... What matters to them is not the words of India's sages, avatars, gurus, wise men and yogis, who live, eat, think and even dream in an Indian spirit, but rather the judgment of the western media, or organizations like Amnesty International. They are not interested at all by what the *Bhagavad Gita*, probably the world's most revelatory, most comprehensive, most relevant sacred book has to say, or how Sri Sri Ravi Shankar, India's 21st century avatar, could help. No, they would rather turn to Thoreau, Marx or Jean-Paul Sartre, people who have even lost relevance in the West, for a solution to their immense problems.

Thus, when one reads certain Indian magazines, one has the impression that they could be written by foreign journalists, because not only do they tend to look at India in a very critical manner, but often, there is nothing genuinely *Indian* in their contents, no references to India's past greatness, no attempts to put things in perspective through the prism of

India's ancient wisdom. Therefore, most of the time, their editorial contents endeavor to explain the present events affecting India, such as Ayodhya, or the problem of Kashmir, or the Christian missionaries' attempts at conversion of tribal Hindus, by taking a very small portion of the subcontinent's history—usually the most recent one—without trying to put these events in a broader focus, or attempting to revert back to India's long and ancient history. In a gist, one could say—although things have been changing in the late nineties—that there is hardly any self-pride among India's intellectual elite, because they are usually too busy running down their own country. It is done in a very brilliant manner, it is true, because Indian journalists, writers, artists, high bureaucrats are often intelligent, witty and talented people—but always with that western *slant*, as if India was afflicted by a permanent inferiority complex. One then has to try to *analyze* the underlying reasons of this negative self-perception that India has of herself, probe the unconscious impulses which give many Indians—Hindus, we should say, as the majority of India's intelligentsia are born Hindus—the habit of always depreciating their own culture and traditions. And certainly, Nehru, his daughter Indira, Rajiv and the subsequent Congress leaders must be held partly responsible for this lack of confidence.

It is true that since Narendra Modi came to power in 2014, India has witnessed a growing wave of national pride and cultural resurgence. For many Indians, this marks a long-awaited moment of self-affirmation after centuries of colonial rule, historical distortions and economic subjugation. Modi's leadership has sought to instill a renewed confidence in India's civilizational legacy, its spiritual traditions, and its global potential. His government has promoted the celebration of ancient Indian knowledge systems, from yoga and Ayurveda to the Vedas and Sanskrit, fostering a deeper connection with the country's roots. Symbolic gestures such as International Yoga Day, the promotion of Indian festivals on the global stage, the construction of the grand Ram Mandir in Ayodhya, or efforts to bring back stolen Indian artifacts from foreign museums, have all contributed to this cultural revival. There is a new pride in being Indian, a sense that India can speak in its own voice and no longer needs to be defined by Western narratives or colonial frameworks. This national awakening has also been driven by India's economic rise and increasing influence in global affairs. From space exploration to digital innovation, India's achievements are no longer ignored or downplayed. Many Indians, particularly the younger generation, now see their country as a rising power capable of shaping its own destiny. Yet, this surge in nationalism is not without its critics. Some worry that the emphasis on cultural identity can sometimes lead to a narrowing of the national conversation. They argue that true pride must be inclusive and rooted in the diversity that defines India. The challenge remains to balance cultural revival with democratic values, ensuring that this renewed sense of nationalism unites rather than divides. Nonetheless, what is undeniable is that a deep emotional shift has taken place—India is learning to walk tall again. Nevertheless, there is still in many upper class and westernized Indians a denial of Bharat's greatness, mainly because Indian education does not teach the young to be proud of their own history. This is why, yesterday and today, we see that the greatest brain drain in the world is still that of Indians (majority of Hindus), particularly towards the United States, the UK, Canada and Australia. We hope that the exorbitant prices now of the H-1B visa, set by Donald Trump, will apply a brake to this talent exodus.

THE HUMILIATION OF 1962

One of the reasons for this self-denying among India's elite has been the war that China launched in 1962 against India, where Nehru's Gandhian non-violent philosophy led to a humiliating defeat. A nation needs warriors, it needs soldiers to defend itself and protect its women, children, and its borders from hostile and *asuric* elements, which throughout history have negated the Good and the Holy. It is fine to be Gandhian and non-violent, but in the tough and rough world of today, one cannot be too naïve: you need a strong and well-equipped army to be able to defend one's dharma. But a well-equipped army is not enough—we have seen how today the United States' army, or Israeli forces, the most modern and high-tech of the world, are only capable of fighting from a distance, using today mostly drones which are remote controled from far away, or shooting from boats off-shore, a coward's war, as its soldiers have lost the sense of Kshatriya, of honor, of dying for one's country. In Kargil, India saw the selflessness of its soldiers, with all the officers in front, climbing in the cold under enemy fire and wrestling peaks in impossible conditions, with little more than blood and tears.

But not only Indians lack self-confidence in their dealings with the West, but they seem to have a permanent fear of the Chinese. Is it because of the humiliation of 1962, and the fact that since then, the Chinese always seem to have the upper hand in their conflict with India? India's first Prime Minister, Jawaharlal Nehru, had decided that India and China were the natural 'socialist' brothers of Asia. Shortly before China's attack, the Indian Army Chief of Staff had drafted a paper on the threats to India's security by China, along with recommendations for a clear defence policy. But when Nehru read the paper, he said: "Rubbish. Total Rubbish. We don't need a defence plan. Our policy is non-violence. We foresee no military threats. Scrap the Army. The police are good enough to meet our security needs." We know the results of this very foolish assessment.

India has also to wake up to the plain fact that China needs space and has hegemonic aspirations: it got Tibet, it got Hong Kong, it got part of Ladakh; now it wants Taiwan, Arunachal Pradesh, the Spratly islands and what not! Fifty years ago, during the Korean war, Sri Aurobindo had understood clearly the Chinese game: "The first move in the Chinese Communist plan of campaign is to dominate and take possession first of these northern parts and then of South East Asia as a preliminary to their manoeuvres with regard to the rest of the continent in passing Tibet as a gate opening to India."

India should overcome its awe of China and be ready to eventually face once more the Chinese army. The nuclear tests of India, which have been highly criticized, because ideally you have to get rid of nuclear weapons if you want a safe world, should be seen in that light. Today, successive governments, including that of the BJP, continue to pay visits to China with great fanfare... and come back empty-handed, as the Chinese have perfected the art of smiling while stabbing you in the back. Narendra Modi received twice the Chinese President, Xi Jinping, with great fanfare and warmth, once in Ahmedabad and once in Mahabalipuram, thinking that it will win him over and convince him of

India's goodwill towards China. Yet, we see today how China has managed to encircle India.

China's growing influence in South Asia is not limited to its control over water or military posturing along the Himalayan borders. Through a calculated and aggressive strategy of economic expansion, Beijing has entrenched itself deeply in the internal affairs of India's neighbors—most notably Sri Lanka and Pakistan—creating a circle of pressure around India. In Sri Lanka, Chinese investments have reached such a scale that the island nation has fallen into a debt trap. Major infrastructure projects like the Hambantota Port, the Colombo Port City, and highways and power plants were built with massive Chinese loans. When Sri Lanka was unable to repay its debts, it was forced to lease the strategic Hambantota Port to China for 99 years—giving Beijing not just economic leverage but a potential military foothold in the Indian Ocean. This is not just business; it is a deliberate strategy of encirclement.

At the same time, Pakistan remains China's closest and most compliant ally in the region, often described as a "client state" or "iron brother." The China–Pakistan Economic Corridor (CPEC), which cuts through the disputed territory in Kashmir, is a clear sign of how deeply Beijing has tied Pakistan into its strategic ambitions. But the cooperation has gone beyond infrastructure. During recent Indian security operations, such as the Sindoor operation (7 May 2025), there are credible reports that China provided tactical, reconnaissance and possibly even aerial surveillance support to Pakistan. This would mark a new level of collaboration—one that directly threatens India's sovereignty and security. Together, these developments form a dangerous pattern. China is surrounding India not only with infrastructure and economic pressure but with a growing network of allies, client states and strategic assets. From ports in Sri Lanka to military partnerships with Pakistan, and now the control of vital rivers in Tibet, Beijing is building a framework of dominance designed to contain and challenge India on every front—economic, military and geopolitical.

India must view these moves not in isolation, but as parts of a coherent and long-term Chinese strategy. The threat is real, and the time for strategic complacency is over.

India as usual is getting bypassed, because of inertia, indifference and a lack of a forceful will, although Burma (Myanmar) falls within her natural sphere of influence. The Chinese may not directly do anything in Kashmir, but they hold a million square meters in Aksai Chin, given to Pakistan, but which rightfully belong to India.

China and the Water War

China has begun constructing, in occupied Tibet, what is projected to be the world's largest hydroelectric dam on the Brahmaputra River, known to Tibetans as the Yarlung Tsangpo. Construction started in July 2025, near the remote and strategic town of Medog in southeastern Tibet. Once completed, the dam is expected to produce around 300 billion kilowatt-hours of electricity annually—three times more than the Three Gorges Dam. But behind the claim of clean energy and economic development lies a far more serious and threatening reality.

For India, this dam represents a direct and growing danger. The Brahmaputra is not just a river; it is a lifeline for millions of people in northeastern India. By gaining control over its upper reaches, China is effectively placing a hand on India's water supply. In the event of military conflict or even heightened tensions, China could turn off the tap—cutting water flow to India's northeast, crippling agriculture, causing drinking water shortages and shutting down hydroelectric stations. Or, worse, it could release massive volumes of water all at once, triggering flash floods and destroying entire regions. This is not mere speculation. Indian officials have openly called the dam a "ticking water bomb." It introduces a new weapon into the already fraught India-China relationship—a weapon that does not fire bullets but strikes at the heart of India's water security. In the face of an aggressive and expansionist China, this dam adds a powerful tool of coercion, giving Beijing the ability to strike without having a single soldier cross over the border.

The danger is amplified by the fact that this region is highly seismic. A powerful earthquake could crack the dam, unleashing a catastrophic flood downstream. Even without deliberate action, the environmental and geological risks are enormous. The damage to ecosystems, farmland and the livelihoods of millions would be irreversible. China has refused to share full details of the project or agree to any meaningful water-sharing agreements. Its secrecy and unilateralism have only deepened mistrust. India has begun developing its own dams in Arunachal Pradesh as a defensive measure, but it remains highly vulnerable.

This dam is not just a threat to the environment or to river systems; it is a potential instrument of war—an asymmetric weapon that could devastate India without a single shot being fired. In the context of rising border tensions, skirmishes in Ladakh, and an increasingly assertive Chinese foreign policy, this project must be understood for what it truly is: a geopolitical provocation, and possibly the most dangerous new front in the India-China conflict.

INDIRA GANDHI (1917-1984)

Indira certainly had a better understanding of the deeper, rural India than her father. But her legacy is still very bleak: she institutionalized the way the Congress still functions today, with its totally centralized pyramid-like system, with one person at the top wielding absolute power—and paved the way for Sonia Gandhi's absolute one-woman rule and the sycophancy surrounding her in the '90s and early 2000. Punjab and the Sikh problem, however, proved the undoing of Indira; it poisoned the last years of her reign and finally killed her in the most frightful manner.

Wonderful religion of Sikhism: the only true attempt ever to synthesize Hinduism and Islam—and who knows what would have happened if it had succeeded. "The Sikh Khalsa," writes Sri Aurobindo, "was an astonishingly original and novel creation and its face was turned not to the past but to the future. Apart and singular in its theocratic head and democratic soul and structure, its profound spiritual being, its first attempt to combine the deepest elements of Islam and Vedanta, *it was a premature drive towards an entrance into the third or spiritual stage of human society*, but it could not create between the spirit and the external life the transmitting medium of a rich creative thought and culture. And thus hampered and deficient it began and ended with narrow local limits, achieved intensity but no power of expansion..." (*Foundations of Indian Culture*, p. 380)

Unfortunately, the Sikhs, because they had to defend themselves against the terrible persecutions by the Muslims, became a *militant* religion, adopting hawkish habits, which even in times of peace they kept. And they also retained some of the more negative side of Islam: intolerance, or feeling of persecution, thus cutting themselves from the mainstream spirit of Hindu tolerance and width—from which they anyway came, and where they might ultimately go back.

Today, but even more during Indira Gandhi's time, Sikhism is on the defensive, or rather displays an aggressive spirit of defence. Why? As Sri Aurobindo points out, Sikhism was a wonderful attempt at synthesizing Islam and Hinduism, but because the conditions were not right, it faltered. And today, whatever the loveliness of Sikh rites, the incredible beauty of the Golden Temple and its wonderful atmosphere; Sikhism, like Zoroastrianism of the Parsi community, may be a stagnating religion—whereas Hinduism, from which Sikhism sprang in greater part, is very much alive and remains the Dharma, the source of all religions in India. It may be this unconscious realization by the Sikhs that their religion is being slowly absorbed back into Hinduism that triggers their militancy and fundamentalism. And after all, what is fundamentalism, but going back to the fundamentals, the foundations! And Sikhism strove *best* when it was militant, when it fought the Muslims; thus unconsciously, the separatists of the late '70s went back to that crease, to that glorious epoch to regain their identity. That is all what separatism is, a desperate attempt to regain Sikh identity in the face of the all-pervasive and subtle Hindu onslaught. The fact that the British had planted that seed of separatism and that later it was fueled, financed and armed by Pakistan, certainly did not help. But can the British, or Pakistan, or even Indira Gandhi be credited with having FABRICATED Sikh separatism? Mrs Gandhi was also accused of having 'created' Bhindranwale and made thus responsible for the whole Punjab problem. This is going to extremes; she may have helped politically Bhindranwale and thought of using him later to counterbalance her opponents in Punjab. That's bad enough; but Bhindranwale's fanaticism and violence was his own; he was just an embodiment of Sikh militancy and frustration; if he had not been there, another Bhindranwale would have sprung up, with or without Mrs Gandhi's help.

Finally, Sikhs and many other Indians have not forgiven Mrs Gandhi for giving the order of storming the Golden Temple. History will judge. But think of it this way: would the French government have tolerated that for months, Basque separatists, for instance, be holed up in the Notre Dame Cathedral in Paris, the holiest of all Christian shrines, with their weapons, issuing deaths warrants against politicians, and receiving journalists, as Bhindranwale did? Certainly not. These Basque militants would not have lasted three days in Notre Dame; the army would have been called—and although great care would have been taken that no harm be done to the wonderful 1000-year-old church, it would have been a fight to the finish. Remember also what happened to the 350 militants who took over the Kaba in Mecca in 1989! Most of them were killed when the Saudi government sent its special forces against what is *the most sacred place* of worship in the world to all Muslims. It is a credit to Indira Gandhi and the inherent Indian tolerance that Bhindranwale and his followers were allowed to hole up for so long in the Golden Temple. No democratic government in Europe or any Arab state would have allowed such a situation to continue. It was unfortunate that the Golden Temple got damaged and so many were killed during the assault; but as the head of government, Mrs Gandhi took the correct decision. It was not her fault that the Sikhs allowed their holiest shrine to be turned into a refuge for armed men carrying weapons and death in their hearts.

It is shameful that many Sikhs rejoiced when she was murdered in such a terrible way by her own Sikh bodyguards, men she had trusted, even though she had been told earlier to have all Sikhs removed from her personal security. To kill a woman lying on the ground with bullets is a curse to any race that condones it. And ultimately, whatever her faults, Indira Gandhi—as she had predicted a few days before her assassination-did give her blood and her life for the country she loved in her own way. The vengeance of Hindus, backed by Congress leaders, was equally shameful and the culprits should be punished, it is never too late. It is also sad that the Shiromani Gurdwara Parbandhak Committee (organization in India responsible for the upkeep of gurdwaras) declared in 2007 Jarnail Singh Bhindranwale as a "martyr," coinciding with the anniversary of Operation Blue Star. Even more surprisingly, Indira Gandhi's murderers were also made into saints by the SGPC.

One can observe today a drifting away of the Sikhs from the mainstream Hindus—that is even more worrying and it should be addressed quickly by the mainstream community, as there are very few differences between these two people. This is why, FACT-India, an organization which highlights human rights abuses, which I head, mounted a project on Sikhism. The objective is to show the Sikhs as the defenders of Indian Dharma. Throughout the ages, Sikhs have protected India from numerous onslaughts by foreign invaders—whether the Mughals or the British. This has not been recognized by society today.

We also need to bring the spirit of Kshatriyas back into the people of India, as today it again faces a threat to its culture and traditions from globalization and conversions. This will and courage to defend one's dharma from threats, both within and without, is still very strong in the Sikh community and this should be brought to the forefront and shared with the rest of the people of this country.

The Exhibition, "Sikhs, the defenders of Indian Dharma," was inaugurated on 22 January 2008 at Delhi's Bangla Sahib Gurdwara by His Holiness Sri Sri Ravi Shankar and the Sikh Gurdwara Management Committee. It ran for twelve days and was viewed by more than a lakh people. It is now permanently exhibited in the Shivaji Maharaj Museum of Indian History, Pune.

Canada's Accusation Against India: The Facts and the Context

India maintains innocence as no evidence has been made public

In June 2023, Hardeep Singh Nijjar, a Canadian citizen and known Khalistan separatist, was killed outside a Sikh temple in British Columbia. In a dramatic move, then Canadian Prime Minister Justin Trudeau accused Indian intelligence of being involved in the assassination, claiming "credible allegations." The Indian government firmly denied the charge, calling it baseless and politically motivated.

Nijjar had been designated a terrorist by India for his alleged involvement in violent separatist activities. He was accused of recruiting extremists and plotting attacks under the Khalistan movement, which seeks to break Punjab away from India. Despite this, Nijjar lived openly in Canada and remained politically active. India has long warned Canada about Khalistani extremists operating on its soil—people who openly call for the disintegration of India and glorify violence. Yet these groups have often found protection under Canada's broad definition of free speech. India believes that Trudeau's accusation reflects a deeper failure to address these threats. Importantly, Canada has so far provided no public evidence to support its claim. No Indian official has been charged, and no documents have been shared with India or released internationally. The investigation is still ongoing, and until facts are presented, the accusation remains just that—an accusation. India has responded firmly but responsibly, urging Canada to act against extremist elements and respect international norms. New Delhi remains open to dialog but insists on facts, not speculation.

In short, there is no proof of Indian involvement, and the presumption of innocence must stand. Responsible diplomacy demands evidence—not political posturing.

RAJIV GANDHI (1944-1991)

Rajiv Gandhi was typical of a certain breed of westernized Indians, totally ignorant about their own country, yet full of goodwill. It must be said to his defence that he was never interested in power, content to be a pilot, hobby around and live a quiet life with Sonia and his two children. But fate and his mother's distrust for everybody, but her own sons, decided otherwise. It must also be said that the man (and his wife and children) demonstrated poise and dignity at his mother's assassination—and what a horrible way to lose one's mother—which could fill one's heart with hatred and ideas of vengeance. Rajiv showed in his early years goodwill and a sincere aspiration to transform the Indian system. But there were two problems: one was that being totally cut off from the Hindu reality of his country, he applied to his effort misconceived ideas about what India should be. And two, that like Don Quichotte battling the windmills, he had to fight the Congress system, its corruption and bureaucracy. In the end he gave up this unequal battle and had to fall back on advice from the old guard. His ill-advised judgment in the Shah Bano case or his pandering to Palestine were certainly more in tune with the old Congress policy of flattering the Indian Muslim community, as in the pre-independence Khalifa movement, than his own opinions, for everything in his upbringing was pro-Western and Israel certainly was no enemy of his. He must have also secretly agreed with the Supreme Court judgment in the Shah Bano case.

If his mother's downfall and ultimate death was due to the Sikh separatist problem, his undoing was Sri Lanka and the Tamil separatist factor there.

In the late 1980s, Prime Minister Rajiv Gandhi made a bold but ultimately fateful decision to intervene in the Sri Lankan civil war. His aim was to support peace and protect the Tamil population, which had long suffered discrimination under Sri Lanka's Sinhala-dominated state. However, what began as a diplomatic effort quickly turned into a strategic trap. In 1987, Rajiv signed the Indo–Sri Lanka Accord with President J. R. Jayewardene. The agreement promised to devolve power to Tamil regions while also calling on Indian-backed Tamil militants, especially the Liberation Tigers of Tamil Eelam (LTTE), to disarm. In return, India sent the Indian Peace Keeping Force (IPKF) to enforce the agreement and oversee the transition. But the plan backfired. The Sri Lankan state remained unwilling to fully share power or implement the promised autonomy. At the same time, the LTTE, which had once seen India as a supporter, turned against the IPKF and India itself. Fierce fighting broke out between Indian troops and LTTE rebels, costing over 1,000 Indian lives.

For the LTTE and its leader Velupillai Prabhakaran, Rajiv Gandhi was a figure of betrayal. In their view, he had turned from ally to occupier. In 1991, two years after Rajiv left office, and just as he was preparing a political comeback, he was assassinated in Sriperumbudur, Tamil Nadu, by an LTTE suicide bomber. What began as a mission of peace turned into an unwinnable conflict, worsened by Colombo's intransigence and the LTTE's rigid extremism. His assassination was not just a personal tragedy but a grim reminder of how easily noble intentions can be twisted by the unforgiving logic of regional politics.

Sri Lanka Today

Sri Lanka is attempting a bold economic rebound after the devastating 2022–23 financial crisis, betting heavily on luxury tourism. Beneath this drive for prosperity, unresolved ethnic tensions remain. The Tamil community, though participating in politics and holding parliamentary seats, continues to face systemic discrimination and surveillance. Laws such as the Prevention of Terrorism Act are still used to silence activists, and commemorations for victims of the civil war are often restricted. Although the Liberation Tigers of Tamil Eelam (LTTE) were militarily crushed in 2009 and there are no signs of a renewed armed rebellion, frustration among Tamils persists. Their demands today focus on justice, equality and accountability rather than separatist violence. The Sinhalese majority continues to dominate most of the state apparatus, though some Tamils and Muslims maintain a presence in local politics and civil society.

On the international stage, relations with India are deeper than they have been in years. In April 2025, Prime Minister Narendra Modi's visit to Colombo marked a turning point, resulting in major agreements on defence, energy, trade and debt restructuring. India is not only Sri Lanka's largest trading partner but also a critical investor, backing renewable energy projects, maritime cooperation and infrastructure connectivity. Naval exercises, coast guard meetings and the acquisition of a controlling stake in Colombo Dockyard by India's Mazagon Dock Shipbuilders underscore India's expanding presence. While Sri Lanka continues to balance ties with China, the trajectory under President Dissanayake suggests a growing strategic embrace of New Delhi.

MANMOHAN SINGH: THE PUPPET PRIME MINISTER (1932-2024)

The term "puppet Prime Minister," often associated with Dr.Manmohan Singh does not reflect his intelligence or integrity, but rather the unusual political arrangement that existed within the Congress Party during his tenure. After the Congress Party won the 2004 elections, its president Sonia Gandhi chose not to take the role of Prime Minister. Publicly, Sonia Gandhi explained her decision as an act of sacrifice for the nation. Privately, there were deeper currents. Her foreign birth had been a constant target during the campaign, and the BJP had mobilized widespread opposition to the idea of a naturalized citizen of Italian origin leading India. Behind closed doors, it is said that President A.P.J. Abdul Kalam (1931-2015) met with her and raised a critical legal concern. Reports suggest that he had received information indicating Sonia Gandhi had not surrendered her Italian passport at the time she acquired Indian citizenship. If true, that would mean her citizenship status could be challenged in court, making her ineligible to assume the highest executive office. Kalam, known for his constitutional integrity, is believed to have told her discreetly that appointing her could trigger a national crisis. Hence, Sonia Gandhi nominated Dr. Singh, a respected economist and former finance minister. While Singh held the top post in government, Sonia Gandhi remained the true power center within the party, leading the United Progressive Alliance (UPA) and chairing the influential National Advisory Council. This created a situation where many key decisions were believed to come from her and her inner circle, rather than from the Prime Minister's Office.

Dr. Singh lacked a strong political base of his own. He had never won a Lok Sabha seat and entered Parliament through the Rajya Sabha. Without grassroots political influence or a personal mandate, his authority depended entirely on the support of the party leadership. This limited his ability to act independently. During his second term, the government faced major scandals such as the 2G spectrum case, the Commonwealth Games irregularities, and the coal block allocations. Though Dr. Singh was personally honest, his silence and inaction during these crises were widely criticized. Many believed he had neither the freedom nor the strength to tackle corruption within his own ranks, reinforcing the view that he was not fully in control. Publicly, he appeared soft-spoken and cautious, especially when compared to the more assertive image of Sonia Gandhi behind the scenes. Reports often suggested that key policy choices and ministerial appointments were influenced or decided by the Congress leadership, not by the Prime Minister himself. Some Congress leaders even claimed that the real power resided at Sonia Gandhi's residence, not in the Prime Minister's Office.

In conclusion, while Dr. Manmohan Singh was a man of economic knowledge and personal honesty, the unique structure of power within the Congress Party made him appear less like a leader and more like a caretaker. The perception of him as a "puppet" was shaped by his dependence on the party high command, his limited political authority and his unwillingness to challenge the real sources of power during his time in office.

CHAPTER 21

The BJP Vajpayee Years

The hostility that much of the Western media and intelligentsia show toward the BJP and the RSS is rooted in a combination of ideological prejudice, historical misunderstanding and geopolitical bias.

First, many Western academics and journalists come from liberal and secular traditions that are often deeply skeptical of nationalism—particularly when it is tied to religion. The BJP and the RSS promote a vision of India grounded in its ancient Hindu civilization and cultural identity. In the West, this is often reduced to simplistic labels like Hindu nationalism or majoritarianism, without a deeper understanding of the Indian context. What is seen in India as cultural self-respect and civilizational awakening is often misinterpreted abroad as religious extremism or exclusion.

Second, a lingering colonial mindset persists in some Western intellectual circles. Many Western scholars continue to interpret India through frameworks inherited from the British Raj, which depicted Hindu traditions as backward and India itself as a chaotic society in need of Western intervention or reform. These outdated lenses continue to influence how modern Indian political movements are perceived. The RSS, which has always promoted self-reliance, national pride and a rejection of colonial narratives, does not fit comfortably within these inherited assumptions.

Third, there is the issue of global geopolitics. A strong, assertive India that defines itself on its own terms rather than through Western ideological models is unsettling for some Western institutions. The BJP's push for strategic autonomy, its resistance to foreign interference in domestic matters and its growing global influence challenge older power dynamics where the West set the tone for global discourse.

Finally, the rise of the BJP and the RSS coincides with the decline of the traditional Nehruvian and left-leaning intellectual elite that the West has long been familiar with. The new political and cultural leadership in India speaks a different language—one rooted in history, faith and national pride. It challenges the dominant Western narrative that equates progress only with Western-style secularism and liberalism.

In summary, the discomfort with the BJP and the RSS among Western media and intelligentsia is less about facts and more about perception. It reflects a clash between an India that is reclaiming its own voice and a Western world that is still trying to understand what that voice really means. Hindus—who let us remember, are 850 millions today, and constitute the overwhelming cultural and political majority of this country—have not only shown that they are extremely tolerant, but Hinduism is probably the only religion in the world which never tried to convert others or conquer other countries to propagate their own religion. This historical tolerance of Hinduism is never taken into account by foreign correspondents covering India and even, unfortunately, by Indian journalists.

On the other hand, Hindus suffered immensely at the hands of the two greatest "monotheistic" religions of the world. And it is only in the last eighty years that some "nationalist" movements were born to try to preserve Hindu culture in the face of conversions by Christian missionaries and the rising influence of the Muslim League. These movements, whose descendants today are the RSS, the Shiv Sena or the VHP, may make preposterous statements—although that is debatable—but they have never killed anybody, never massacred anybody in the name of their God. Burning down a few makeshift churches under Vajpayee Prime Ministership, however reprehensible these acts were, does not make them Nazis or even dangerous fundamentalists. Let's respect the proper use of words.

In 1984, the Bharatiya Janata Party bagged only two seats in the general elections, a total humiliation. Twelve years later, in 1996, it became the largest party in India with 186 MPs and came briefly to power, even though its government was unfairly toppled ten days later. After the disastrous governments of H.D. Deve Gowda and I.K. Gujral, a well-meaning but largely ineffective man.

This is why, after Sonia Gandhi—assisted by Jayalalithaa (1948-2016)—toppled the BJP government, once again, with the covert support of the President of India and the Election Commissioner, the Indian electorate returned the BJP and its allies to power with a resounding majority. However, the BJP itself did not perform as strongly as expected, particularly in Uttar Pradesh, perhaps because it had compromised some of its original ideals in order to placate its allies. Regrettably, the BJP of Atal Behari Vajpayee, in its desire to appear "secular," forsook many of the ideals which had made it dear and unique in the eyes of many of India's voters, thus taking the road charted by the Congress before him. It did not take advantage of the unprecedented popularity it enjoyed once upon a time, of a new feeling of "nationalism" to come up with some hard decisions, so as to "Indianize" the nation that it may manifest again its true unique soul: give back the power to the villages in the form of Panchayats; reintroduce Sanskrit as the national language; rewrite Indian history, which had mostly been devised by White Masters; revive ancient traditional systems such as *pranayama,* yoga, and incorporate them in the education system and everyday life; change the Constitution so that democracy may not be perverted as it is today; privatize the numerous "White Elephants," such as many of the Indian banks, SAIL, ITDC, etc. Many of the Hindu groups, like the RSS, were disappointed with the BJP leaders, although some of the ministers, such as Dr Murli Manohar Joshi did try their best to Indianize culture and education in the face of much resistance.

Chapter 22

Narendra Modi's Three Mandates

2014-2019

Narendra Modi's first mandate was marked by a wave of ambitious reforms, bold initiatives and a strong push to modernize India's economy and governance. It reflected not only determination, but also a remarkable political intuition. One of the most notable achievements was the implementation of the Goods and Services Tax (GST), a long-pending reform that simplified India's complex indirect tax system into a single nationwide tax, enhancing ease of doing business and promoting greater tax compliance. Another key reform was the Insolvency and Bankruptcy Code (IBC), which gave India, for the first time, a clear legal framework to resolve bad debts and bring discipline to the financial sector. It helped strengthen banks and sent a strong signal to corporate defaulters. Modi also launched the Jan Dhan Yojana, a massive financial inclusion drive that brought over 300 million people into the formal banking system. Linked with Aadhaar (see box below) and mobile technology, it laid the groundwork for direct benefit transfers, reducing leakages in welfare schemes and empowering the poor. The government also took bold steps like demonetization (see Chapter 25) in 2016, aimed at curbing black money, fake currency and informal cash economies. Though controversial, it reflected a willingness to take risks in the fight against corruption.

In foreign policy, Modi strengthened India's global image, engaging assertively with world powers while pursuing stronger ties with neighboring countries and the Indian diaspora. His frequent visits and strategic diplomacy projected India as a confident and rising power. The first mandate also saw a renewed focus on infrastructure development, with record-breaking construction of highways, rail modernization and rural electrification. Programs like Swachh Bharat Abhiyan not only improved sanitation but also created a cultural shift around cleanliness and public health. In essence, Modi's first term was driven by vision, speed and scale. His leadership combined economic reform with political stability and a strong narrative of nationalism and development. It was a period when India began to move away from slow bureaucratic consensus and embraced a more decisive and transformative style of governance.

2019—2024

Narendra Modi's second mandate was marked by significant political decisions and continued development efforts, but it was not seen as inspired or reform-driven as his first term. While the government remained active and determined, the second term focused more on consolidating power, addressing national security, and cultural identity, rather than launching major new economic reforms. One of the most defining actions was the abrogation of Article 370 on August 2019, which removed the special status of Jammu and Kashmir. It was a bold move that fulfilled a long-standing promise of the BJP and was met with widespread support in India, though it drew criticism internationally. The government also passed the Citizenship Amendment Act (CAA), which sparked protests and debates over its impact on India's secular fabric, especially when viewed alongside the proposed National Register of Citizens (NRC). In terms of economic reform, Modi's second term was more cautious. The economy faced serious challenges, including a slowdown that began in 2019 and deepened with the COVID-19 pandemic, which brought health and economic crises. The government responded with the Atmanirbhar Bharat (Self-Reliant India) initiative, focusing on boosting domestic manufacturing, supply chains and reducing dependency on imports, especially from China. Though important in spirit, many of these initiatives took time to translate into clear outcomes. There were continued investments in infrastructure, including highways, digital connectivity and renewable energy. India became the third-largest producer of solar energy and pushed for clean technology. The Digital India campaign expanded, and the Unified

Payments Interface (UPI) grew into a global model for digital transactions. Agricultural reforms were attempted through three new farm laws aimed at liberalizing the market, but they triggered year-long protests and were eventually repealed. This episode was seen as a rare retreat for a government otherwise known for standing firm.

On the international front, India maintained its strong global engagement, standing up to China during the Galwan border clash (see box) and strengthening ties with key partners like the U.S., Japan, and France. Modi's image as a global statesman remained intact. Socially and politically, the second term reinforced the Hindu cultural narrative, with key moments like the start of the Ram Mandir construction in Ayodhya, fulfilling another long-held promise. However, critics argue that freedom of expression, dissent and institutional autonomy suffered during this period.

In summary, Modi's second term focused more on national identity, security and consolidation, rather than launching groundbreaking reforms as in 2014–2019. It was a period of major decisions, some deeply symbolic, others contentious, but it lacked the same visionary economic momentum of the first mandate. Still, Modi remained the dominant figure in Indian politics, with an ability to set the national agenda and maintain high public support.

The Galwan Border Clash: A Modern Flashpoint in India–China Relations

The Galwan Valley clash, which took place on the night of 15 June 2020, was the deadliest military confrontation between India and China in over four decades. Located in eastern Ladakh, the Galwan Valley lies near the Line of Actual Control, the de facto border that separates the two countries. The incident marked a sharp escalation in tensions that had been brewing for weeks following Chinese incursions into areas traditionally patrolled by Indian troops. During the clash, twenty Indian soldiers were killed, including Colonel Santosh Babu. Though China officially acknowledged only four deaths, independent reports suggest their losses may have been higher. Unusually, the skirmish involved no firearms—in keeping with bilateral agreements—so soldiers fought hand-to-hand, using rocks, sticks and improvised weapons. The clash triggered a wave of national outrage in India and a strong response from the Indian government. In the following months, India increased its military presence in the region and imposed economic measures, including banning Chinese apps and tightening scrutiny on Chinese investments.

For India, Galwan became a symbol of Chinese aggression and betrayal, especially since the clash occurred during disengagement talks. For China, it was framed as a defense of sovereignty. The incident underlined the fragile nature of the border peace and revealed how quickly a local standoff could spiral into a national crisis. Though both sides have since held multiple rounds of talks and partial disengagement has occurred in some areas, tensions remain high. The Galwan clash has fundamentally altered India–China relations, pushing India to strengthen its military posture and deepen strategic partnerships with like-minded countries. It also reminded the world that Asia's two nuclear-armed giants remain locked in an unresolved and potentially dangerous border dispute, one that still simmers beneath the surface.

2024—2029

Narendra Modi's third mandate continues to be marked by his strong leadership, strategic vision and firm control over the government and BJP party. The Prime Minister remains a dominant force in Indian politics, with widespread public support and a global presence. However, some critics, particularly among the Western media, feel that this phase has seen a notable shift toward more centralized authority and there are, even in India, growing concerns over autocratic tendencies and personality-driven governance. Modi's political brand remains however powerful—rooted in nationalism, development and a promise of a strong, self-reliant India. His communication style, direct outreach to the people, and control over the narrative have helped maintain his popularity. Major policy decisions continue to be executed swiftly, with minimal opposition resistance and efficient coordination between the central government and key institutions. Decision-making is increasingly concentrated within the Prime Minister's Office (PMO), with less room for internal debate or cabinet-level dissent. The media landscape is also marked by growing alignment with the government, and critical voices face legal and political pressure. The personality cult around Narendra Modi has grown stronger, even though he himself keeps on working tirelessly without seeking limelight. But this does not stop government campaigns, welfare schemes and even international diplomacy, to be frequently branded with his image and name. This said, for many Indians, Sri Narendra Modi represents not just a Prime Minister, but a symbol of national pride and progress. While this gives the government a clear identity and unity of purpose, it also fosters a culture where loyalty to the leader sometimes overrides institutional process or diversity of opinion. Economically, India continues to grow, with major investments in infrastructure, digital innovation and defence. The "Viksit Bharat" vision for 2047—an ambitious road-map for a developed India—is driving long-term planning.

On the world stage, Modi's third term further cements India's role as a key geopolitical player. He balances relations with the U.S., Russia, the Middle East, and Asian neighbors, while projecting India as the voice of the Global South. Narendra Modi is playing an increasingly important role in BRIC, which is an acronym that stands for four major emerging economies: Brazil, Russia, India, and China. The term was first introduced in 2001 by economist Jim O'Neill from Goldman Sachs. He predicted that these countries would play a growing role in the global economy due to their large populations, strong economic growth and increasing political influence. Each of these nations has unique strengths. Brazil is rich in natural resources and agriculture. Russia has vast energy reserves. India has a young, tech-savvy population and a growing services sector. China is a global manufacturing powerhouse with significant trade influence. Though different in political systems and regional interests, the BRIC countries share a common goal of challenging the dominance of Western powers in global decision-making. They began holding annual summits in 2009 to promote cooperation in areas like development, finance, trade and international governance. In 2010, South Africa joined the group; in 2025,

Ethiopia, Iran, Egypt, Indonesia, and United Arab Emirates joined too; expanding it to BRICS+. Since then, the alliance has launched initiatives like the New Development Bank and has aimed to create a more balanced and multipolar world order. BRICS+ represents a major shift in global dynamics, as these rising economies continue to demand a stronger voice on the international stage. However, ties with China remain tense, and regional rivalries, especially with Pakistan, persist.

In August 2025, U.S. President Donald Trump imposed a 50% tariff on Indian goods, citing national security concerns. The primary reason for this decision was India's continued import of discounted Russian oil, which Trump argued undermined global efforts to economically isolate Russia during its conflict in Ukraine. He also accused India of unfair trade practices, claiming that American products faced high tariffs in India while Indian goods enjoyed easier access to the U.S. market. The tariffs affected exports worth about forty-eight billion dollars, including textiles, footwear, jewelry, and seafood, and created significant economic uncertainty. Analysts estimated that India's GDP could shrink by up to half a percent and that supply chains might be disrupted, leading to job losses, especially in labor-intensive industries. In addition, exporters faced challenges such as double taxation and stricter visa rules. India condemned the move as unjustified and unfair, asserting its right to procure energy based on national interests. Experts warned that the escalating tensions could push India closer to Russia and China, weakening U.S. influence in the Indo-Pacific region. Despite hopes that the tariffs would be temporary, they remained in effect as of early October 2025, leaving both countries locked in a deepening trade and diplomatic crisis.

The BJP Govt Takeover of Auroville: A Visionary Push or Centralised Control?

In recent years, Auroville—the international township founded in 1968 near Puducherry with the blessing of the Mother (Mirra Alfassa) and inspired by the philosophy of Sri Aurobindo—has witnessed growing tension between its founding ideals and the changing political landscape of India. Since Prime Minister Narendra Modi's second term, and more visibly during his third, there has been a clear effort by the central government to assert greater control over the functioning and development of Auroville. This has sparked both optimism and concern. The Modi government sees Auroville not just as a spiritual experiment or an isolated community, but as a potential model for sustainable living, national pride and cultural revival. The Prime Minister has openly expressed admiration for Sri Aurobindo's vision and philosophy, especially during the celebrations of the philosopher's 150th birth anniversary. Under his leadership, Auroville has received increased attention, funding and strategic support from various ministries, including environment, education and culture.

However, this renewed focus has not come without controversy. In late 2021 and into 2022, the Auroville Foundation—which is under the Government of India—began pushing forward infrastructure projects, such as roads and construction aligned with the original "Galaxy Plan" for the township, an architectural plan, made in the '60s by a French architect, long dead. This plan is not environmentally friendly, as it strives to build high rise flats, with millions of tons of concrete, huge roads cutting through the forests of Auroville and a massive lake, when there is water scarcity. This is being pushed through, despite objections from long-standing residents, who feared that ecological damage and authoritarian management were overriding the community's core values of consensus, experimentation and slow organic growth. Several members of the Auroville community alleged that decisions were being made unilaterally, bypassing established internal consultation processes. Protests, legal challenges and public statements from international supporters followed. Trees were felled, bulldozers moved in and a deep divide emerged between those who welcomed the development as long overdue and others who saw it as a betrayal of Auroville's soul. Supporters of the government's intervention argue that Auroville had, for too long, become stagnant, inward-looking and resistant to necessary evolution. They see the Centre's push as a way to finally implement the original master plan envisioned by the Mother—a Utopian urban model based on harmony, not chaos.

Artificial Intelligence Today in India

India's software story, once told through the rise of outsourcing and call centers, is now entering a second act shaped by artificial intelligence. The industry already generates about USD 254 billion annually and employs over five million people. Yet the model that fueled this growth—vast armies of coders and service staff—is beginning to show signs of strain. Machines are learning to do what India once sold as cheap labor: writing code, testing software and answering queries. What looks like a threat is also a vast opening. Consultants predict that generative AI could raise productivity in India's tech sector by nearly 45 percent within the next five years. In some fields, the leap could be even sharper: software development might gain 60 percent, outsourcing and BPO work over 50 percent. Surveys suggest six in ten Indian companies are using AI in some form, the highest rate among major economies. The money flowing into this shift is extraordinary. From less than USD 700 million in 2022, AI spending in India is forecast to touch USD 8 billion by 2025 and perhaps USD 17 billion by 2027.

Sri Narendra Modi has sensed the moment. A new IndiaAI Mission, backed by more than ten thousand crore rupees, has been launched to build skills, research and infrastructure. Global firms are following suit: OpenAI has set up shop in the country and promised half a million free ChatGPT licenses for students; Kyndryl is putting USD 2.25 billion into a new AI lab in Bengaluru. These are not side stories—they are signals that the center of gravity in Indian software is shifting. If outsourcing was India's first revolution, AI may become its second. The challenge lies not in adoption, but in preparing people: fewer than half of engineering graduates today are considered employable for AI and machine learning. The industry's future will depend on whether it can turn a workforce once valued for numbers into one prized for imagination and invention.

CHAPTER 23

The Threats from Within

KASHMIR

Sri Aurobindo wrote in 1940: "In Kashmir, the Hindus had all the monopoly. Now if the Muslim demands are acceded to, the Hindus will be wiped out again." (*India's Rebirth,* p. 220) How prophetic! Because nobody cares to remember today that Kashmiris were almost entirely Hindus or Buddhists, before they were converted by the invading Muslims six centuries ago. True, today these Muslims in Kashmir have not only accepted as their own a religion which their ancestors had rejected, but they have also often taken up the strident cry of Islam. Does anyone remember too, that at the beginning of the century, there still were 25 percent Hindus in the Kashmir valley and that today the last 350,000 Kashmiri Pandits are refugees in their own land, they who originally inhabited the valley, at least 5,000 years ago, a much bigger ethnic cleansing than Armenians in Turkey, or the Druze in Syria?

It is a common refrain today in most Western newspapers to say that since Independence India alienated Kashmiris through years of wrong policies. But those who have been in close contact with Kashmir, even in its heydays of tourism, know for a fact that as a general rule, Kashmiris **never** liked India. There was only one thing that attached them to India—the marvellous financial gains and state bounties that they made out of tourism. Even those Kashmiris who are now settled in India make no bones about where their loyalty lies. Talk to them, specially if you are a Westerner, and after some time, they will open their hearts to you; whether it is the owner of this Kashmir emporium in a five star hotel in Chennai, or the proprietor of that famous travel agency in Delhi:

suddenly, after all the polite talk, they burst out with their loathing of India and their attachment to an independent Kashmir.

The successive governments of India, including this one, have also often given the illusion that ordinary Kashmiris are fed up with the militants after years of fighting, militants' abuses and the partial drying up of tourism revenues. Indeed, if you meet the Kashmiris of today, from the lowly unemployed *shikara* boatman, to the retired High Court judge, you will find that they are all unanimous in their hatred of the Indian army and their support of the militants. Kashmiris will stick together—and their family system ensures that they will support each other when in need. Nowadays Omar Abdullah, or Ghulam Nabi Azad want us to believe that with a certain degree of autonomy, or with the demilitarization of the Valley, Kashmiris will be appeased. This may be true in most Indian states, who are often rightly fed up with the Centre's constant interference in their internal affairs, but basically, there is only one thing which Kashmiris are craving for and that is a plebiscite on whether they want to stay with India or secede... The answer in the Kashmir valley, would be a massive "**no**" to India (90 percent?). And as for Omar Abdullah, or Ghulam Nabi Azad, they would be quickly eliminated by the militants, who would immediately seize control of Kashmir and attach it to Pakistan.

Amnesty International and other human rights bodies often highlight "the Indian atrocities" in Kashmir. But Amnesty, which does otherwise wonderful work to keep track of political atrocities worldwide, can sometimes become a moralistic, somewhat pompous organization, which in its comfortable offices in London, judges on governments and people, the majority of whom happen to belong to the Third World. Its insistence on being granted unlimited access to Kashmir is a one-sided affair. Does Amnesty bother at all about the atrocities committed by Hamas militants on Israeli men, women and children on 7 October 2023? Amnesty also criticized the removal of Article 370 by the Narendra Modi government, without understanding what it was all about.

Article 370 was a provision in the Indian Constitution that granted special status to the former state of Jammu and Kashmir. It was introduced in 1949 as a temporary arrangement after the state acceded to

India following the partition in 1947. Under this article, citizens from other parts of India were not allowed to settle or buy land in Jammu and Kashmir, even though Kashmiri Muslims could enjoy all the rights and privileges available elsewhere in the country. Indeed, the Souvenir market in India is today cornered by Kashmiri Muslims, whom you find all over the country, from Delhi to Auroville. This arrangement led to several problems; first, it created unequal rights. Indian citizens living outside Jammu and Kashmir were denied basic rights in one part of their own country; second, there was clear discrimination against women. Women from the state who married outside lost certain rights, including property inheritance, while men who did the same did not face such penalties ; third, it prevented full national integration. The special status set Jammu and Kashmir apart, both legally and emotionally, creating a sense of separateness; fourth, it blocked development and progress. Many central welfare schemes and reforms could not be implemented in the region. This held back growth, limited investment and hurt the most vulnerable sections of society. In August 2019, the Government of India decided to revoke Article 370. The move was justified as a step towards unity, equality and long-term peace. It was seen as a way to bring Jammu and Kashmir into the mainstream of Indian democracy, law and development.

Operation Sindoor was a high-precision retaliatory strike carried out by India on the night of 6-7 May 2025, in response to the brutal terror attack in Pahalgam, Jammu & Kashmir, on 22 April that killed 26 civilians, including tourists and locals. Over nine terrorist camps in Pakistan and Pakistan-occupied Kashmir were targeted, with four located deep within Pakistan's Punjab region—a first since the 1971 war.

The operation was executed jointly by the Indian Army, Navy, and Air Force from Indian territory. It utilized advanced precision weapons such as SCALP cruise missiles, HAMMER guided bombs, BrahMos, and loitering munitions to minimize collateral damage while neutralizing core terrorist infrastructure. India reported that more than 100 terrorists, including high-value targets like Yusuf Azhar and Abu Jundal, were eliminated in the operation. The strikes were characterized as focused, measured and non-escalatory, with no Pakistani military installations hit. India's leadership, including Foreign Secretary Vikram Misri, emphasized that the operation was a direct and proportionate response designed to dismantle terror networks rather than provoke escalation. It reinforced the country's zero-tolerance policy toward terrorism while maintaining strategic restraint. The strategic depth of the operation—penetrating up to 100 km into Pakistani territory, including deep into Punjab—marked it as one of India's boldest military responses in decades and conveyed a strong deterrent message to terror sponsors and planners across the border. Despite Pakistan denouncing the strikes as an act of war, India maintained that civilian targets and national infrastructure were deliberately avoided, demonstrating professionalism and self-restraint.

In the aftermath, India also faced cyber and drone retaliation, including attempted drone incursions and misinformation campaigns. Indian forces successfully neutralized drone waves and thwarted cyberattacks, further showcasing their preparedness across domains. Operation Sindoor stands as a watershed moment in India's counter-terrorism posture—showing advanced capability, swift response and an unwavering stance: terrorists will be held accountable, wherever they are found. During Operation Sindoor, China was reported to have provided Pakistan with tactical intelligence, satellite imagery and limited air surveillance support.

THE INDIAN MUSLIMS

Since the early 21st century, radicalism seems to have gripped some Muslim communities in the world. We see today that not only immigrants, who are welcomed in many Western countries, often turn to bite the hands that fed them. There are worrying ethnic cleansing in the Muslim world, whether it is the Jews in Iran, the Yazidis in Irak, or the Druzes in Syria. It is true that there is also a karma factor and the West which did colonize, often ruthlessly Third World countries, is experiencing what the Dalai Lama calls 'Black Karma'.

In India, the situation is very different. Over the ages, the majority Hindu community has given refuge to every persecuted religious community in the world: the Zoroastrian from Iran, the Jews from Israel—indeed India is the only country in the world where Jews were never persecuted—the Armenians from Turkey, or today the Tibetans fleeing Chinese persecution. Arab traders were freely allowed to do commerce in India, before the first Muslim invasions which became massive and bloody from the 10th century onwards.

Unfortunately, the tolerance of Hindus was, and is today, a one-way traffic. Is not only, as we said in the previous chapter, that the holocaust of Hindus, at the hand of Muslim invaders, is unparalleled in world history, but even today, a majority of the Indian Muslim community continues to consider Hindus as infidels and regularly attacks their gathering and possession in every city of India. This intolerance is also of course very present in Pakistan, or even Bangladesh (see box), forcing Bangladeshi famous writer, Taslima Nasreen, to take refuge in India. The intolerance of a certain portion of Indians Muslims today shows how much they are influenced by the hard Wahhabite streak that most of them pick up when they work in Gulf countries. Yet, they find it normal when M.F. Husain (1915-2011), one of India's most prominent modern artists, stirred significant controversy by portraying Hindu deities in the nude or in intimate sexual poses in several of his paintings. While his supporters defended these works as expressions of artistic freedom and rooted in classical Indian art traditions, many Hindus found them offensive and disrespectful. The backlash led to legal cases, protests, and eventually, his self-imposed exile. The episode raised enduring debates in India around the limits of artistic expression, religious sensitivity and freedom of speech.

After Sheikh Hasina's ouster in 2024—driven by student riots, orchestrated by the Jamaat-e-Islami—Nobel laureate Muhammad Yunus assumed the role of interim leader of Bangladesh and swiftly redirected the country's foreign policy away from India. While Hasina had maintained strong ties with New Delhi, Yunus distanced himself and began aligning with Pakistan and China. His government accused India of interfering in internal affairs and made statements that challenged India's territorial integrity and influence in the region. The return of Islamist groups, including Jamaat-e-Islami, and rising attacks on Hindu minorities signaled a move away from the secular legacy of 1971. India expressed concern, but Yunus dismissed these warnings and accused India of spreading misinformation. At the same time, Bangladesh revived military and trade ties with Pakistan and welcomed Chinese investment near India's borders, raising alarms in Delhi. Yunus's government also downplayed India's role in Bangladesh's liberation and pushed a new narrative that glorified pro-Pakistani forces. Relations with India deteriorated further when the interim government sought the extradition of Sheikh Hasina from Indian soil. The shift under Yunus represents a clear break from decades of cooperation. India now views his leadership as openly hostile, with serious implications for regional security and balance.

Coming back to Indian Muslims, the question they should ask themselves now is simple: "Who are we?" Among the 205 millions of Muslims in India, only a tiny percentage descends from the Turks, Afghans, or Iranians who invaded India. The majority of them are converted Muslims. And converted how? By terror, coercion, force, bloodshed. The ancestors of today's Indian Muslims are probably those who suffered the most from the Arab and Muslim invasions. Those Hindus and Sikhs who chose not to convert, took refuge in their faith, fought together and kept their pride and honor. The first two generations of those who converted must have endured hell: for they certainly did not convert out of conviction, but because they had no choice: their daughters and wives were raped, sons taken into slavery, parents killed. It is sad today that their descendants have sometimes made theirs the intolerant cry of Islam.

It is true that many Indian Muslims were Hindu untouchables. Marxists would like us to believe that they converted because they thought that they would access the more egalitarian society of Islam. What rubbish! Does one think in that way in times of war, terror and tears? Do today's Hindu lower castes convert to Islam when there is no more violent coercion? More likely, the untouchables were the most vulnerable, the least apt to defend themselves; they had neither the faith of the Brahmins, nor the riches of the Vaishiyas, nor the military skill of the Kshatriyas.

Do Indian Muslims understand that they were part of the richest, most advanced, most tolerant and generous civilization of ancient times? That their culture was so advanced that it had spread all over the world? Do they realize that more and more archaeological and historical discoveries are pointing out that the genocide of Hindus by Muslim invaders is without parallel? Surely, many of present-day Indian Muslims' ancestors must have been among those slaughtered.

Islam cannot be wished away. As Sri Aurobindo said, "Mahomed's mission was necessary, else we might have ended by thinking, in the exaggeration of our efforts at self-purification, that earth was meant only for the monk and the city created as a vestibule for the desert...." Thus, Indian Muslims have to keep their faith and any attempt by Hindus to convert them back is not only futile but counterproductive. But Dara Shukoh's example says: "What kind of Islam do you want to practice? An Islam which looks westwards, towards a foreign city, Mecca, swears by a Scripture, the Koran, which is not only not relevant to India, but which was meant for people living 1500 years ago, in a language which is not Indian? Or do they want to practice an Islam which is tolerant, which accepts the reality of other Gods, as Hinduism and Buddhism accept that there have been other avatars than Ram or Buddha?"

Do Indian Muslims want to worship Babar, a man who destroyed everything which was good, beautiful and holy and lived by the power of violence, or do they want to imbibe the qualities of Dara Shukoh, who believed that Islam needed to accept others to survive, and even that Islam has borrowed from other religions like Hinduism or the Jewish faith? Do Indian Muslims want to participate in that great Indian adventure set up by Narendra Modi? Do they want to feel that they are first Indians and then Muslims, and not the opposite? Do they want to live in peace with the Hindu, Sikh and Buddhist brothers and sisters?

Nowadays it is politically incorrect to say anything against Islam. You are immediately labeled as an Islamophobe or dismissed as a "rightist." No matter if you are only reporting the fact that there is a real problem with Islam in South Asia: that India is surrounded by fundamentalists states: Afghanistan and Pakistan, while more moderates like Bangladesh, radicalized in time and tend to close an eye to anti-Indian activities; that

Indian Muslims sometimes tend to put their religion before their country; and that Kashmiris, far from being the persecuted that the foreign press likes to portray, are actually paying the price for having allowed Afghan and Pakistani Sunnis radicalize what used to be a more gentle and tolerant Islam and left their Hindu brothers and sisters being butchered and chased away from their ancestral land.

AYODHYA IS REBUILT, BUT WHAT ABOUT KASHI VISHWANATH?

How many of those who have lambasted so many times the "Hindu fundamentalists" and lamented the destruction of the Babri Masjid mosque as the "death of secularism in India," have been to Ayodhya? (Not Faizabad, mind you, which is Ayodhya's twin Muslim city.) When one arrived in Ayodhya before the destruction of the mosque, one was struck by the fact that it was a Hindu town "par excellence." More than Benares even, it is dotted everywhere with innumerable temples; it has all these old Hindus houses and this lovely river with its ghats which runs through the lower town. And then, forlorn on the top, there was this lone mosque with its two ugly domes, which looked so out of place and unused, that anyone with a right sense—and that includes the Muslims—should see that it was not worth making an issue of.

The reconstruction of the Ram Mandir by the Narendra Modi government was widely seen as justified for several historical, cultural and legal reasons. Ayodhya is one of the most sacred and ancient pilgrimage sites for Hindus. Hindus firmly believe that it is the birthplace of Lord Ram, one of the most revered figures in Hinduism and a symbol of dharma, virtue and righteous rule. For centuries, Hindus have regarded the site as Ram Janmabhoomi, as extremely sacred, and many ancient texts, devotional songs and traditions point to Ayodhya's deep spiritual significance. Historical records and accounts suggest that a grand temple once stood at the site, but in the 16th century, the Mughal emperor Babur's general demolished it and built a mosque, the Babri Masjid, in its place. This act was viewed by many as an insult to Hindu faith and as part of a broader pattern of destruction of indigenous temples by foreign invaders. Over time, the site became a point of conflict between Hindu and Muslim communities. Despite restrictions, Hindus continued to worship at the site, often under difficult conditions. Legal disputes began during the British era and intensified after independence. The tension erupted in 1992 with the demolition of the Babri Masjid by *kar sevaks*, leading to nationwide riots and a prolonged legal battle.

In 2019, the Supreme Court of India delivered a landmark judgment, recognizing the Hindu claim to the site based on centuries of worship and archaeological evidence that confirmed the existence of a pre-Islamic structure beneath the mosque. The court acknowledged the deep emotional and cultural significance of the land for Hindus, and it ordered the construction of the Ram Mandir while also allotting land for a mosque elsewhere in Ayodhya. The Modi government, following the court's verdict, facilitated the formation of a trust to build the temple and oversaw the beginning of its construction in a peaceful and organized manner. For many, this marked the correction of a historical injustice and the restoration of a sacred space that had been taken by force.

Thus, the construction of the Ram Mandir was justified not only by religious sentiment and historical memory but also by legal validation and a desire to bring closure to a centuries-old conflict. It is seen as a moment of spiritual healing and national renewal, rooted in India's civilizational identity.

The new Ram Mandir in Ayodhya is considered glorious, because it stands as a symbol of spiritual resurgence, national pride and the fulfillment of a centuries-old dream for millions of Hindus. Built with intricate craftsmanship and traditional architecture inspired by ancient Hindu temple design, the temple radiates a sense of sacred grandeur. The temple is constructed using high-quality sandstone without iron or steel, reflecting a timeless and enduring vision. Every detail, from the pillars to the sanctum, is designed to reflect the ideals of dharma, devotion and Hindu heritage. The structure is not only a place of worship but also a work of art that represents the depth of Indian civilization. Since its opening, millions of Hindus from across India and the world have already visited the temple. For many devotees, the pilgrimage is a once-in-a-lifetime experience, offering the chance to connect with their faith at its most sacred origin. The temple has become a unifying space, drawing people from all walks of life, including saints, scholars, farmers and youth, all coming together in reverence for Lord Ram. The joy and devotion seen in Ayodhya today are the result of generations of hope, struggle and unwavering belief. The new Ram Mandir is more than a temple—it is a living symbol of Hindu endurance, a cultural renaissance and a reminder of the timeless values Lord Ram represents. It is true that most major mosques in India were built over destroyed Hindu, Buddhist or Jain temples, and that some of them, such as the Krishna Mathura temple, or the Kashi Vishwanath temple, also some of the most ancient and sacred Hindu pilgrimages, should be handed back to the Indian government.

A recent archaeological survey in Benares has uncovered significant remnants of Hindu religious heritage at the Gyanvapi Mosque complex. The Archaeological Survey of India (ASI) identified 55 stone sculptures, among them two figures of Lord Vishnu, along with depictions of Ganesha, Hanuman, Nandi, Krishna, and fifteen Shiva *lingas*. The findings also included a fragment showing a half-human, half-snake figure believed to represent Vishnu's Varaha avatar, and a broken slab of a four-handed Vishnu seated regally, holding the sacred *chakra* (discus) and *shankha* (conch). These discoveries indicate that the site was once a multi-deity Hindu worship center, with evidence of reverence for Vishnu and Hanuman alongside traditionally dominant Shaiva imagery. The Vishnu idol fragments were particularly notable for their iconographic detail—such as the *chakra* and conch, attributes closely associated with that deity. The results of the excavation have ignited renewed legal and cultural discussions. A Hindu group has petitioned the Supreme Court to authorize further archaeological investigations akin to those undertaken at the Ayodhya Ram Temple site. However, a Varanasi court rejected a request to conduct 'invasive' excavations at Gyanvapi, citing Supreme Court directives, shielding the structure from such actions.

Do Some of India's Elite Look Down upon Their Own Country?

As we saw earlier, when the British invaded India, they quickly set upon trying to destroy what they perceived as paganism, but which was in reality India's many-sided perception of truth, Hinduism, the Santanam Dharma of the Vedic sages. Fortunately for India, they never succeeded in their task, but they did manage to win over a small portion of India's elite population. These people, whether maharajas, lawyers, or journalists, were made to feel ashamed of their own ways and thus tried to become more British than the Britishers, be it in their dress, in their thinking... or in their Hinduism-bashing. It is they who upon getting independence, denied India its true identity and copied blindly from the West to frame its Constitution, unfit to India's own ways and needs. It is they who today are ready again to split India at the seams, let go of Kashmir, of Punjab, of Assam, of Gorkhaland, Jarkhaland, and tomorrow Tamil land, all in the name of democracy and human rights, of course.

Nothing symbolizes more this lack of nationalism and love for one country than the exodus of Hindus towards the West. The greatest brain drain in modern history is that of the Hindu population from India, especially from the 1960s onward. Over the past few decades, millions of highly educated Indians—primarily Hindus—have migrated to the West in search of better professional opportunities, education and quality of life. By some estimates, nearly 5 million Indians live in the United States alone, and a large majority of them are Hindus. According to the Pew Research Center, approximately 94 percent of Indian Americans have a college degree, and nearly one in ten doctors in the U.S. is of Indian origin. In the Silicon Valley, Indian-origin CEOs and engineers play key roles in major companies like Google, Microsoft, Adobe and IBM. As of 2023, over 70 CEOs of global companies are of Indian origin, many of them from Hindu backgrounds. This migration pattern began during a period when India's economy was tightly controlled by bureaucracy and licenses, leading to limited job prospects for highly educated individuals. The U.S. Immigration and Nationality Act of 1965 opened doors for skilled professionals, and tens of thousands of Indian doctors, engineers and scientists—most of them Hindus—began moving abroad. For example, by 1990, over 25 percent of Indian Institute of Technology (IIT) graduates had emigrated to the U.S. or Europe. The impact of this brain drain was twofold. On the one hand, countries like the U.S., U.K., and Canada benefited from a highly skilled and disciplined workforce grounded in Hindu cultural values like education, discipline and family, and on the other, India suffered a significant talent loss during a critical time in its development. While India produced brilliant minds, many of them ended up contributing to foreign economies instead of helping build the nation.

In recent years, the trend has begun to shift. With India's rise as a global tech and innovation hub, many Indian professionals abroad are now investing back into the country through remittances, startups and mentorship. In 2024 alone, India received USD 135 billion in remittances, the highest in the world. Some professionals are returning home, driven by new opportunities and a sense of giving back. Still, the Hindu brain drain remains one of the most significant migrations of intellectual and spiritual capital in the modern era. It reflects both the extraordinary talent of the Hindu community and the challenges India faced in retaining it during crucial decades. As written earlier, because Mr Trump wants to give back jobs to Americans, he has instituted huge fee for skilled workers of India. So there is hope after all.

THE CONGRESSIZATION OF THE BJP

When the BJP came to power, most of its cadres, future ministers, MPs, presidents, vice presidents, came from the RSS, which has a culture of humility and working with the people. Unfortunately, they had to function in a system made by the Congress, where a minister has 60-70 people at least working for him or her, who bow down, sometimes touch the feet of their masters, and never offer any constructive criticism—but just plain bhakthi or adoration. For a while, the BJP, particularly Sri Narendra Modi, resisted this Congress legacy, particularly favoritism: the Prime Minister telling his ministers not to endorse anyone or their families, unless they had genuine work. Also efforts were made by Mr Modi to minimize the huge inconvenience to the public by this unless caravans of cars, and police with blaring sirens, whenever a minister or a prime minister travels. But it was a losing battle. The VVIP and favoritism system is so entranched, that most BJP, MP and ministers, not only made do with it, but started enjoying it. Today, the tamasha of lower ranked BJP workers touching the minister's feet, posting for photos with them and asking them for favors, seems to have taken over the BJP cadres, from the highest to the lowest ranks, bare for a few exceptions. As with gurus, the disciples—in the case of Mr Modi, his workers and cadres, use his image and photos at every turn, for every campaign, which gives the impression now in India that everything turns around Mr Modi, which might or might not be the case.

CHAPTER 24

The Threats from Without

It would be bad enough if India had to suffer threats from within only, at the hands of Kashmiri secessionists, at the mercy of the sometimes doubtful allegiance of its 205 million strong Muslim community, under the onslaught of its westernized "elite" minority, or from its missionary contingent. But India is also under attack from without, not only from its Muslim neighbors, who are all offspring of a once Greater India; but also from her non-Muslim neighbors, from China—and even further away, from the West, particularly the USA, who does not always grasp India's problems and its relevance to Asia and the world.

PAKISTAN

Ah, Pakistan, finally! Everything reverts to Pakistan, whether you talk about Kashmir, Ayodhya, or Kargil. Everywhere the Indian government says it sees the "Pakistani hand" behind it. It is a hostile hand, they add, active, militant, whose ultimate goal is the destruction of India. Is actually Pakistan the continuing incarnation of those Muslim invaders who raped India from the middle of the 7th century onwards? Militant Hindus contend that nothing has changed: "Their cry is still the same: 'Dar-ul-Islam,' the house of Islam. Yesterday they used scimitars, today they have the atomic bomb; but the purpose is identical, only the weapons have evolved: to conquer India, to finish what the Mughal Emperors were not able to achieve." To reason with Pakistan is useless, they conclude, "for once again they are only putting in practice what their religion teaches them every day—that 'the Pagans shall burn forever in the fire of hell. They are the meanest of creatures.' Or, 'slay the infidels, wherever we find them and take them captive and besiege them and prepare them for all kinds of ambush.' Or again: 'Choose not thy friends among the infidels till they forsake their homes and the way of idolatry. If they return to paganism then take them whenever you find them and kill them.' All these quotations are taken from the *Quran* and are read everyday to the faithful by their mullahs.(*Quran* 98:51-9:5-4:89)

Is Pakistan's war against India then a Muslim *jihad*, the ultimate *jihad* against the infidel, which if necessary will utilize the ultimate weapon, nuclear bombs? And as in the case of Ayodhya, the whole of Islam might side with Pakistan, for to their eyes India is still the infidel, the idolater, which the *Quran* asks them to slay. Says Elst: "If tomorrow the Pakistani start the Prophet's first nuclear war against an Infidel country (India), a billion Muslims will feel compelled to side with this *muhajid* struggle and dissenters will be careful not to protest aloud."

But then you also have to understand the Pakistani point of view: take Kashmir for instance. If one goes by the logic of Partition, then at least the Kashmir valley, which is in great majority Muslim (and it should be emphasized that for long the Hindus Pandits in Kashmir exploited and dominated the Muslims—who are getting back at them today), should have reverted to Pakistan. It should be clear also that Pakistan never forgot the humiliating loss of Bangladesh at the hands of India, although India only helped Bangladesh to gain its freedom in the face of what the Bangladeshis say was Pakistani genocide. Zia's emergence, as well as the next militant Prime Ministers of Pakistan, was a result of that humiliation, and the whole policy of proxy war by supporting the separatist movements in Punjab and Kashmir is a way of getting back at India. The same can be said about the nuclear bomb, for Pakistan has realized, after having lost three wars (four if you count Kargil), that both numerically and strategically, it can never beat India in a conventional conflict.

The enmity between India and Pakistan has remained one of the most enduring and complex rivalries in modern geopolitics. Rooted in the traumatic Partition of 1947 and the unresolved issue of Kashmir, tensions have continued well into the 21st century, marked by military conflicts, cross-border terrorism and shifting alliances in the region.

The first major conflict of this century was the Kargil War of 1999, which, although beginning in the last year of the 20th century, cast a long shadow into the new millennium. Pakistani soldiers and militants occupied strategic peaks in the Kargil sector of Indian Kashmir. India launched a determined military operation to flush them out. Though it eventually succeeded, the conflict exposed Pakistan's role in sponsoring irregular forces and attempting to alter the Line of Control by stealth. The war caused hundreds of casualties and re-ignited public anger and mistrust on both sides of the border. In the years that followed, India faced a series of devastating terrorist attacks, many of which were traced back to Pakistan-based militant groups. One of the most tragic was the 2001 Indian Parliament attack, which brought both nations to the brink of another war. This was followed by the 2008 Mumbai attacks, carried out by members of the Lashkar-e-Taiba, a group operating from Pakistan. These attacks killed more than 170 civilians and caused international outrage. Investigations and global pressure exposed the complicity or at least tolerance of such groups by sections of the Pakistani establishment, particularly its intelligence agency, the ISI. Meanwhile, Kashmir remained a volatile region. Cross-border infiltration, local radicalization, and frequent ceasefire violations along the Line of Control added fuel to the fire. The Pulwama suicide bombing in 2019, which killed 40 Indian paramilitary personnel, was a turning point. India responded with airstrikes in Balakot, deep inside Pakistani territory, targeting a militant training camp. This was unprecedented and marked a significant shift in India's defence posture. Pakistan retaliated by sending fighter jets into Indian airspace, and the region briefly teetered on the edge of full-scale war.

Another key element in this rivalry has been China's growing support for Pakistan, as the Chinese long time President, Xi Jinping, has skilfully managed to encircle India from all sides, particularly making use of Pakistan Islamist hostility towards its Hindu-majority neighbor. China and Pakistan share a long-standing strategic partnership based on military cooperation, economic ties and a mutual distrust of India. China has become Pakistan's largest arms supplier and a key investor, particularly through the China-Pakistan Economic Corridor (CPEC), which passes through parts of Kashmir which rightfully belong to India. This has added a new dimension to the conflict, as India sees CPEC not only as a violation of its sovereignty but also as a sign of deepening China-Pakistan cooperation against Indian interests. Furthermore, China has often shielded Pakistan on the global stage. For example, at the United Nations, China repeatedly blocked India's attempts to designate certain Pakistani-based individuals as international terrorists. This diplomatic protection has allowed Pakistan to avoid greater international isolation despite evidence of supporting or harboring terrorist groups. In recent years, India has taken a firmer stance, both diplomatically and militarily. It has increased its surveillance, modernized its armed forces and sought stronger international alliances. At the same time, India has consistently tried to isolate Pakistan in international forums as a sponsor of terrorism, while deepening its own ties with the United States, Europe and several Gulf countries.

Despite moments of dialog and backchannel communication, the latest beeing Mr Modi meeting president XI in Tianjin (31st August 2025), on the sides of the Shanghai Cooperation Organisation (SCO) Summit, peace remains elusive. The shadow of nuclear weapons continues to hang over the subcontinent, making every flare-up potentially catastrophic. The enmity between India and Pakistan in the 21st century is not just about land or ideology; it is a struggle shaped by history, religious identity, geopolitics and external influences like China. Until deeper trust is established and cross-border terrorism is fully dismantled, relations between the two neighbors are likely to remain tension and uncertain.

On the opposite spectrum, Indians can cry themselves hoarse about Pakistani treachery and see the evil hand of Islamabad everywhere, even sometimes behind events where Pakistan is not even involved. But then the Indian government should only blame themselves. For have they not recognized at independence the geographical and political reality of Partition and have they not continued to do so up to now? Is there any political leader in India who dares say today that India and Pakistan are ONE? **Is there any voice to proclaim the truth in a loud and clear voice, as Sri Aurobindo** did in 1947: "But the old communal division into Hindu and Muslim seems to have hardened into the figure of a permanent division of the country. It is hoped that the Congress and the nation will not accept the settled fact as forever settled, or as anything more than a temporary expedient. For if it lasts, India may be seriously weakened, even crippled: civil strife may remain always possible; possibly even a new invasion and foreign conquest. THE PARTITION OF THE COUNTRY MUST GO."

The menace from within cannot be tackled unless the menace from without is solved. India and Pakistan (+ Bangladesh) are ONE. And as long as Partition remains, India will not be able to live in peace: Ayodhya, Kashmir, Kargil, Bangladeshi infiltration and a potential (nuclear?) war with Pakistan is always possible.

However, many Hindu leaders fear that a reunion between Pakistan and India would create a huge Muslim community, which would rapidly become the majority in India and impose the Sharia. But why can't we envision a kind of South Asian Common Market, where each country would retain its autonomy, but with free borders and a common currency? The Kashmir problem, for instance, would immediately vanish, because both Kashmir would become one.

THE OTHER NEIGHBORS

It remains one of the paradoxes of modern geopolitics: despite its democratic values, rich cultural heritage, and largely peaceful history, India is still viewed with suspicion, hostility, or even open dislike by many of its neighbors. Whether Muslim-majority Bangladesh, Buddhist Sri Lanka, or Hindu Nepal, the narrative of India as a regional "bully" persists, widely propagated by both domestic and foreign journalists. But is this image justified? Historically, India has never shown expansionist or hegemonic tendencies. Unlike Western colonial empires, Islamic conquests, or even Buddhist missionary campaigns, India's influence spread through its culture, spirituality, art, and ideas—not by force. From Cambodia to Indonesia, from Iran to China, India's soft power once shaped entire civilizations. Hinduism never tried to convert others by the sword, and Indian armies rarely invaded foreign lands. Even today, remnants of this civilizational influence remain embedded in Southeast Asia. So where does this hostility stem from? Perhaps the key word is fear—a deep, unconscious fear among India's neighbors that they are historically, culturally and even spiritually tied to her, and that one day this magnetic pull might reassert itself. This subconscious recognition of India's vast civilizational weight often manifests as resentment, stoked further by opportunistic politicians and external powers.

Take Nepal for example. Culturally and religiously, it is India's closest kin—the only other Hindu-majority nation in the world. Yet anti-Indian sentiment often flares up, carefully cultivated by political factions eager to blame India for internal failures. Over the years, successive governments in Kathmandu have leaned increasingly toward China, using its support as leverage against India. Beijing has been quick to exploit this rift, investing heavily in Nepal's infrastructure and influencing its domestic politics. Recently, after the September 2025 storming of the Nepalese Parliament & the violent large-scale anti-corruption protests and demonstrations that took place across Nepal, predominantly organized by Generation Z students and young citizens, there has been suggestions that there was an Indian 'hand' behind it—though nothing was ever proved.

In Bangladesh, which owes its very creation to India's military and diplomatic intervention in 1971, the relationship is ambivalent. While people-to-people ties remain strong and economic cooperation has improved, political rhetoric often turns hostile. As mentioned above, the rise of Islamist forces, after the advent of Muhammad Yunus, combined with narratives of water disputes and border tensions, fuels this animosity. China has capitalized on this dynamic, emerging as Bangladesh's largest trading partner and arms supplier. Sri Lanka presents another paradox. Despite cultural and historical ties, India is often blamed for meddling in its affairs, especially due to its support for Tamil militancy in the 1980s. While Sri Lanka's tragic ethnic conflict was a result of its own flawed policies, successive leaders found it convenient to scapegoat India.

Today, like we explained earlier, Sri Lanka is deeply indebted to China after taking massive loans for infrastructure projects. The infamous Hambantota Port, leased to China for 99 years, is a potent symbol of Beijing's strategic hold over the island nation. Even the Maldives, once firmly in India's sphere of influence, has seen political oscillations between pro-India and pro-China governments. While India has provided crucial support during political crises and natural disasters, China's financial clout continues to grow.

Pakistan remains the most overtly hostile of India's neighbors. From the Kargil War to repeated terrorist attacks in Kashmir and beyond, Pakistan has used proxy warfare to bleed India. China's all-weather alliance with Pakistan, symbolized by the China-Pakistan Economic Corridor (CPEC), is both strategic and ideological. Beijing backs Islamabad diplomatically, economically and militarily, using Pakistan as a counterweight to India in the region. The situation is further complicated by the Arab Gulf nations. Millions of Indian workers—mostly Muslims—send home remittances, but they also sometimes bring back more radical strains of Islam. The blasts in Mumbai in 1993 and 2006 showed how extremist ideologies can travel and mutate across borders, funded and encouraged by hostile entities.

So, is India a bully? Or is she a civilizational giant surrounded by smaller nations, often insecure, sometimes manipulated, and frequently under the shadow of a rising China? India's size, success and civilizational self-confidence are not easy to digest for neighbors still defining their national identities. It is not so much India's assertiveness, but her sheer presence that unsettles them. And China, with its long-term strategic vision and deep pockets, is carefully deepening these divisions, offering an alternative to Indian influence. In doing so, Beijing is creating a ring of nations where anti-India sentiment can be exploited to serve its own ambitions in South Asia and the Indian Ocean.

India has also sometimes to account for the hostility of the Gulf countries, although since Mr Modi came to power, things have improved. However, India's hands are still tied, because of its 9 million citizens, most of them Muslims, who work in the Gulf countries and regularly send home precious foreign exchange. But does India realize that this foreign exchange is sometimes a poisoned gift, that these Indian Muslims often bring home a more militant Islam? The Bombay blasts that followed the destruction of the Babri Masjid were a stark example of the threat India faced from the Gulf countries. The attacks were carried out by Indian Muslims who had received training, arms and funding from Pakistan, while some Gulf countries almost certainly had prior knowledge of the plot. The fact that the perpetrators were able to transit through two of these Gulf countries after their deed is proof enough: the police of these countries are everywhere and are totalitarian tools to the monarchies;

they must have known when the Memons entered the country and exactly where they were staying. It would have been a simple matter to stop them from leaving both the countries till an extradition was officially asked for. Yet they chose to let them go and now "Tiger" Memon has gone into hiding in Pakistan and India will probably never see him again and solve the mystery of the Bombay blasts. Why did Dubai and Jeddah let him go? And why did the Indian government do nothing to prevent it?

CHINA

Today, the future of Asia is increasingly being shaped by the rise of two rival powers: India and China. These two civilizations—vast in population, ancient in history and ambitious in their visions—stand at the heart of a new geopolitical order. As the United States and much of the Western world experience a slow but undeniable decline, both economically and morally, the era of Western dominance appears to be drawing to a close. The liberal international order, forged in the aftermath of World War II and sustained through decades of American military and financial hegemony, is fraying under the weight of its own contradictions. With this retreat, many Asian economies that once relied on Western markets, technology and protection are now grappling with uncertainty. The so-called "Asian Tigers"—Singapore, South Korea, Taiwan, and others—built their prosperity on the back of global trade and Western security guarantees. But in an era of de-globalization, rising protectionism and strategic realignment, they find themselves vulnerable, caught in the growing gravitational pull of China's expanding influence.

The Chinese Communist Party, under Xi Jinping, has made its ambitions unmistakably clear, as often repeated in this book. After crushing the spirit of freedom in Tibet and extinguishing democratic aspirations in Hong Kong, Beijing now casts a long and menacing shadow over Taiwan. What was once a slow diplomatic squeeze has become overt military intimidation, with frequent airspace violations, cyberattacks, and naval encirclement. The possibility of a full-scale invasion, unthinkable a decade ago, now looms as a real and present danger. And if Taiwan falls—either through war or coerced capitulation—it would mark a seismic shift in the global balance of power, signaling the triumph of authoritarianism over democratic resilience in Asia.

In this turbulent landscape, it is increasingly evident that only two giants will be left standing as we are going to enter the third decade of this century: India and China. But while their size may be comparable, their systems, values, and worldviews could not be more different. India, for all its imperfections, remains a pluralistic democracy. Its institutions may be flawed, its bureaucracy often sluggish, but its civilizational ethos is rooted in dialog, diversity and spiritual depth. Its rise is not marked by territorial conquest or ideological imposition, but by soft power, innovation and a growing commitment to global partnerships based on mutual respect. China, by contrast, is a one-party authoritarian state with a relentless appetite for control—of its people, its neighbors and the global narrative. It has fused advanced technology with totalitarian surveillance, built a military capable of projecting power far beyond its borders, and reshaped global institutions to suit its interests. Its Belt and Road Initiative has drawn dozens of countries into a web of economic dependency. Its diplomacy is aggressive. Its ambitions are imperial.

Both India and China are nuclear-armed. Both are permanent members of the Shanghai Cooperation Organisation. Both seek influence across Africa, Latin America, Southeast Asia, and beyond. But only one offers the world a vision of freedom, coexistence and sustainable development. The other promises order through obedience, prosperity through silençe and stability through suppression. The West now faces a critical choice. If it truly believes in the values it has long espoused—liberty, democracy, human dignity—it must recognize that India is not just a market or a counterweight to China. It is a civilizational partner. In this great Asian chessboard, the outcome is not merely about territorial disputes or trade wars. It is a civilizational contest between *Dharma* and dictatorship, between open society and totalitarian control. India must prepare itself for this role—not with arrogance, but with clarity and confidence. Its strength lies not only in its military or economy, but in its soul, its culture of tolerance, and its ancient wisdom that sees unity in diversity. The world is watching. And the stakes could not be higher.

What makes this more alarming is that China continues to push its territorial claims through a mix of military aggression, infrastructural buildup and cartographic revisionism. It builds roads, helipads and outposts in disputed regions, often attempting to change facts on the ground before India can respond. Even as diplomatic dialogs carry on in Geneva and Delhi, Chinese troops test the Line of Actual Control, probing for weakness and exploiting ambiguity. Meanwhile, Beijing's strategic embrace of Pakistan has only intensified India's security dilemmas.

The New Silk Road

Under the guise of the China–Pakistan Economic Corridor (CPEC)—a flagship arm of Beijing's vast Belt and Road Initiative—China has funneled tens of billions of dollars into Pakistan's infrastructure, building highways, power plants and special economic zones. Yet this is no simple economic partnership. Much of CPEC's route passes directly through Gilgit-Baltistan, a region that India claims as part of Jammu and Kashmir. By entrenching itself in this disputed territory, China has not only strengthened Pakistan's grip but also has also challenged India's sovereignty, setting the stage for simmering tensions across the Himalayas.

Even more concerning than bricks and asphalt is Beijing's steady military patronage of Islamabad. For decades, China has been the silent architect behind Pakistan's defence capabilities. From providing advanced JF-17 fighter jets, stealth frigates and submarines, to offering direct assistance in Pakistan's missile and nuclear programs, China has ensured that its "iron brother" remains armed to the teeth. This support means that India's western border is never quiet, never fully stable—just as its northern frontier with Tibet and Xinjiang remains under constant Chinese pressure.

The implications are clear: while India invests heavily in balancing development with security, Beijing guarantees that Pakistan can punch above its weight militarily. This two-front challenge—Pakistan in the west, China in the north—creates a strategic vice intended to stretch India's resources, divide its focus and undermine its rise as a regional power. For New Delhi, the CPEC is not merely an economic corridor but a creeping encirclement strategy. Each road laid in Gilgit-Baltistan, each submarine delivered to Karachi, tightens the knot of dependency between Pakistan and China, and simultaneously reinforces a geopolitical trap for India. The real question is not whether this alliance will destabilize South Asia—it already has—but how far India can adapt and respond to an axis designed to keep it perpetually off balance.

THE IGNORANCE AND SOMETIMES HOSTILITY FROM THE WEST TOWARDS EMERGING INDIA

In recent years, a peculiar pattern has emerged in the way Western governments, media and academic circles engage with India. Despite the country's rise as a global economic power, a stable democracy and a vital player in international geopolitics, India is often viewed with suspicion, if not outright disdain, by many Western institutions. This attitude becomes even more pronounced when it comes to Hinduism, the Bharatiya Janata Party (BJP), and Prime Minister Narendra Modi. There is a striking ignorance in the West about Hinduism, a religion older than most civilizations still in existence. Rather than being understood as a diverse and tolerant spiritual tradition that has given rise to profound philosophies, meditation practices and non-violent ideals, Hinduism is often reduced to caste, cow worship, or caricatured as majoritarian nationalism. Little effort is made to explore its subtleties, its internal pluralism, or its spiritual depth. The BJP, the ruling political party of India, and its leader Narendra Modi, are typically portrayed in stark, negative terms. Modi is frequently described in Western outlets as an authoritarian populist, a Hindu nationalist, or even a threat to democracy. These labels rarely capture the nuance of Indian democracy or the reasons behind Modi's enormous popularity among Indians, especially the poor and marginalized who see in him a voice that finally speaks for them.

Much of this bias stems from a postcolonial hangover, where Western observers still struggle to view India as a civilizational power with its own logic and agency. There is also an entrenched discomfort with the idea of a proud Hindu identity asserting itself politically. In contrast to the West's embrace of multiculturalism, the assertion of Hindu civilizational values is often misinterpreted as religious extremism. The irony is that India remains one of the most tolerant and diverse societies on earth. Despite its challenges, it has absorbed countless cultures, languages and faiths, maintaining a robust electoral democracy in a subcontinent of 1.4 billion people. Indian Muslims have held top constitutional posts, including president and vice president. Sikh, Christian and Parsi minorities thrive in various spheres of life. Yet these facts are rarely acknowledged in narratives shaped by Western commentators.

Another point of friction is India's strategic autonomy. New Delhi's refusal to align blindly with Western policies, particularly on issues such as Russia, the Middle East, or trade, is often seen as defiance. But in truth, India is asserting its sovereign interest, just as any major power would. This independence unsettles the Western diplomatic establishment, which still tends to expect compliance from countries of the Global South. Prime Minister Modi's foreign policy, including India's strong ties with the Global South, its leadership in the G20, and its growing partnership with Africa and Southeast Asia, often goes under-reported or is overshadowed by controversies. His domestic policies, aimed at empowering the poor through digital infrastructure, sanitation, housing and access to banking, receive scant coverage, while every tension is magnified. Ultimately, the West's discomfort with Hinduism and the Modi-led BJP may reflect a deeper unease with a non-Western civilization rising on its own terms, proud of its heritage, and unwilling to play by old rules. India is not perfect, nor is its leadership beyond criticism. But any honest critique must begin with an understanding of India's unique history, culture and democratic evolution. Until the West makes that effort, it risks continuing to misread one of the world's most important and enduring civilizations.

The Tariff War

When Donald Trump imposed these tariffs of up to 50 percent on Indian goods in 2025, the decision sparked sharp resentment in India and a deep sense of injustice. For decades, India had maintained a relatively cooperative trade relationship with the United States—one often described as mutually beneficial. The sudden decision to target Indian exports—ranging from textiles to pharmaceuticals and steel—was seen not simply as an economic policy, but as a political blow to a country that had long considered itself a strategic partner to Washington. For Indian exporters, the tariffs were devastating. Industries like textiles and leather, which rely heavily on access to the American market, found themselves priced out overnight. Small and medium-sized enterprises, particularly in states like Gujarat, Tamil Nadu and Uttar Pradesh, suffered immediate losses. For India's growing pharmaceutical industry, which supplied affordable generic medicines to millions of Americans, the measure seemed particularly unfair, as it punished a sector that was addressing public health needs in the United States itself.

However, it is also true that the American side had a point. While the United States does not levy duties on Indian goods valued up to USD 800, India's own customs system is notoriously heavy. Duties on imported cars, electronics and agricultural products can be exorbitant, sometimes reaching more than 100 percent. To Washington, this imbalance looked like hypocrisy: India enjoyed the openness of the American market while maintaining formidable barriers of its own.

This dual reality explains both the bitterness and the defensiveness in India's reaction. The tariffs hurt, and they felt unjust, but they also exposed the asymmetry at the heart of Indo-U.S. trade. In global commerce, fairness is rarely absolute; it is often a negotiation between perception, leverage and necessity.

THE BLACK KARMA OF TURKEY

In AD 732, one of the most decisive battles in European history took place near Poitiers, where Charles Martel, king of France (688-741) halted the advance of Arab armies into Western Europe. Known as the Battle of Tours, this victory preserved Europe's Christian identity and ensured that Greco-Roman traditions could flourish into the Renaissance. Without Martel's triumph, the Arab campaign might have swept into the heart of Europe, reshaping its spiritual and cultural destiny. The Islamic wave, however, did succeed in two corners of the continent. Spain, conquered in the 8th century, witnessed centuries of Muslim rule and a rich cultural fusion in Córdoba and Granada, before the Reconquista ended with the fall of Granada in 1492. The Balkans, later conquered by the Ottomans, retained deep Islamic roots that endure in Bosnia and Albania. Yet, beyond these regions, Islam never penetrated the European core, thanks to moments like Poitiers and the long Serbian resistance after the Ottoman victory at Kosovo in 1389. Serbia endured centuries under Turkish rule but never lost its Christian soul, and by the 19th century, leaders like Milos Obrenovic restored independence. Europe owes much of its distinct identity to these pivotal struggles.

India's story runs parallel, though on an even greater scale. From the 8th century onward, waves of invasions—from the Delhi Sultanate to the Mughal Empire—brought destruction, enslavement and forced conversions. Temples were razed in Mathura, Somnath and Vijayanagar; sacred texts were burned, and countless Hindus were massacred or enslaved. Yet unlike Persia, Central Asia, or much of the Middle East, India did not succumb to Islamization. Hinduism endured because millions resisted—Rajput warriors, Marathas, Sikh Gurus, and countless anonymous villagers. For a thousand years, India fought for survival, preserving *dharma* through sacrifice and memory. This resilience is one of history's greatest untold epics: a civilization rooted in peace withstanding relentless violence without losing its essence. Today, echoes of those struggles return in modern geopolitics. Turkey, under President Erdoğan, has embraced Neo-Ottomanism, projecting pan-Islamic solidarity across the world. Once hailed as a secular republic, Turkey now seeks to revive influence in former Ottoman lands and position itself as a defender of Muslim causes. From Gaza to Myanmar, Erdoğan has cast himself as a champion of Islam, but his rhetoric has also targeted South Asia—particularly Kashmir.

At the United Nations and the Organisation of Islamic Cooperation, Turkey routinely echoes Pakistan's narrative, portraying Kashmir not as a postcolonial dispute but as a Muslim grievance. This selective solidarity reveals deeper motives. Ankara has been silent on the plight of Uyghur Muslims in China, unwilling to jeopardize economic ties with Beijing, yet vocally aggressive on Kashmir, where its interests align with Pakistan's strategy of destabilization. Through diplomacy, media and cultural outreach, Turkey is steadily planting influence in South Asia, from Bangladesh to the Maldives.

For India, this alliance between Turkey, Pakistan and even China is a serious concern. While China presses militarily in Ladakh and supports Pakistan's military programs through the China–Pakistan Economic Corridor, Turkey adds an ideological front. By offering Pakistan diplomatic cover and invoking pan-Islamic identity, Ankara strengthens separatist propaganda and emboldens jihadist networks. The "ghost" of the Ottoman Empire thus lingers, reemerging not through conquest but through religious populism and soft power. India has not remained passive. It has built stronger ties with Saudi Arabia, the UAE, and Israel— nations increasingly wary of Turkey's ambitions. Strategically, India aligns with the U.S., Europe and Japan to balance both Chinese authoritarianism and Turkish Islamic populism. At home, India asserts its pluralist identity, aware that external pressures seek to weaken its cohesion.

The parallels with Europe's past are striking. Just as Charles Martel and Serbian kings held back Islamic expansion, India must now defend itself against modern encirclement—military, ideological and cultural. History teaches that civilizations survive not by retreating but by clarity of vision and unity of purpose. India is one of the world's oldest and proudest civilizations, with nothing to be ashamed of. From Poitiers to Kosovo, from Panipat to Haldighati, history reminds us that survival demands strength, memory and resolve. The Ottoman Empire may have vanished, but its shadow resurfaces in modern forms. India's enduring task is to confront history's challenges with *dharma*, courage and with the confidence of a civilization that has weathered the fiercest storms—and still stands tall.

THE NUCLEAR DILEMMA: SOVEREIGNTY AND THE INDO–U.S. EQUATION

In the corridors of Indian policy-making, few issues have stirred as much debate, passion and division as the Indo–U.S. civil nuclear agreement. First unveiled in 2005 and signed in 2008 under the UPA government led by Dr. Manmohan Singh, the deal was hailed by some as a landmark strategic partnership and condemned by others as a subtle surrender of sovereignty. Today, nearly two decades later, the fundamental questions it raised remain just as relevant—perhaps even more so, as India navigates an increasingly hostile world order marked by Chinese aggression, Western ambivalence, and shifting geopolitical alliances.

At its core, the deal allowed India to gain access to American nuclear technology and fuel for civilian energy purposes, despite not being a signatory to the Nuclear Non-Proliferation Treaty (NPT). For a country that had faced decades of nuclear isolation following its 1974 and 1998 tests, this was seen as a breakthrough. It not only signaled global recognition of India as a responsible nuclear power, but also opened the doors for collaboration with other nations, such as France and Russia, in the civil nuclear domain. Yet the fine print of the agreement raised concerns that continue to echo today. The Hyde Act, passed by the U.S. Congress to enable the deal, clearly stated that if India were to conduct another nuclear test, sanctions would automatically kick in. Critics rightly asked: Was India now boxed in, unable to modernize or test its nuclear arsenal if regional threats escalated? Was the deal an invisible chain, binding India to American expectations and restricting its sovereign right to strategic self-defence? These questions acquired a new urgency in recent years as China's assertiveness has grown on India's northern borders, and Pakistan continues to develop its nuclear capabilities in tandem with its deepening alliance with Beijing. In this scenario, India's ability to maintain and advance a credible minimum deterrent is not a matter of abstract policy—it is a matter of national survival.

The BJP, which was in the opposition at the time of the deal, initially opposed it. Its concerns were rooted not in anti-Americanism, but in a firm belief in India's sovereign decision-making in defence matters. Leaders like Atal Bihari Vajpayee, who had ordered the 1998 tests, saw India's nuclear independence as a civilizational imperative. The idea that strategic autonomy could be traded for technology or diplomatic favors was, to many, an unacceptable compromise. However, time—and power—have nuanced these positions. After coming to office in 2014, Prime Minister Narendra Modi's government did not roll back the nuclear agreement. Instead, it quietly expanded strategic cooperation with the

United States, strengthening military, intelligence and technological ties through agreements such as LEMOA (Logistics Exchange Memorandum of Agreement), COMCASA, and BECA. These pacts, while not directly related to the nuclear sphere, show a broader convergence between India and the U.S., driven not by ideology but by shared concerns over China. At the same time, the Modi government has taken visible steps to assert India's strategic independence. It has refused to join the NPT or the Comprehensive Nuclear-Test-Ban Treaty (CTBT), both of which would permanently cap India's nuclear options. It has maintained a deliberate ambiguity on further testing, keeping the door open should circumstances demand it. In 2019, India's former National Security Advisor Shivshankar Menon subtly hinted that the "no first use" policy could be subject to change—conveying to adversaries that India's doctrine remains dynamic.

So, should India test again if required? Would the U.S. impose sanctions? Would India buckle under pressure? The answer is more complex than it appears. The United States needs India as a strategic counterweight to China. Its own priorities in the Indo-Pacific are deeply tied to India's rise. In such a context, it is unlikely that Washington would risk alienating New Delhi over a single test—especially one justified by regional security imperatives. Moreover, in a world where even treaty-bound powers violate norms when convenient, India must retain the right to act in national interest, irrespective of external consequences. Yet, the dilemma persists. India's energy needs are massive. Nuclear energy offers a clean, long-term solution to power shortages and fossil fuel dependence. Access to international nuclear markets through the 2008 waiver from the Nuclear Suppliers Group (NSG) was a gain not to be dismissed. But the price of that access—strategic restraint under the watchful eyes of global powers—remains deeply uncomfortable for many in India's strategic community.

The question, then, is not whether India should scrap or embrace the nuclear deal. The real question is: Can India leverage it without becoming beholden to it? A confident, self-assured India must walk this tightrope—using the tools of diplomacy, technology and strategic depth to ensure both energy security and defence autonomy. It must modernize its deterrent without being reckless. It must deepen partnerships without becoming dependent. It must test, if needed, without apology. And it must remind the world that India's nuclear journey did not begin with a handshake in Washington—it began with a civilizational ethos of *shakti* balanced by *dharma*, of power anchored in responsibility. As India emerges as a great power in its own right, it will no longer have to ask for recognition. It will command it.

All weapons of war are a manifestation of human greed and the ultimate symbol of mankind's dominance over matter. Ideally, they should all be banned—or at least gradually phased out until we inhabit a world without weapons, a world where they are no longer needed because humanity has outgrown such folly.

Therefore, more than anything, the atom bomb symbolizes that folly, because at a single stroke, at the simple push of one button by a misguided hand, or though the order of a mad leader, thousands of lives can be obliterated in a single second, entire cities be wiped out in a single flash.

The film, *The Day After* (1983), has given us an inkling of that terror, a glimpse of that horror. The atom bomb also demonstrates the limit of man's command over matter. For what use is that material mastery to man, when he has no control over his impulses, when he is still unable not only to love his human brothers, but even to reason with himself not to use his domination over matter to harm others. And ultimately, his might may slip out of his hands, because material mastery without inner control is incomplete and dangerous.

For this and many other reasons, should not India then voluntarily forsake nuclear power and cap its missile program and become a true non-violent country, in the spirit of Mahatma Gandhi?

But have those who are pushing this theory forward read the *Bhagavad Gita*? For once more, what does the *Bhagavad* tell us? It does not say, as Christians do, or as the Mahatma purported, that all violence is wrong. It asserts that when violence is absolutely necessary, when it is used for defending one's country, one's wife, brothers, sisters, then it becomes *dharma (*duty) and is acceptable, as long as it is done with the right attitude in one's heart. India, as we have just seen, is facing multiple threats from hostile nations, armed with both conventional and atomic weapons. The Islamic bomb, assembled by Pakistan with Arab financing, is the first one of these.

It is to be hoped that India will realize that surrendering to America's pressure would jeopardize her unity and open her for dismemberment. For her nuclear and missile programs are not meant for aggression—once again in her 7000 year history, India was never an aggressor—but as a deterrent to protect herself, to show her enemies that she means business and that she will retaliate in case of the first attack. It is a sad reality of the world today, and India needs to take it into consideration. Let India be strong, powerful, nuclear even, but as *dharma*, because it is her duty to protect her children.

Chapter 25

From Wonder to Wasteland? The Betrayal of India by Indians Themselves

There was once a time when travelers from China, Greece and Persia marveled at the magnificence of India. They spoke of her cities, cleaner and more organized than anything in Europe; of her spiritual vision that transcended material desire; of her science, art, and architecture that dazzled the senses. India, then, was not only a land of wealth but of wisdom, where kings lived modestly, sages advised rulers, and life followed the subtle rhythm of *dharma*. Today, however, a far less flattering image confronts both the visitor and the native: a land staggering under the weight of her own neglect, confusion and decay, borne out of centuries of oppression and enslavement. The miracle that was Bharat seems in many places to have become the nightmare that is India. And while colonialism, invasions and foreign manipulations have certainly contributed to her degradation, the uncomfortable truth remains: Indians themselves have played no small role in the unraveling of their own civilization. At the beginning of this 3rd millennium, one is forced to ask—how did the spiritual cradle of mankind, with its ancient wisdom and inner richness, become a country where garbage piles fester in every corner, where officials sell their signatures to the highest bidder, where public servants act like petty tyrants, and where crass materialism has replaced timeless culture?

Let us examine some spheres where this slow rot is most apparent: garbage and ecological neglect, corruption and bureaucratic sclerosis, and the lack of industrial dignity and efficiency.

SWACHH BHARAT: A NOBLE VISION IN RUINS?

When Prime Minister Narendra Modi launched the Swachh Bharat Abhiyan (Clean India Mission) on 2 October 2014, it ignited a national movement unlike any before. The campaign aimed to eliminate open defecation, clean up cities and villages, and instil civic responsibility among citizens. It was more than a cleanliness drive; it was a call to action, a Gandhian tribute meant to transform the way India sees hygiene, sanitation and public spaces. In the initial years, Swachh Bharat achieved impressive milestones. Millions of toilets were constructed in rural areas, many cities became officially "open defecation free," and for a while, it felt as if India was on the brink of a genuine civic revolution. Urban centers saw volunteers, students and even celebrities wielding brooms. The mission became a symbol of New India's aspiration to shed centuries of squalor and take pride in public hygiene. But ten years later, the shine has faded.

Many of the toilets built have no running water or sewage connections. Urban waste continues to pile up in ever-growing garbage mountains on the outskirts of cities. Public toilets remain unhygienic, and litter lines the roads of even the most prosperous towns. In rural India, some families have reverted to open defecation due to lack of maintenance or cultural resistance. So what went wrong? And more importantly—who is to blame? The fault, sadly, lies not with one person or party, but across multiple levels of society and governance. Yes, the government must answer for the lack of sustainable planning. Too much emphasis was laid on infrastructure (building toilets) and not enough on behavioral change, waste management systems and maintenance. Funds were often misused or left unspent. Municipalities lacked the manpower and technology to implement long-term cleanliness solutions. But the public too bears responsibility. Civic apathy runs deep. For all the slogans and social media campaigns, many citizens continue to dump trash in public spaces, spit on sidewalks, or misuse public amenities. There is still a disturbing disconnect between cleanliness at home and cleanliness in public.

Swachh Bharat was not meant to be a ten-year project—it was meant to ignite a permanent shift in civic consciousness. That transformation has only half-bloomed. Yet, it is not too late. The foundation has been laid, the vision is powerful. What is needed now is a second wave: one that emphasizes education, responsibility, local accountability and long-term maintenance. Cleanliness is not a one-day event or a once-a-decade mission. It is a daily act of national devotion. Only then can we resurrect Swachh Bharat—not as a forgotten campaign, but as an enduring legacy.

THE EMPIRE OF CORRUPTION AND BUREAUCRACY

If garbage is the most visible symptom of decline, corruption is its moral core. It is now no longer shocking but expected that bribes must be paid for birth certificates, driving licenses, school admissions, or electricity connections. This in spite of Narendra Modi's initial fight against corruption in India's bureaucracy, especially at the grassroots where citizens suffer most. His government launched the JAM trinity (Jan Dhan bank accounts) which enabled direct benefit transfers and cut out middlemen who used to siphon off subsidies and welfare funds. Many government services were moved online, reducing face-to-face dealings where bribes were common. In 2016, demonetization, as we will say below, pushed the shift to digital payments, limiting cash-based graft. The administration also introduced e-tendering and online procurement, making contracts more transparent. Officials accused of corruption were compulsorily retired, while regular performance reviews increased accountability. Modi's motto, *Na Khaunga, Na Khane Doonga* ("I won't take bribes, nor allow others to"), reinforced his message. Unfortunately, corruption persists: political leaders embezzle development funds. Police officers extort the vulnerable. Officials delay files for months until "tea money" is offered. This normalization of corruption has eaten away at India's moral fibre. It has created a nation where honesty is punished, where ethical businesses lose to cronies, and where merit is buried under nepotism. Bureaucracy compounds this sickness. The Indian administrative system, inherited from colonial masters, was designed not to serve but to control. It remains fossilized, opaque and hierarchical. Files are lost, signatures delayed, rules contradicted. Innovation is stifled. Foreign investors are scared away. Indian entrepreneurs flee to more efficient countries. And worst of all, citizens no longer trust the state. This breakdown of trust is catastrophic for democracy. A nation where the people fear or disdain their own institutions becomes fertile ground for chaos, extremism or authoritarian shortcuts.

DEMONETIZATION: A BRILLIANT VISION, DERAILED BY AN ENDURING VICE

When Prime Minister Narendra Modi announced the demonetization of ₹500 and ₹1000 notes on the evening of 8 November 2016, it was nothing short of revolutionary. For the first time in independent India, a sitting government had dared to strike directly at the heart of black money, corruption and terror financing by removing 86 percent of the currency in circulation overnight. It was a bold gamble, one that aimed to shock the corrupt ecosystem and force the informal economy into the light.

In the initial weeks and months, the results seemed promising. Mountains of unaccounted cash flooded the banks. Shell companies went under scrutiny. Fake currency networks were disrupted. Small digital transactions surged dramatically, and many Indians, especially the youth, welcomed this long-overdue cleansing of the system. For a brief moment, it felt like a national reset—a mass purging of economic impurities. The middle class bore the brunt of the queues and inconveniences with patience, even pride, believing they were part of something greater than themselves: a war on corruption. But then, as the months turned into years, old habits resurfaced. Indians are ingenious, especially when it comes to circumventing bureaucracy. *Benami* transactions, cash hoarding and under-the-table dealings slowly found new forms. Black money that once flowed in ₹1000 notes now moved in gold, real estate, or simply in newer ₹2000 denominations. Those with political connections or advance notice found ways to convert their illicit wealth even before the public announcement.

Moreover, much of the money that was supposed to "disappear" actually returned to the banks, raising questions about the effectiveness of the operation. While the formal economy did grow in terms of digitization and transparency, the informal sector—where most Indians earn their living—was badly hit. Millions of small traders, laborers and rural businesses struggled to recover from the cash crunch.

So, was demonetization a failure? Not entirely. It was a bold, visionary step—and in many ways, it did achieve temporary discipline in the system. It forced India to have long-overdue conversations about black money, cash economy and digital transactions. But its long-term impact was diluted not by the policy itself, but by the resilience of corruption in Indian society. In the end, systems can change, but if human nature does not evolve with them, the old ways find new expressions. Demonetization remains a turning point in India's modern economic history—an audacious attempt to change the DNA of a corrupt system. But like all revolutions, its success depends not just on policy, but on the moral will of the people it seeks to transform.

INDUSTRIAL INEFFICIENCY

Despite its vast talent pool, India remains a country that often fails to build with precision, speed, or pride. Public infrastructure projects take decades and are riddled with cost overruns and poor quality (see box). Trains are still slow. Roads are dangerous, though it must be said that Nitin Gadkari, the present Road and Transport Minister, has drastically improved the roads infrastructure in India, building multiple 4 lane highways, which have considerably reduced the traveling time of cars in India. Public buildings are ugly and poorly maintained. Even in the private sector, many industries function without standards. Electric wires hang perilously from poles. Air conditioners leak. Plumbing fails. Customer service is erratic. Workers are not trained to take pride in their tasks, and management is often indifferent. India has shown flashes of brilliance—in space, in IT, in pharma—but this remains an exception, not the norm. What is missing is an ethic of excellence, a spirit of perfection. In Japan, a worker polishing a train window does so with reverence. In Germany, an engineer double-checks every bolt. In India, the painter drops his brush mid-job and walks off to drink chai. This is not just an industrial issue—it is spiritual. When one's work becomes only a means to money and not an offering to something higher, decay follows. In the Indian ethos, *karma yoga* taught that every act, however small, is sacred. That vision is lost. Here comes Shri Narendra Modi!

The Tejas White Elephant

Hindustan Aeronautics Limited's Tejas fighter jet has often been dismissed by critics as a white elephant. The project began in 1983 under the Light Combat Aircraft program with the aim of developing an indigenous fighter jet and reducing India's dependence on foreign suppliers. Yet, after four decades of development and investment, the project has struggled to deliver on its promise. Progress was hampered by technical hurdles, shifting design requirements, and delays in acquiring advanced technology. The Tejas, while lighter and smaller than many modern fighter jets, suffers from limitations in combat range and payload capacity. Additionally, its radar, engine and weapons systems have been considered inferior to those of rival aircraft. Although it was formally inducted into the Indian Air Force in 2016, production numbers have remained limited, and the aircraft's cost has risen due to imported components and maintenance needs. Critics argue that the money spent on the program has not translated into adequate defense capability, and that the Tejas consumes vast resources while failing to meet strategic demands. Supporters, however, view it as a vital step toward self-reliance in defense manufacturing—an investment in capability that will mature over time. Yet, until performance improves and production scales up, the Tejas remains, for many, an ambitious but underperforming project.

THE PRIVATISATION OF INDIA'S WHITE ELEPHANTS: NARENDRA MODI'S BOLD RESTRUCTURING

One of the most striking reforms undertaken by the Modi government has been the privatization of public sector undertakings (PSUs)—especially those long considered "white elephants": bloated, loss-making, inefficient government-owned enterprises that consumed massive taxpayer funds while delivering little value in return. For decades, India carried the legacy of Nehruvian socialism, where the State owned everything from airlines and banks to hotels and steel plants. These behemoths were created with good intentions—to serve the people, to generate employment and to build infrastructure in a newly independent nation. But over time, many of them became symbols of inefficiency, nepotism and corruption. Their financial losses were propped up year after year by government subsidies, draining the exchequer and hindering economic dynamism. When Narendra Modi came to power in 2014, he inherited a sluggish economy burdened by these unproductive giants. Unlike previous governments, which hesitated to act for fear of political backlash or ideological criticism, Modi moved decisively. He framed privatization not as an abandonment of responsibility but as a necessary correction—"Government has no business to be in business," he famously declared.

Under his leadership, a clear strategy was drawn: the government would retain control over strategic sectors such as defence, atomic energy, and railways, but would exit non-strategic and chronically loss-making sectors. Several major enterprises were identified for sale or disinvestment, including Air India, BPCL, Shipping Corporation of India and IDBI Bank.

Perhaps the most symbolic was the sale of Air India, which had become a monument to mismanagement. Once the pride of India, it was reduced to a debt-ridden burden on the taxpayer. After multiple failed attempts by earlier governments, Modi's administration finally succeeded in selling it back to the Tata Group in 2021—the same industrial house that had originally founded the airline before it was nationalized in 1953. The transaction was not just financial but symbolic: it marked a break from the past and a return to private entrepreneurship.

Privatization under Modi was also accompanied by efforts to improve corporate governance, consolidate public banks and make PSUs more accountable. While some critics argued that selling national assets would lead to monopolies or job losses, the government maintained that these enterprises had already become unsustainable, and their continued survival required a professional, competitive environment that only the private sector could offer.

Yet, the process was not without its challenges. Trade unions resisted, bureaucratic delays persisted, and in some cases, valuation controversies emerged. But the direction was clear: the Indian economy was being freed from its socialist baggage and pushed toward greater efficiency, innovation and global competitiveness. Modi's privatization drive has not yet reached its final goal, but it represents a paradigm shift in India's economic thinking. No longer is the government seen as the omnipotent provider of jobs and goods—it is being reshaped as a facilitator of opportunity, empowering private players while focusing on governance and infrastructure.

In doing so, Modi has tackled one of the thorniest legacies of independent India: the myth that the State must own everything to serve the people. Instead, his reforms suggest that leaner governance and vibrant enterprise can coexist—and that India, to rise, must finally shed its white elephants. Despite the bold vision behind Narendra Modi's privatization drive, the results have fallen short of expectations. While the successful sale of Air India to the Tata Group was hailed as a landmark achievement, it remains the lone major success story. Many other planned disinvestments—such as BPCL, IDBI Bank, and Shipping Corporation of India—have faced repeated delays, valuation issues and lack of investor interest. Bureaucratic hurdles, political resistance and global economic uncertainty further slowed momentum. What began as a promising effort to offload white elephant public sector units has, so far, yielded modest results, exposing the persistent difficulty of reforming India's entrenched public sector.

POLITICIANS

"Spirituality is India's only politics, the fulfilment of Sanatana Dharma, it's only Swaraj," wrote Sri Aurobindo in 1911 (*India's Rebirth,* p. 89).

In the old times, princes and kings were Kshatriyas, their duty was to serve the nation and high ideals were held in front of them by the Brahmins and rishis who advised them. The Buddha's father for instance, was a king *elected* by his own people Yet what has happened to Indian politicians? Today we see, particularly in the small regional parties, or in the Congress, corrupt, inefficient men, who have lost track of the good of the nation they are supposed to serve, who are only interested in minting the maximum money in the minimum of time. Before Narendra Modi's advent, Indian politicians had often become a caricature, which was made fun of by the whole country. They were frequently uneducated, gross people, elected on the strength of demagogic pledges, such as promising rice for Rs.3 a kilo, a folly which drained many states' coffers, or of playing Muslims against Hindus, Harijans against Brahmins, as in UP and Bihar. Politicians in India were most of the time ignorant; ministers had customarily no idea about the department they were overseeing. It is the civil servants who controlled matters, who knew their subject thoroughly. You have to work hard to become a civil servant, study, pass exams, then slowly climb up the hierarchy, hereby gaining experience. The politician just jumps from being a lowly clerk, or some uneducated zamindar to become a powerful minister, lording over much more educated men. There should also be exams to become a politician (but what if they are rigged like in UP!); a minimum of knowledge and skills should be required of the man who says he wants to serve the nation.

The rise of the Bharatiya Janata Party, under the leadership of Prime Minister Narendra Modi, marked a significant turning point in Indian politics, particularly in how citizens viewed their leaders. Modi's ascent to power in 2014 carried the promise of change, of a government that would be both accountable and transparent, with leaders who were dedicated to service rather than personal enrichment. One of the most striking changes under the Modi administration has been the emergence of a core group of ministers whose reputation for integrity and hard work stand in sharp contrast to the corruption-tainted image of many of their predecessors. Nirmala Sitharaman, the Finance Minister, is often cited as an example. Known for her diligence and straightforward approach, she has built a reputation as a politician who focuses on results rather than power or privilege. Similarly, Nitin Gadkari, the Minister for Road Transport and Highways, has been widely respected for his efficiency and for overseeing some of the most ambitious infrastructure projects in modern India. His ability to deliver on projects has won praise across party lines. Amit Shah, the Home Minister, is another example of a leader whose image is not that of a traditional politician enjoying privileges, but of a strategist and administrator who works tirelessly to ensure the government's agenda is implemented.

These ministers symbolize a broader transformation in the perception of Indian politicians. The BJP has consciously cultivated an image of being a party of service-oriented leaders, contrasting itself with the Congress Party, which for decades was associated with dynastic politics and entrenched corruption. This change has resonated strongly with ordinary Indians, who have long demanded leaders that reflect integrity and competence. However, it would be misleading to suggest that the challenges of governance in India have been completely overcome. The BJP, despite its efforts, still operates within a political and administrative framework largely shaped by the Congress Party during its decades-long dominance. In Delhi, as repeatedly stated, the heart of political power, old habits die hard. The culture of privilege, often referred to as the VVIP system (see previous chapter), continues to linger. This system, marked by red-beacon cars, special access and a sense of entitlement among those in power, has been deeply entrenched for generations and cannot be dismantled overnight.

Moreover, the higher bureaucracy remains a formidable force. India's administrative machinery—shaped first by the colonial era and later by decades of Congress rule—retains its hierarchical, rigid, and change-resistant character. Senior bureaucrats continue to wield significant influence over both policy and implementation. While Modi has pushed for greater accountability and efficiency, the reality is that systemic reform in such a vast and entrenched structure takes time. In this context, the BJP's achievement lies not in completely eliminating corruption or privilege but in setting a new standard for political leadership. By elevating leaders who are hardworking and clean in their public image, Modi has shown that politics in India can be about integrity and performance. At the same time, the persistence of old systems serves as a reminder that while leadership can inspire change, institutional reform is a gradual process. The journey is far from complete, but the shift in perception itself is significant. For many Indians, seeing, particularly during Modi's first mandate, but much less now, ministers who work long hours, travel without ostentation and deliver tangible results has rekindled faith in the possibility of good governance. The BJP has succeeded in planting the seeds of change, even if the soil of India's political system is still resistant to transformation.

The VVIP Syndrome

There is nothing which symbolizes better the degradation of Indian politics than the VVIP syndrome. The protection that most politicians enjoy today, was born out of the trauma of seeing Indira Gandhi killed by her own bodyguards and Rajiv Gandhi wasted by a human bomb; it sprang from a sincere desire to protect future Indian VIPs from such a fate. But *once again perversion has taken over, and man, the political animal, has misused what was in the beginning a genuine movement*. Today, no leaders in the world are as protected as some of the Indian politicians. France, which has got its fair share of Islamic fundamentalism—there have been numerous deadly attacks against its railways, shopping plazas, airlines even—has learnt to cope with security in an efficient and discreet manner. President Macron, for instance, does not move around with an army of rude and brutish security men; and one still remembers how Francois Mitterrand, one previous President, used to go out at night to his favorite restaurant with only two bodyguards. The so-called "VVIP curse"—India's deep-rooted culture of privilege, entitlement, and special treatment for politicians, bureaucrats and the wealthy—has long eroded public trust. When Narendra Modi came to power in 2014, he vowed to break this feudal legacy. He banned red beacons on official cars, flew economy class on occasion and emphasized *"Sabka Saath, Sabka Vikas"*—governance for all, not just for the elite. In the beginning, there was a real shift. Ministers were seen standing in airport queues, and the Prime Minister projected himself as a servant of the people, not a ruler above them. But over time, the old habits crept back. VIP enclosures still thrive, security convoys still snarl traffic and the culture of deference to power remains alive and well. Worse, the centralization of power and the rise of a new political elite around Narendra Modi have simply replaced the old with the new. Despite good intentions, the VVIP mindset has proved resilient—cemented not by policy but by psychology, and difficult to dislodge in a society where status often trumps service. Thus, Modi's attempt to end the

VVIP culture remains a work in progress—symbolically powerful, but only partially successful.

PEOPLE

Individually, Indians are among the most generous and spiritual people in the world, full of warmth and hospitality. But collectively, something goes wrong. The gap between the rich and the poor has widened dramatically since liberalization, and compassion often fails to translate into action. In Mumbai, luxury towers stand next to sprawling slums, yet few among the privileged notice their neighbors. Surat, enriched by the diamond trade, once allowed filth to accumulate until decisive administration intervened. Unless wealth is shared and civic responsibility embraced, the nation risks not only social and human tragedy but also ecological disaster in the years to come.

Indians also show very little civic sense in other domains of their life. Look how they drive. Truck and bus drivers in India routinely overtake in curves endangering not only their passengers' lives, but also those of incoming traffic. They often stop right in the middle of the road, with little concern for those behind them. Their incessant horn-blaring deafens us, and their driving habits reveal a general disregard for others. After all, does not the way one drives reflect the vital soul of a nation? When an Israeli, who said that everything happens in his country with guts, asked his Indian counterpart how it was done in India, he was told: "With luck!" And it is true that there is some divine grace in India, borne out of the centuries of *tapasya* of its yogis, to reach safely on its roads from one point to another. And the bus driver who overtakes at the curve must be unconsciously knowing it.

Look also at how Indians are in the habit of pushing other people, whether it is to enter a plane, or exit a cinema. Or how they so innocently ignore those who have been queuing for hours at some railway counter, by jumping at the head of the queue. And it is not only the poor, but also the rich, who display this habit; witness the checking-in at airports.

Dishonesty is also a lack of collective discipline. Glimpse, even after the Prime Minister's demonetization and drive against corruption, how the Indian man is often cheating, whether it is the cement which is mixed with ashes, the change not tendered exactly, or the rich man who swindles the income tax, by keeping lakhs of black money, gold and jewels in his house, when he could very well afford to pay a little more taxes and put his money in his bank. It is often said that a third of India's wealth lies in the black economy. Make no mistake—India is a **wealthy** nation. Its poverty persists not from a lack of resources, but from mismanagement, dishonesty, *tamas* and the burden of flawed inherited structures. For Indians, like the Jews, are among the world's best savers. But they do not save in abstractions—they turn to solid assets: gold, land and cash, whether they are small shopkeepers or powerful business magnates. The question remains: where is all this money going? Too often, it is held back or misused, reflecting a lack of discipline, a weak sense of national responsibility, and an indifference to how unchecked individualism can harm the country as a whole.

Cricket's Monopoly and India's Lost Sporting Spirit

One of India's greatest failures has been in sports. A nation's vitality often reflects in its sporting achievements. Yet, in India, cricket has become not just a game but a national obsession. Since the rise of the Indian Premier League in 2008, cricket has dominated the country's imagination, attracting massive sponsorships, media coverage and global power through the BCCI. This success, however, has come at a heavy cost: other sports are left neglected, underfunded and invisible. While crores flow into cricket, Olympic athletes often struggle with poor facilities and meager rewards. A bronze medallist may fade into obscurity while an average cricketer earns millions. Schools and colleges now push cricket at the expense of other disciplines, and government initiatives like *Khelo India* remain too marginal to reverse the imbalance.

India is a land rich in natural talent—from wrestlers in Haryana to archers in Jharkhand—but without systemic support, much of it is wasted. The government must curb the over-saturation of cricket, reduce international matches and boldly invest in other sports, possibly through privatization of training. Only then can India break cricket's monopoly and emerge as a true sporting superpower.

IS INDIA HEADING TOWARDS AN ECOLOGICAL DISASTER ?

All right: India, after three mandates of *vibhuti* Narendra Modi might overcome its colossal indiscipline, her people will rise, her politicians will change; she will also last through all internal and external threats. Thus, whatever foreigners and India's own "secular" Indians say, the land of Bharat, the cradle of the mighty Vedas, the Mother of so many saints, poets, great artists, philosophers, revolutionaries, **will survive**. After all, it has already passed through the unspeakable barbarism of countless Muslim invaders, the soul-stifling British colonial rule—and 60 years of "secular" socialism.

But for what purpose, one may ask? India strides ahead in technology, arms itself with nuclear power, sends missions to the Moon and Mars, and boasts a growing GDP. Yet, beneath the surface of this remarkable ascent lies a silent, swelling catastrophe. By the middle of this century, India may well be home to over 1.6 billion people, making it the most populous country in the world by a wide margin. This sheer demographic pressure is no longer just a challenge—it is an existential threat. Forests are vanishing at alarming rates, replaced by sprawling cities, roads, mines and farmland. The green canopy that once covered vast stretches of the subcontinent is now reduced to fragmented patches. If the current trends continue, there may be no meaningful forest cover left in India within a few decades—except in protected sanctuaries, themselves increasingly under siege from development and encroachment. This relentless human expansion is not just overwhelming nature; it is beginning to stifle the very mechanisms of progress. Overpopulation drains resources, multiplies waste, and spreads pollution across land, water and air. Infrastructure is perpetually behind demand. Cities swell into unmanageable sprawls, rivers run black with industrial toxins, and villages become unlivable due to lack of water and employment. Efforts at reform and innovation, however sincere, are suffocated under the weight of numbers and bureaucratic lethargy. Education, healthcare, sanitation—all suffer. The environment is degraded not only by poverty, but by middle-class consumerism and elite indifference. And yet the nation continues to add nearly twenty million people every year, a number equivalent to the population of a medium-sized country.

What will India be when its forests are gone, its wildlife extinct, its groundwater depleted, and its cities choked? Will democracy, innovation and tradition survive the crush of unchecked growth? Or will the very idea of India collapse under its own weight? This is not a prophecy of doom, but a wake-up call. The future can still be shaped. But without bold action—on population control, environmental preservation and sustainable development—India's greatest threat may not be China, Pakistan, or any external enemy, but herself. India's cities will be so polluted by their millions of cars that it will be impossible to breathe any more. India's rivers will be so poisoned by industries, that all living life will long have disappeared from it. There will be no drinking water left, except imported mineral water. And India will be littered with so much plastic (bags, bottles, buckets, etc.) that it will be materially impossible to ever get rid of them (indeed the land of Bharat should be renamed "the civilization of plastic"). This is 21st century India for you.

But ultimately, is it fair to blame only the politicians, or even the British, who started the massive deforestation for their railways and killed hundreds of thousands of tigers? Is there not something else in the Indian psyche that is to blame? Where is the root of this massive unconcern for one's environment; this total disregard for beauty, whether it is the terrible ugliness of the cities in Punjab, or the appalling filthiness in Tamil Nadu? And, maybe, for once, the Hindus are to blame. The Ganges seems to be the perfect illustration of a religion which enjoins a thousand purification rites and yet has allowed her own Mother earth to be defiled. Here is a river that Hindus have held most sacred for centuries, nay millenniums; to bathe in it is to purify oneself of all bad karma; to die here is to be reborn in Light. Yet what do all Hindus do with their sacred Ganges? They defecate in it; they throw in all their refuse; they let their dead float down the mighty river, AS IF THEY THOUGHT THAT THE SPIRITUAL PURITY OF THE WATER CAN NEVER BE OBLITERATED BY MATERIAL DIRTINESS. But ask any scientist about the degree of pollution in the Ganges today and he will tell you that it is near the point of no return. Did you know for instance that the Ganges has shrunk by half since the Tehri dam was built? How could the Central Government approve of a dam so harmful to India's interests? What will happen to India if it loses the Ganges, which is its very soul?

So, for once, India should copy the West, which has grown a tremendous ecological concern and developed various ways of fighting against the physical degradation of our planet. We have seen for instance how India has been forced to adopt certain environmental measures just out of greed, when European countries refused for instance to accept any textile export which was not free, or leather which was not chemically poisoned. Look at Auroville (see box above), the greenest place in the plains of Tamil Nadu, which is being deforested at this moment, to build huge unnecessary roads, camps for IT colleges, or training centers for the NCC. Without its land and a minimum forest cover and some unpolluted rivers, India will be like a great soul without a body, unable to manifest itself.

CHAPTER 26

Success Stories

The previous chapter should not suggest that India is doomed. On the contrary, Narendra Modi has emerged as a transformative leader, potentially the instrument through which Bharat may redeem itself and rise as a true superpower in the 21st century. Below are some of the Prime Minister's notable success stories.

AADHAAR AND THE DIGITAL GOVERNANCE REVOLUTION

Though Aadhaar was launched in 2009 under the UPA government with Nandan Nilekani as the founding chairman of the Unique Identification Authority of India (UIDAI), it remained, until 2014, largely an identity project with limited practical application. By the time Narendra Modi came to power in May 2014, over 60 crore Aadhaar numbers had already been issued, but their integration into governance, banking or welfare systems was limited and lacked clear direction. What Modi saw—and seized—was the vast potential of Aadhaar not just as a biometric ID, but as a foundational platform for India's digital future. His government aggressively expanded its scope and functionality. The number of Aadhaar holders soared past the 100-crore mark by 2016, and the infrastructure to integrate Aadhaar with various government services was laid at breathtaking speed. The real game-changer came with the creation of the JAM trinity: Jan Dhan (bank accounts for the unbanked), Aadhaar (biometric identity), and Mobile (digital connectivity). This model was conceptualized to eliminate corruption, middlemen and inefficiencies in the distribution of welfare benefits. By 2017, nearly 80 percent of all central government subsidies and welfare schemes—from LPG to

MGNREGA wages—were being routed directly into beneficiaries' bank accounts linked with Aadhaar. The Pratyaksh Hanstantrit Labh (PAHAL) scheme for LPG subsidy, relaunched in late 2014, became the world's largest cash transfer program by 2016. It alone saved the exchequer over ₹14,000 crore by eliminating bogus connections and ghost beneficiaries. In parallel, the government used Aadhaar-based e-KYC (Know Your Customer) to make it easier to open bank accounts and access digital wallets, especially post-demonetization in November 2016, when cash vanished and digital transactions boomed. Aadhaar authentication allowed rural citizens and the poor to transact securely, receive wages, pensions, or subsidies without relying on agents or brokers.

By 2018, Aadhaar was powering over 300 crore authentications per month—a staggering number that reflects its deep integration into Indian life. Critics continued to raise alarms about privacy, security and the risks of surveillance, particularly after the Supreme Court's 2018 judgment that upheld Aadhaar's validity but barred its use by private corporations. Nonetheless, Aadhaar's success is visible on the ground. Today, more than 99 percent of adults in India possess an Aadhaar card, and the system supports over 1,200 government schemes across states and ministries. Financial inclusion, once a dream, has become a reality for hundreds of millions, thanks in large part to the Aadhaar ecosystem. Modi's vision of a Digital India, launched on 1 July 2015, found its foundation in Aadhaar. Without it, the UPI boom, the fintech revolution, and the success of DBT schemes would have been far slower and more fragmented. In many ways, Aadhaar is to 21st-century India what the railway system was to the British Empire—an infrastructure of integration and control. But under Modi, it has largely served the cause of empowerment rather than exploitation.

MODI'S FOREIGN DIPLOMACY: A NEW CHAPTER IN INDIA'S GLOBAL IMAGE

One of the most striking transformations in India's international standing over the past decade has come through the personal diplomacy of Prime Minister Narendra Modi. Since assuming office in May 2014, Modi has placed foreign policy at the center of his agenda, not merely as a matter of statecraft, but as a powerful tool to reshape India's global image. His frequent travels, personal rapport with world leaders, and bold articulation of India's interests have significantly altered how the world perceives India today. In his first five years alone, Modi visited over 60 countries—a record unmatched by any previous Indian prime minister. These visits were not symbolic; they were strategic, aimed at revitalizing ties, attracting investment, signing defence and technology agreements, and positioning India as a leading voice in global governance. Modi's approach was clear: India must no longer be a passive participant in international affairs, but an assertive and respected global player.

Modi developed a visible and warm personal chemistry with several world leaders. His camaraderie with French President Emmanuel Macron led to deeper cooperation in defense, climate change and technology. The India–France strategic partnership was further cemented with joint efforts on solar energy and naval security in the Indo-Pacific. Modi's dynamic relationship with U.S. President Donald Trump brought the two countries closer on trade, counter-terrorism and military cooperation. The "Howdy Modi" event in Houston (2019) and the "Namaste Trump" event in Ahmedabad (2020) showcased a new kind of diplomacy—public, confident, and people-centered. These friendships were not limited to the West. Modi also built strong ties with leaders across Asia, Africa and the Middle East, especially with Gulf states like the UAE and Saudi Arabia, who now see India not just as a labor source but as a trusted strategic partner. His emotional addresses, often invoking shared cultural or historical values, helped India connect beyond formal diplomatic channels.

The result of this high-octane diplomacy has been a dramatic improvement in India's image, particularly in Western capitals. No longer seen merely as a developing nation struggling with internal contradictions, India is now recognized as a civilizational power, a technological innovator and a key democratic ally in a shifting world order. Modi has positioned India as a bridge between the Global South and the West, between tradition and modernity, and between emerging economies and established powers. India's confident presence in forums like the G20, Quad, BRICS, and COP summits, combined with Modi's consistent visibility and statesmanship, has contributed to a new perception: that India is not just rising—it has arrived.

Narendra Modi's Love and Hate Story with Donald Trump

Narendra Modi and Donald Trump share one of the most unusual political relationships of recent times. Both leaders project themselves as strong nationalists, proud of their cultures and unafraid of breaking conventions. At first, their encounters radiated warmth. As mentioned above, Modi's grand "Howdy, Modi" rally in Houston in 2019, attended by more than 50,000 Indian-Americans, became a symbol of this camaraderie, with Trump himself walking hand in hand with Modi before an electrified crowd. It was rare for an American president to so openly endorse a foreign leader on U.S. soil. Trump, in turn, was given a massive reception in Ahmedabad in early 2020, with Shri Modi welcoming him to a packed stadium of over 100,000 people. Yet beneath the public spectacle lay tensions. Trump's "America First" policy often clashed with India's economic interests. He imposed steep tariffs on Indian goods and revoked India's special trade status, accusing the country of unfair practices (see above). On defence and foreign policy, too, disagreements lingered. Trump pushed India to curb ties with Iran and Russia, while New Delhi sought to preserve its strategic autonomy. The immigration debate was another thorny issue, with Trump tightening H-1B visa rules, directly affecting thousands of Indian professionals in the U.S.

Their bond was therefore a mix of admiration and suspicion. Narendra Modi admired Trump's bluntness and ability to disrupt established norms, while Trump saw Modi as a kindred nationalist who could deliver spectacle and votes through the Indian diaspora. But neither was willing to compromise on national interest. In the end, what remained was not a steady alliance, but rather a series of love and hate episodes—friendship when the cameras flashed, friction when the real business of trade, defence and diplomacy began.

THE ECONOMY

In 2025, India stood at the forefront of global innovation in artificial intelligence, having surpassed many traditional tech powerhouses in both talent and implementation. With a vibrant startup ecosystem, a growing digital infrastructure, and a massive pool of skilled engineers and data scientists, the country has become an indispensable player in the fourth industrial revolution. Its economy, once sluggish and over-regulated, has now grown manifold over the past decade, emerging as one of the most dynamic on the planet. Yet, just as India seemed poised to fully assert itself on the world stage, a jolt came from across the Atlantic, in the form of the 50% taxes imposed by Trump.

However, as history has often shown, adversity can spark transformation. The Trump tariffs may, in the long run, serve as a boon in disguise. Faced with punitive trade barriers, Indian industry and policymakers are being forced to rethink their over-dependence on the U.S. market and re-imagine the structure of the Indian economy. Instead of lobbying for concessions, India is using the moment to further liberalize its internal markets, encourage domestic consumption, strengthen regional trade partnerships and boost manufacturing self-reliance under the *Atmanirbhar Bharat* (Self-Reliant India) vision. New free trade agreements with Europe, Southeast Asia and Africa are in the works. The government is pushing through long-pending reforms in logistics, labor laws and capital markets to make India not just a tech leader but a true global manufacturing and services hub. Thanks to Mr Modi, GST rates were also cut on a wide range of products to ease costs and boost consumption. Essentials like milk, paneer, ghee, soaps, and toothpaste were exempted or taxed at 5 percent, while durables such as TVs, air conditioners, washing machines, and small cars saw rates fall from 28 percent to 18 percent. This made everyday life more affordable and encouraged domestic spending. In a way, the Trump tariffs may do for India what earlier Western pressures have occasionally done: provoke a leap forward. Just as the 1991 balance-of-payments crisis triggered sweeping economic reforms, the 2025 tariff shock may catalyze a new phase of Indian resilience, competitiveness and global positioning.

The question remains: will India seize this moment, rise above reactive politics, and push forward with long-term vision? If it does, the very attempt to isolate or punish India may end up helping her become what she is destined to be—a true economic superpower, not dependent on the goodwill of any single nation, but standing tall on the foundation of her own strength.

CHAPTER 27

India, Spiritual Leader of the World

Has Western civilization reached the end of the road? As we know, each culture has its own uniqueness: the Greeks were great thinkers, the Indians unsurpassed spiritualists, the Egyptians superb occultists. The West's genius is undoubtedly *materialism*, its immense capacity to achieve material perfection and its great vitality. But materialism has its shortcomings and ultimately, because it blanked out spirituality, except in a superficial and ritual manner, it may bring in the decline of Western civilization. The first signs of weaknesses have already been seen in the first quarter of the 21st century: the collapse of communism, the erosion of capitalism with recession and unemployment and the on and off raging wars in Ukraine and Palestine; these wars have spilled over in mainstream Europe, even if it is in an indirect manner, by an influx of refugee and rising costs of essential goods.

"For my part," wrote Sri Aurobindo in 1910, "I see failure written largely over all the splendid and ostentatious achievements of Europe. Her costliest experiments, her greatest expenditure of intellectual and moral force have led to the swiftest exhaustion of creative activity, the complete bankruptcy of moral elevation and discouragement of man's once infinite hope... System, organisation, machinery, have attained their perfection. Bondage has been carried to its highest expression, and from a passion to organising external liberty Europe is slaying her spiritual freedom. When the inner freedom is gone, the external liberty will follow it, and a social tyranny more terrible, more inquisitorial, and relentless than any that caste ever organised in India, will take its place. The process has already begun. The shell of external liberty remains, the core is already eaten away. Because he is still free to gratify his senses and enjoy himself, the European thinks himself free. He does not know what teeth are gnawing into the heart of his liberty!" (*India's Rebirth*, p. 75)

The other reason for the failing civilization of the West is that it greatly misused the mastery it had achieved over technology and the material. Instead of putting this mastery to the service of truth, instead of turning it towards the spirit of evolution, it used it for domination and the satisfaction of the Western man's senses.

What about Asia then? In Japan, only codified, externalized forms of the past greatness of Shintoism and Zen Buddhism survive. It is hoped that its success as the most powerful industrial nation today will not totally blank whatever remains of the old inner genius of Japan. But look at China: in spite of its enormous economic successes, communism has killed most forms of Buddhism and Confucianism, making the Chinese one of the most materialistic nations in the world. And behold what the Chinese did to Tibet, eradicating a 2000-year-old tradition of tantric Buddhism in a few decades. This is a karma which China will have to repay one day.

And what of India? Throughout these chapters, the reader has journeyed through the many dangers, threats, aggressions, pitfalls, perils and mistakes that the land of Bharat endured after the glorious Vedic epoch. From the yogis' disdain for matter and the physical—which gave rise to a great *tamas*—to the rigidification of the caste system; the ossification of society; and the first foreign incursion under Alexander, each episode marked a turning point in India's long history. To the successive Muslim invasions, which would have wiped out any culture, any civilization in 10 centuries of furious onslaughts. Yet, India's spirituality survived—it was preserved by its people in their hearts, when their temples were destroyed, in their flesh when it was burnt, in their souls, when they were killed. And they were reborn again and again, to fight for the continuation of true Hinduism. India also survived the immense threat of European colonialism, which has annihilated the souls of so many countries, some more powerful than India. The British came, conquered... understood nothing... left nothing... but India's spirituality remained. It survived the cruel partition of its ancient land, tearing its limbs into Pakistan and Bangladesh; any other nation might never have recovered from such a maiming. It survived the road to socialism charted by Nehru, the stifling oppression of state bureaucracy and corruption. It survived the dangerous politics of non-violence, which Mahatma Gandhi propounded for so long and which activated not only the division of India along Hindu-Muslim lines, but also sowed the seeds of inter-caste fighting. It survived the Mahatma's sterile policies of Charkha, Brahmacharya and Khadi. It survived the Chinese onslaught in 1962. It survives today, thanks to a new nationalism triggered by Narendra Modi, the Hindu-bashing of its Westernized elite, which is all set to wipe out whatever is left of Hinduism, to replace it with prototypes that have already shown the world their total failure. It is also hoped that it will survive economic liberalization, the onslaught of modernity and the egotism of becoming a powerful nation. And finally that it will also survive the ecological holocaust that is taking place in this country.

And if it survives all these dangers, as it survived other dangers for 10,000 years, then India will ride the second part of the 21st century, not only as a world power, industrially, socially and militarily, but also as the only nation in the world where true spirituality is still alive.

For we have lost the truth, we have lost the great sense, the meaning of our evolution, the meaning of why so much suffering, why dying, why getting born, why this earth, who are we, what is the soul, what is reincarnation, where is the ultimate truth about the world, the universe... But India has kept preserved this truth through seven millennia of pitfalls, of genocides and attempts at killing her sanatana dharma.

And this will be India's gift to this planet during this millennium: to restore to the world its true sense, to recharge humanity with the real meaning and spirit of life. India will become the spiritual leader of the world: "It is this religion that I am raising up before the world, it is this that I have perfected and developed through the Rishis, saints, and Avatars, and now it is going forth to do my work among the nations. I am raising this nation to send forth my word... When therefore it is said that India shall rise, it is the Sanatana Dharma that shall rise, it is the Sanatana Dharma that shall be great. When it is said that India shall expand and extend herself, it is the Sanatana Dharma that shall expand and extend itself over the world. It is for the Dharma and by the Dharma that India exists." (*India's Rebirth*, p. 46, Uttara speech)

Rise up, O India of the Vedic ages. Thou livest in the hearts of all thy people. Rise up O Westernised "secular" India, because thou art also the true India. Realize in your hearts the genius of the country which is yours. Stop comparing it to a civilization which is crumbling and cease equating it with parameters that are not hers. Wake up to the greatness of thy country. Not only the past greatness, which thou seekest to repossess in its music or in its temples, but the greatness that IS there, waiting to be grasped again, waiting to be brought down concretely. Rise up O India, to the greatness that IS in you. Rise up O true India.

Ah, we are coming back again full circle to the wonder that WAS India, the India of the Vedas and the Upanishad, which many historians have criticized as being militant and politically disunited. But the truth was that they were united in their diversity, that it was much more democratic and allowed much more freeplay and freedom, individually and collectively, than the India of today allows. Let us again reread history, let us look at India, not through the Western prism, but with the ancient wisdom that she has bestowed upon us.

For indeed, this is one of the most amazing paradoxes of today's world: here you have a country, India, which used to be considered as one of the poorest on this planet, which was, before Narendra Modi, disregarded by most Western nations (and many of its own people), as irrelevant, backward, too bureaucratic—and lately, as a hotbed of Hindu fundamentalism. Yet, India holds the key to the world's future. For India is the only nation which still preserves in the darkness of Her Himalayan caves, on the luminous ghats of Benares, in the hearts of her countless yogis, or even in the minds of her ordinary folk, the key to the planetary evolution, its future and its hope. This knowledge which once roamed the shores of the world from Egypt to China, is today lost everywhere. Europe has now entered a turbulent age; it will take a long time before it unites in spite of the near uniformity of its races and religions. The West, in its thirst for materialism, does not know anymore where it stands and has lost this precious knowledge, which India still holds, alone in the world.

The 21st century then will be the era of the East; this is where the sun is going to rise again, after centuries of decadence and submission to

Western colonialism; this is where the focus of the world is going to shift. And as when India used to shine and send forth Her *dharma* all over the Orient: Japan, Thailand, China, Burma, or Cambodia and influence their civilizations and religions for centuries to come, once more She will emit Her light and radiate, Queen among nations: "India of the ages is not dead nor has She spoken Her last creative word; She lives and has still something to do for Herself and the human peoples. And that which She must seek now to awake, is not an anglicised oriental people, docile pupil of the West and doomed to repeat the cycle of the Occident's success and failure, but still the ancient immemorial Shakti recovering Her deepest self, lifting Her head higher towards the supreme source of light and strength and turning to discover the complete meaning and vaster form of Her Dharma." (Sri Aurobindo)

CHAPTER 28

The Final Dream & AI

The 21st century is witnessing an extraordinary technological surge. Artificial Intelligence, once the realm of science fiction, now will shape more and more the way we live, work, think and even dream. Machines diagnose disease, compose music, drive cars, write poetry and make decisions in ways that once seemed exclusively human. We are told this is progress. And yet, beneath the glitter of data and innovation, something profound is being lost—something essential to our humanity. The more man becomes connected to technology, the more he seems disconnected from his inner being. There is a deepening sense of alienation, anxiety and inner emptiness. The two cars, the satellite phone, the global connectivity, the instant computerization—none of these are taking man any closer to his soul. In fact, they often serve to pull him further away from it. There is a subtle, but growing despair behind the glittering surface of modern life.

Sri Aurobindo saw this long before the age of AI. In his writings, he described the limitations of the mind and the trap of a purely mechanistic, intellectual evolution. "Mind is the highest form in man," he wrote, "but the mind is an ignorant, clouded and struggling power. And even when most luminous it is possessed only of a thin, reflected and pallid light." Man is not the measure of his tools or his intelligence. He is a "littleness that reaches to a wideness and a grandeur beyond him." His life is a striving moment, filled with suffering and longing, cast adrift in the immensity of universal existence. It is this spiritual view that offers the clearest lens through which to understand the rise of Artificial Intelligence. AI is not just a technical phenomenon—it is a philosophical and existential one. It forces us to ask: What does it mean to be human? Is intelligence the same as consciousness? Can machines think, or only simulate thought? And if they simulate it well enough, will we forget the difference?

Artificial Intelligence can replicate many outer forms of intelligence—pattern recognition, language generation, problem-solving, creative mimicry—but it cannot touch the soul. It has no self-awareness, no ethical compass, no intuition of truth, no capacity for love or spiritual yearning. It can analyze and respond, but it cannot experience beauty, or grief, or wonder. It cannot gaze at the stars and ask, "Who am I?" The risk we face is not that machines will become like men, but that men will become like machines. In our drive for efficiency, optimization and control, we have begun to mimic the very logic of the systems we have created. We reduce meaning to metrics, truth to data, wisdom to algorithms. We have become conditioned to speed, addicted to information, and have lost touch with silence. As the mechanical expands, the mystical retreats. Yet this need not be the destiny of humanity. Technology in itself is not evil. AI is not the enemy. The real danger lies in forgetting the higher purpose of human life. Technology must serve consciousness, not replace it. AI can ease the burden of physical and mental labor, freeing human beings to explore deeper dimensions—art, contemplation, self-discovery. But without spiritual orientation, it will only amplify our ignorance.

Sri Aurobindo called for a new evolution—not just of machines, but of man himself. He envisioned a humanity that could rise beyond the limitations of the mental consciousness, into the supramental, where knowledge is direct, will is aligned with divine truth, and life is an expression of a higher harmony. This is not science fiction. It is the true task of human existence. The solution, then, is not to reject AI, but to integrate it into a broader vision of human growth. We must build outer intelligence while cultivating inner wisdom. We must train the mind, but also open the heart. We must master machines without becoming mechanical. We must embrace innovation, but never lose sight of stillness. If this balance is lost, the consequences could be grave. A civilization driven solely by AI, without spiritual anchoring, will eventually collapse under the weight of its own cleverness. It will suffer not from a lack of knowledge, but from a loss of meaning. The more power we give to machines, the more responsibility we have to nurture our humanity.

Today, even as AI advances, depression, loneliness and existential confusion are on the rise. The soul is not nourished by information. It seeks presence, connection, truth. It does not grow through automation, but through attention, devotion, surrender. The real transformation must begin within. In India, this truth has been known for millennia. The seers of the Upanishads did not measure knowledge in bytes. They spoke of the *Atman*, the immortal self, as the source of all wisdom. They knew that man is not just a thinking machine but a bridge between the material and the divine. In the *Bhagavad Gita*, Krishna does not teach Arjuna how to optimize his battlefield strategy, but how to realize the eternal in the midst of action. This ancient wisdom is more relevant than ever. As the world becomes more virtual, India's spiritual heritage becomes more vital. The yogic sciences, the meditative disciplines, the knowledge of *prana* and inner silence—all these are tools not just for personal peace but for civilizational survival. AI may extend our capacities, but it cannot answer our ultimate questions. Who am I? What is the purpose of life? What lies beyond birth and death? What is consciousness? These are not questions for a chatbot or a neural network. They are the eternal questions of the soul.

Sri Aurobindo reminded us that evolution is not finished. The human being is not the last word of creation. We are not here merely to make faster machines, but to become more conscious beings. The future belongs not to the robot, but to the realized soul. In the long arc of time, AI may be a passing wave. Consciousness is the ocean. The challenge before us is immense. We live in a time of dazzling brilliance and deep confusion. We must embrace technology, but not idolize it. We must welcome the future, but remember the eternal. We must build machines, but not forget the soul. The real intelligence lies not in artificial systems, but in awakened consciousness. It is not in the circuits of silicon, but in the still flame within the heart. The age of AI may be upon us, but the destiny of man lies far beyond it—in the unfolding of a divine life on earth. And for that, we must turn inward. For it is only in the silence of the soul that the true light of knowledge dawns.

Conclusion

What is this knowledge that is still alive in this wonderful country which we call India ?

Firstly and foremost: "I accept you; I accept that you may be White or Black, Red or Yellow, Christian, Buddhist, or Muslim. I accept that God may manifest at different times, under different names, using different scriptures. Thus God is Krishna, but also Jesus Christ, Buddha or Mohamed. This an extraordinary statement and a marvellous instrument towards world peace, at a time where terrorism is striking everywhere in the world in the name of One God. It is also a Knowledge that only the body dies, but not the soul, which is born and reborn again till it achieves perfection. A Knowledge that whatever you do bears consequences in this life or another. A Knowledge that all human beings are made out of Love, even beneath the hate and the killings…"

And also: "I have inherited from my ancestors the tools to become a better person, whatever my religion, ethnicity and profession: a better Christian, a better Hindu, a better Muslim." What are these tools? *Hatha-yoga,* India's gift to the world, which has been copied and imitated everywhere. Meditation, this extraordinary technique of coming back to one's Self, of settling the mind and the body, which is today practiced by millions around the world—another bequest of India to humanity. *Pranayama*, the science of respiration, perfected by Indians for three millennia. "Does the breath have any religion," asks His Holiness Sri Sri Ravi Shankar, the founder of the Art of Living movement, which has spread today in 140 countries? "Is the air we breathe around us, Muslim, Christian, or Hindu?"

This knowledge thus does not only belong to Hindus, but also to Buddhists, Jains, Christians and Muslims of India. Once upon a time, the Syrian Christians of Kerala, though they remained faithful to the word of Jesus Christ, had incorporated some of the basic tenets of Hinduism such as reincarnation and karma. Once upon a time, great Sufis, such as Dara Sukoh, Shah Jahan's eldest and preferred son, while remaining true Muslims (and not apostate ones), could translate the Upanishads and step into a temple without thinking they were committing a mortal sin. Once upon a time Sikhism was born out of *dharma*, to defend the Hindu *dharma,* and neither Sikh nor Hindu saw any difference between themselves. Once upon a time, Buddha, although he did strike against ritualism and hereditary Brahmanism, did not find a religion, but a path that led to the same *Ananda* he came from.

This knowledge is unique to India. For the West has lost the truth. We have lost the Great Sense, the meaning of our evolution, of why so much suffering, why dying, why getting born, why this earth, who are we, what is the soul, what is reincarnation, where is the ultimate truth about the universe? And this will be India's gift to this planet during this century: to restore to the world its true sense; to recharge humanity with the real meaning and spirit of life. Thus, if you are an Indian settled abroad, whatever your religion, you should carry that identity in your actions and your aura, that you may shine without words, for it is a great privilege and responsibility to be born an Indian. Yet, too often, Indians in the US or Canada, or even the UK for that matter, hide their identities and try to merge into the mainstream culture, becoming more American than Americans, more British than the British. Sometimes, even Indians are ashamed to say that they are Indians and it is a tragedy to themselves and to their children, who lose the connection with one of the most ancient cultures in the world, which is not a religion but the last living spirituality on this planet.

You should also know that today, this ancient knowledge is under attack from multiple directions. Foremost among them is the relentless wave of globalization and Westernization, which continues to sweep across India at an unprecedented pace. Television channels, streaming platforms and aggressive advertising campaigns are perhaps the biggest culprits. Is white still considered the most beautiful skin tone? Does fair skin automatically make someone more valuable or successful? Do a smartphone, a business suit, or an expensive car truly make someone a better human being? These are the illusions being sold daily to millions of innocent villagers and lower-middle-class families. Through glossy commercials and curated lifestyles, they are being taught to abandon the richness of their roots and aspire to a hollow image of success. There is also an accelerated wave of Christian proselytization taking place in many parts of India—even today. In the tribal belts of Tamil Nadu, Andhra Pradesh, Chhattisgarh, and especially the North-East, entire villages are being converted with the help of vast foreign funding. The real tragedy is that these communities are often encouraged to feel ashamed of their own culture, rituals and ancestral traditions. What replaces them is often not a spiritual upgrade, but a rupture in identity and dignity. Meanwhile, there is a growing radicalization among some sections of India's Muslim youth. This is deeply unfortunate, especially in a country where Islam has enjoyed unprecedented freedom and constitutional protection. Try being openly Hindu, Buddhist, or Christian in countries like Saudi Arabia or even Bangladesh, and you will understand the contrast. And yet, some of the terror attacks that have shaken Indian cities, particularly at the beginning of the 21st century—from Hyderabad to Delhi to Mumbai in 2008—could not have happened without active help from a few Indian Muslims. This is something rarely acknowledged by mainstream politicians or media, but it remains a dangerous truth.

Lastly, Hindu renegades, those intellectuals who want to cut off at any cost India from her past and make a copy—however brilliant—of a Marxism which has died everywhere else, or of the United States of America, where violence, divorce and depression are affecting three persons out of five, are still very active at the moment, thanks to U.S. government, who continues to be so ignorant about India. Yet, it is for this precious knowledge that all Indians, be they Hindu, Muslim, Christian, or Sikh, should retain their *dharmic* identity, while being faithful to their creed or Supreme God. Every Diwali, thus, should symbolize for **all** Indians, the rekindling of this Ancient, Universal, All-encompassing, Non-Religious *Dharmic* Light in their hearts. Let Mother India shine in them and rekindle their common identity beyond their religions.

It is time Indians look again at their own history—IN THE LIGHT OF TRUTH—understand how it is important to save that knowledge.

Bibliography

Books

* *Negationism in India,* by Konrad Elst, Voice of India, New Delhi.

* *The Wonder that Was India,* by A.L. Basham, Rupa.

* *Vande Mataram*, by Sri Aurobindo, Sri Aurobindo Ashram Press, Pondicherry.

* *Histoire de l'Inde,* by Jean Daniélou, Éditions Fayard, Paris.

* *India's Rebirth,* Institut de Recherches Evolutives, Paris.

* *Distributed in India* by Mira Aditi Center, 62 Sriranga 1st Cross, 4th Stage Kuvempunagar, Mysore 570023.

* *The Mother,* by Sri Aurobindo, Sri Aurobindo Ashram Press, Pondicherry.

* *Life without Death,* by Satprem. Mira Aditi Center, 62 Sriranga 1st Cross, 4th Stage Kuvempunagar, Mysore 570023.

* *Indigenous Indians,* by Konrad Elst, Voice of India, New Delhi.

* *The Foundations of Indian Culture,* by Sri Aurobindo, Sri Aurobindo Ashram Press, Pondicherry.

* *Hindu Society Under Siege,* by Sitaram Goel, Voice of India; New Delhi.

* *The Hour of God,* by Sri Aurobindo, Sri Aurobindo Ashram Press, Pondicherry.

* *The Supramental Manifestation,* by Sri Aurobindo, Sri Aurobindo Ashram Press, Pondicherry.

* *The Secret of the Veda,* by Sri Aurobindo, Sri Aurobindo Ashram Press, Pondicherry.

* *The Mother's Agenda,* as recorded by Satprem. 13 volumes. Mira Aditi Centre, 62 Sriranga 1st Cross, 4th Stage Kuvempunagar, Mysore 570023.

* *Mother India and Her Destiny,* by the Mother, Sri Aurobindo Ashram Press, Pondicherry.

* *Arise Arjuna,* by David Frawley, Voice of India, 1994.

** The author is grateful to the Sri Aurobindo Ashram Trust for permission to quote extensively from Sri Aurobindo and the Mother's works.

AHIR D. C., *Aśoka the Great,* B. R. Publishing (Delhi), 1995.

ALLEN Charles, *Ashoka: India's Lost Emperor,* Little Brown and Company, 2012.

AMBEDKAR Bhimrao Ramji, *Annihilation of Caste: The Annotated Critical Edition,* Verso Books, 2014.

ANQUETIL-DUPERRON Abraham-Hyacinthe et KIEFFER Jean-Luc, L'Inde en France au XVIIIe Siècle, Les Belles Lettres, 2001.

ATTALI Jacques, *Gandhi ou l'éveil des Humiliés,* Fayard, 2007.

AYESHA Jalal, *The Sole Spokesman: Jinnah,* the Muslim League and the Demand for Pakistan, Cambridge University Press, 1994.

BERNSTEIN Richard, *Ultimate Journey: Retracing the Path of an Ancient Buddhist Monk (Xuanzang) Who Crossed Asia in Search of Enlightenment,* Vintage (New York), 2001.

BONGARD-LEVIN G. M., *Mauryan India,* Stosius Inc./Advent Books Division, 1986.

BUDGE E. A. Wallis, *The Life and Exploits of Alexander the Great: Being a Series of Translations of the Ethiopic Histories of Alexander* by the Pseudo-Callisthenes and Other Writers, C. J. Clay (Londres), 1896.

CATHERINE CLEMENT, *Pour l'amour de l'Inde,* Flammarion, J'ai Lu, 1993.

CHIROL Valentin, *The Indian Unrest,* Macmillan and Company, 1910.

DALRYMPLE William, *Le Dernier Moghol: La Chute d'une Dynastie,* Delhi, 1857, Broché, 2008.

DANIELOU Alain, *Approche de l'Hindouisme,* Kailash, 2004.

DANIELOU Alain, *Histoire de l'Inde,* Fayard, 1983.

DANIELOU Alain, *Mythes et Dieux de L'Inde,* le Polythéisme Hindou, Champ-Flammarion, 1994.

DEBROY Dipavali, *The Holy Vedas: Rigveda, Yajur Veda, Sama Veda, Atharva Veda,* B. R. Publishing, 2006.

DELEURY Guy, *Le Modèle Indou,* Kailash, 1978.

DELLON Charles, *l'Inquisition de Goa, la Relation de Charles Dellon* (1685), Broché, 2003.

DHAVALIKAR M. K., *Indian Protohistory,* Deemed University (Pune), 1998.

FORREST G. W., *A History of the Indian Mutiny,* William Blackwood and Sons (Londres), 1904.

FRAWLEY David, *Myth of the Aryan Invasion of India,* Voice of India, nouv. éd., 1997.

GHOSH A., *Encyclopedia of Indian Archaeology,* Brill, 1990.

GUENON René, *Introduction générale à l'étude des doctrines hindoues,* Marcel Rivière, 1921.

GUENON René, *La Crise du Monde Moderne,* rééd., Gallimard, " Folio Essais", 1994.

GUENON René, *L'Homme et son Devenir selon le Vêdânta,* Bossard, 1925.

HABIB Irfan, *People's History of India,* Tulika Print Communication Services, 2002.

HAUDRÈRE Philippe, *Les Compagnies des Indes Orientales,* trois Siècles de Rencontre entre Orientaux et Occidentaux, Desjonquères, 2006.

HYDER Mohammed, October Coup, A Memoir of the Struggle for Hyderabad, Lotus/Roli Books, 2012.

JAIN V. K., *Prehistory and Protohistory of India. An India (Palaeolithic-Non-Harappan Chalcolithic cultures),* D. K. Print World, 2006.

KANE P. V., *History of Dharmasastra (Ancient and Mediaeval Religious and Civil Law),* v.5.1, Opensource (1 réédition, 1958).

KATE P. V., *Marathwada Under the Nizams, 1724-1948,* Mittal Publications (Delhi), 1987.

KAUTILYA, *Arthasastra, Traité politique et militaire de l'Inde ancienne,* Le Félin, 1998.

KAUTILYA, *The Arthashastra,* Penguin Classic, 2000.

KENOYER Jonathan Mark, *Ancient Cities of the Indus Valley Civilization,* Oxford University Press and American Institute of Pakistan Studies (Karachi), 1998.

KNAPP Stephen, *The Aryan Invasion Theory: The Final Nail in its Coffin,* The Vedic Friends Association, 2012.

MACPHAIL James Merry, *Aśoka,* The Associative Press (Calcutta)/Oxford University Press (Londres), 1918.

MAJUMDAR R. C., *Ancient India,* Motilal Banarsidass Publishers, 9th ed., 2016.

MEDLICOTT H. B., BLANFORD W. T., OLDHAM, *A Manual of the Geology of India,* Cambridge University Press (New York), 1893.

MEGASTHENES, SCHWANBECK, MCCRINDLE, John WATSON, *Ancient India as described* by Megasthenes and Arrian; being a translation of the fragments of the Indika of Megasthenes collected by Dr. Schwanbeck, and of the first part of the Indika of Arrian, Thacker/Spink (Calcutta), 1877.

MEID Wolfgang, *Celtiberian Inscriptions,* Archaeolingua, S. Bökönyi and W. Meid (ed.), Series Minor, 1994.

MISRA Amaresh, *Mangal Pandey: The True Story of an Indian Revolutionary,* Rupa and Company (Delhi), 2005.

MOORE R. J., *Jinnah and the Pakistan Demand,* Cambridge University Press, 1983.

MÜLLER Friedrich Max, *Rig-Véda-sanhita: The Sacred Hymns of the Brahmans,* Trübner (Londres), 1869.

NIKAM N. A. et MCKEON Richard, *The Edicts of Aśoka,* University of Chicago Press, 1959.

PIGGOTT Stuart, *Prehistoric India,* Penguin Books, 1950.

RADHEY Shyam Chaurasia, *History of Ancient India: Earliest Times to 1000 AD,* Atlantic Publishers & Distributors, 2001.

Raynal Guillaume-Thomas, *Histoire philosophique et politique des Établissements et du commerce des Européens dans les Deux Indes* (1770), ed. Critique.

RONGXI Li, *The Biographical Scripture of King Aśoka,* trad. du chinois, Numata Center for Buddhist Translation and Research (Berkeley), 1993.

SARKAR Nurul Islam, *Sonia Gandhi, Tryst with India,* Atlantic Publishers & Distributors, 2006.

SINGH Upinder, *Governing the State and the Self Political Philosophy and Practice in the Edicts of Aśoka,* South Asian Studies, University of Delhi, 2012.

SRI AUROBINDO, *Le Secret du Véda,* Fayard, 1983.

SRI CHINMOY, *Commentaries on the Védas, the Upanishads and the Bhagavad Gita: The Three Branches of India's Life-Tree,* Aum Publications, 1997.

TALAGERI Shrikant, *The Aryan Invasion Theory, A Re-appraisal,* Aditya Prakashan, 2006.

VOLTAIRE, Œuvres Complètes..., avec des Notes et une Notice Historique sur la Vie de Voltaire, vol. 4, 1836.

WEBER Jacques, *Pondichéry et les Comptoirs de l'Inde après Dupleix,* Denoël, 1996.

WOLPERT Stanley, *Jinnah of Pakistan,* Oxford University Press (New York), 1984.

Other Publications

BAKLIWAL P.C. et Grover, *"Signature and Migration of Sarasvati River in Thar Desert, Western India,"* Records Geological Survey of India, 1988.

BARR Stephen M., *Science and Religion: The Myth of Conflict (Explanations)*, Catholic Truth Society, 2011.

BHADRA B. K., GUPTA A. K. et Sharma, "Sarasvati Nadi in Haryana and its linkage with the Vedic Sarasvati River, Integrated Study Based on Satellite Images and Groun-based Information," Jour. Geological Society of India, 2009.

BISWAS Soutik, *India's Dark History of Sterilization*, BBC, 14 November 2014.

FURBER Holden, *Rival Empires of Trade in the Orient, 1600-1800,* University of California Press, 1983.

GOSWAMI M. C. et BHAGAVATI A. C., "A Preliminary Report on a Collection of Neolithic Toll Types from West Assam ," *Man in India,* 1959.

KENOYER Jonathan Mark, *New Perspectives on the Indus Tradition, Contributions from Recent Research at Harappa and Other Sites in Pakistan and India, in Sindhu-Sarasvati Valley Civilization,* Nalini Rao, 2014.

KHAN Yasmin, *The Great Partition: The Making of India and Pakistan,* Yale University Press, 2008 (1se ed., 2007).

KUMAR Vikrant, "Y-chromosome Evidence Suggests a Common Paternal Heritage of Austro-Asiatic Populations," *BMC Evolutionary Biology,* 2007.

N. J. ALLEN, "How to Kill a Dragon: Aspects of Indo-European Poetics by Calvert Watkins," *The Journal of the Royal Anthropological Institute,* 2000.

POUCHEPADASS Jacques, "La révolte des cipayes," *L'Histoire (mensuel),* n° 27 October 1980.

PRINSEP, "Interpretation of the Most Ancient of Inscriptions on the Pillar Called Lat of Feroz Shah," *Journal of the Asiatic Society,* 1837.

SAHOO S., "A Prehistory of Indian Y Chromosomes: Evaluating Demic Diffusion Scenarios," Proceedings of the National Academy of Sciences, 2006.

SASTRI K. A. Nilakanta, *A History of South India,* Oxford University Press, 1958.

SMITH V. A., *« Oxford History of India »,* Maharaja's College Magazine, 1922.

UNDERHILL PA, MYRES NM, ROOTSI S, METSPALU M, ZHIVOTOVSKY LA, KING RJ, LIN AA, CHOW CE, SEMINO O, BATTAGLIA V, KURTEV I, JÄRVE M, CHAUBEY G, AYUB Q, MOHYUDDIN A, MEHDI SQ, SENGUPTA S, ROGAEV EI, KHUSNUTDINOVA EK, PSHENICHNIKOV A, BALANOVSKY O, BARANOVSKA E, JERAN N, AUGUSTIN DH, BALDOVIC M, HERRERA RJ, THANGARAJ K, SINGH V, SINGH L, MAJUMDER P, RUDAN P, PRIMORAC D, VILLEMS R, KIVISILD, *« Separating the post-Glacial coancestry of European and Asian Y chromosomes within haplogroup R1a »*, Pubmed,US National Library of Medicine/National Institutes of Health, 2009.